THORNS
and
THISTLES[1]

---

[1]   See Gen. 3:17-18. To the man he said: "Because you listened to your
wife and ate from the tree of which I had forbidden you to eat,
"Cursed be the ground because of you! In toil shall you eat its yield
all the days of your life. **Thorns and thistles** shall it bring forth to
you, as you eat of the plants of the field." Scripture teaches that we
are born into sin because of disobedience; the soil of our heart is
cursed with weeds, and thorns and thistles. In the same vein, its
spiritual significance tells us that the Word of God is not a seed that
we can simply scatter in the field that is full of thorns and thistles.
We need to commit and partake of the flesh that involves the call of
discipleship.

THORNS
and
THISTLES

PATHWAYS TO DISCIPLESHIP
CYCLE C

MARK A. ESCOBAR

InspiringVoices®
A Service of Guideposts

Inspiring Voices books may be ordered through booksellers or by contacting:

Inspiring Voices
1663 Liberty Drive
Bloomington, IN 47403
www.inspiringvoices.com
1-(866) 697-5313

ISBN: 978-1-4624-0596-1 (sc)
ISBN: 978-1-4624-0595-4 (e)

Library of Congress Control Number: 2013907140

Printed in the United States of America.

Inspiring Voices rev. date: 5/22/2013

To my Scalabrinian confreres

CONTENTS

ORDINARY TIME

LENT

HOLY WEEK

EASTER SEASON

ORDINARY TIME

ADVENT SEASON

CHRISTMAS SEASON

FOREWORD

"What do you remember about last Sunday's homily?" I remember my professor of homiletics several years ago in South America sharing with his students that this was a question he regularly asked people in his parish during the week. The answer that most stayed with him, he jokingly said, was that of an older lady who never missed Sunday Mass: "not much, Father, but you spoke wonderfully." This is perhaps what every preacher fears most after delivering a homily. Yet, the consolation is that something stays in the minds and hearts of those who listen. After smiling at the woman and asking more specifically whether she liked any of the readings or the stories he told, she replied: "ah yes, I liked what you said about . . . ," and on she went to recall a few interesting details. Not all listeners remember the same message or remember in the same way. This calls for homilies well prepared and well delivered; homilies that bring us into conversation with the complexity of the biblical world in which the readings that inspire them are rooted and our own contemporary experience. Preachers and educators are always up to be surprised by what stays with the people we address.

Preaching is an art and as such it must be mastered through constant discipline, preparation, and intentionality. We must never underestimate the value of this important dimension of the ministry of the Word in the life of the Church. The homily is for many baptized the primary means to enter into the depths of the Scriptures and the Church's Tradition. It is in listening to the preacher that many discover that God has something important for us in the everyday of our lives. Homilies have the potential to transform not only how we live our lives, but also how we understand God becoming present in our midst. St. Paul clearly reminds us that there is an intimate connection between faith and good preaching: "But how can they call on him in whom they have not believed? And how can they believe in him of whom they have not heard? And how can they hear without someone to preach?" (Rom 10:15). Christian preaching is then an art that carries the weight of a very unique responsibility: to bring women and men to faith, namely to an encounter with the person of Jesus Christ in whom we partake of God's salvific love.

The preacher plays an amazingly important role in the liturgical celebration and in the life of the Church. One metaphor that I believe captures well what the preacher does is that of a mediator. Preaching mediates the many worlds and meanings that converge at the moment of the liturgical celebration in which a homily is delivered. When the Scriptures are proclaimed, we hear the echo of voices and experiences that emerged thousands of years ago. Those voices and experiences are now to make sense in the lives of people who also have their own experiences, as shaped by the historical reality of the present, and live in the particularity of their cultural-historical location. The preacher stands before the congregation as the person who mediates these realities. It falls upon the shoulders of the preacher to know as much as possible about the world of the Scriptures and about the world of those who are listening. Mediation in the context of preaching is about interpreting, making connections, identifying differences, and insightfully showing how faith and life are mutually related. But perhaps the most important task of the preacher as mediator is that of empowering listeners to do their own interpreting and make those connections that only they can in their own lives.

Christianity enjoys a centuries-old tradition of assembling collections of homilies and sermons for this particular purpose, beginning with Jesus's own discourses in the gospels. These collections are indeed great resources to learn from the theological wisdom of the preacher and how this person has wrestled with the questions of a particular time in conversation with God's Word and Revelation. I have always admired, for instance, the depth and structure of Thomas Aquinas' Summa Theologica as well as his various other philosophical works, but am uniquely fascinated by his sermons. There one encounters a somewhat more personal side of the Angelic Doctor, a theologian in love with the Scriptures and the person they reveal. Augustine's Sermons are alluring; John Henry Newman's ever insightful. No history of Christian missions or religious education or even theology would be complete without a serious study of available sermons and homilies delivered at various moments in history.

Thorns and Thistles is Fr. Mark Escobar's gift to preachers, Christian educators, parishioners, and readers interested in the wisdom shared through his homilies during 2010 as part of Year C of the Sunday cycle of readings. It takes time and discipline to write a good homily, conviction to deliver it in a persuasive manner, and courage to publish them. Here we find a sample of all the above. In this well-crafted collection of homilies, Fr. Escobar walks us through an entire liturgical year of Sunday preaching deeply rooted in the weekly readings from the Scriptures. I had the pleasure to carefully study each one of these homilies. First started reading them as an intellectual exercise but soon found myself mediating upon the readings and the reflections as in a personal retreat guided by the hand of a master preacher.

The present collection of homilies is an invitation into a journey. First, it is a journey into the Scriptures, the heart of every homily. Fr. Escobar carefully explains each biblical passage providing key details to better understand the context of the texts in the Bible and in the cultural moment in which they were written. This is a unique sensibility that surely flows from his experience as a missionary in various continents. Second, it is a journey into the mind of a well-read person. One cannot but admire the depth and breadth of Fr. Escobar's intellectual interests. His homilies constantly intersperse references to the world of literature and the history of thought. The choir of voices from poets like William Cowper, Homer, and John Milton; those of writers such as William Blake, Frederick Buechner, Charles Dickens, Fyodor Dostoevsky, Nathaniel Hawthorne, Ernest Hemingway, Abraham Heschel, C.S. Lewis, Henri Nouwen, Mary Flannery O'Connor, Ovid, Karl Rahner, Leo Tolstoy, Mark Twain, Victor Hugo; and those of Christian champions such as Thérèse of Lisieux and John Henry Newman, among others, join Fr. Escobar's own voice to invite his listeners to a life of Christian authenticity by searching for the truth and the good of which every human person is capable. Finally, it is a journey into our present reality with its complexity and demands. Fr. Escobar's homilies are not mere intellectual abstractions or spiritual meditations that ignore the questions that people in his congregation are asking or hearing. The connection of his homilies to recent news and current events remind us that the Good News must become incarnate in our everyday lives. Such incarnation or inculturation is what truly leads to transformed lives in the confines of history. And in the present historical reality, for us today, it is imperative that as Christians we do all it is possible to address the needs of the poor and most vulnerable in our midst and around the world.

Whether you are a preacher or someone searching for a good resource to reflect on the readings for Year C in the Sunday cycle of the lectionary, Thorns and Thistles is definitely an excellent resource worth exploring.

Hosffman Ospino, PhD
Professor of Theology and
Religious Education, Boston College
March 23, 2013—Feast of St. Toribio
Alfonso de Mogrovejo

ACKNOWLEDGMENTS

O ver the years the lens through which I have viewed my ministry has always been a learning experience. The roller coaster of attention and sacrifice has molded my perspective in the priesthood vis-a-vis the mixture of peoples of diverse cultures. The competing trends of secularization and missionary endeavors have challenged me more to further my understanding of God's Word, mission, culture, and my prayer life. They have helped me grow more deeply in the sacramental priesthood as the "alter Christus" who acts "in persona Christi Capitis."

Keenly aware of those people who have been part of my ministry as a missionary priest, I am pleased to thank for their continuous support, presence and care for the Church, along with the Scalabrinian Order.

With the growing numbers of migrants across the country, I cannot help but be mindful of a world that is marked by a yawning gap between rich and poor; a world which continues to witness afflictions in the midst of the ongoing migration of people searching for a better place to live and quality of life towards the future. On the strength of this idea, Pope John XXIII saw a basis for a right to emigrate in the legitimate desire of people to acquire the humanly necessary level of material goods.[1]

In the summer of 2010 I have been greatly assisted by Susan and Jim, along with Dominic, with their patience in helping me understand the dynamics of human concerns and priorities being at home in the world with others. I am thankful to my parishioners who have inspired and challenged me, too, to write my Sunday homilies. Heartfelt thanks are extended to my friends for being a source of information, strength and guidance.

My deep appreciation, however, goes to Professor Hosffman Ospino for taking the time to read the manuscript, for his advice, and kind words in seeing this book through to completion. My own community, Scalabrinian Missionaries, has been a great source of encouragement over the years, as well as of challenge. I am also grateful to Fr. Volmar Scaravelli, my pastor at St. Tarcisius Church in Framingham, MA, for his fraternal concern and comprehension especially for all the days and hours I have spent on the computer.

I am grateful to Mrs Nancy Marotta, a member of the Lay Scalabrinian Movement and former Assistant Principal of Public School 50 on Staten Island, New York, for her editorial assistance. She continues to be of great help in my writing and allows me to trust in prayer that "all shall be well."

And the last but not least, to my deceased parents who have been my inspiration. I thank them for their steadfast love and humility which helped me mold that vision within me to live a kind of life—simple and focused in many settings. I thank God for the gift of parents like them.

---

[1]   John XXIII, "Mater et Magistra," par. 45

INTRODUCTION

T he impact of revolutionary information technology and globalization has brought diverse values in multicultural settings and shaped that perspective that has an engaging portrait for all people of faith today. Over the years people across cultures have lived their lives the way they want to live it. It follows that with many sources of information and interaction through the mass media, entertainment and other social networks, their faith commitment has changed; a popular culture that assumes the rightness of all that is relative or trendy, no matter how evil, has brought engagement of today's context, and their conversation with practices of genuine witnessing has been headed in a different direction.

From the perspective of faith, our efforts to draw others to friendship with God start with experience. No lesson is more persuasive than good example—especially when it comes with a personal touch.[2] While it is much easier to talk about the reality of our people in the poor countries than it is

---

[2]   cf. Editorial. *A Personal Touch*. The Tablet. Vol. 103, No. 35. December 4, 2010. p 13.

to answer why this reality happens, I am convinced that from many angles of the gospel, we can find certain connections that provide a pathway of hope, justice, and mission that responds to a vital need in the church and society.

I believe that the call we have been given is larger than we are. The starting point makes us aware of the world within us and around us through our human encounters in many forms, including our participation in the healing, loving and creative way this process can generate.

Carl Anderson's "A Civilization of Love: What Every Catholic Can Do to Transform the World" comments on the vision of human existence of Blessed John Paul II.[3] He quotes the Holy Father that we are created by Love and we are called to love. In a similar vein, Pope Benedict XVI, in his first encyclical letter, stressed our commitment to love others as a gift from God and this has to be shared in a deeper way, both at a personal and social level. Hence, we are challenged to love one another. Jesus, for instance, was executed because he refused to stop loving his people. He denounced cruelty and injustice that deprives others of their rights to love. He refused to stop challenging the world's *status quo*. And he made it known to everyone that his mission in life was to keep on loving without limits. It's a biblical imperative to love others, welcome a stranger and commit to helping those who are poor.

By the same token, there are many ways to shed light on the broader phenomenon of wonders and the mysteries present in the lives of people. They are part of a human web that ought to be seen and painted like any portrait of

---

[3]   quoted from Fr Robert Lauder. *Every Truth Helps to Set a Person Free*. <u>The Tablet</u>. Vol. 104, No. 16. February 5, 2011. p 20.

our innermost thoughts and feelings as reflected in our experiences.

These compiled homilies, while not intended for an ideal way of preaching for a community called to worship on Sundays, is an attempt to serve only as a form of sharing. Some stories within familiar historical and biblical contexts make us cognizant of the lessons of the past and other issues which explore specific events, along with the growing literature on human relationships.

It is of interest, however, to appreciate the value and importance of shaping the perspective on discipleship and interaction of old-world heritage and cultural conditions in the contemporary life.

As this book stands, with its biblical reflections, along with its considerable mosaic of allusions on literary works and other disciplines, it brings to mind that we are called upon to spread the word of God and to be good examples of what it means to be Christian. It also allows us to open the hearts of others to faith in Jesus Christ through our prayer and mutual exchange of experiences that people of faith may seek by word and example.

Nothing can be more convincing than sharing our life with others with a great deal of faith and trust in God. It has a core value of mission that has its founding vision from the flesh and blood of faith experience where transformation occurs. Given our understanding of how faith brings us closer to the Trinitarian presence of God, we are called to go through the process of conversion—experiencing the living God in different forms of poverty in diverse situations.

As we now live in a radically different world replete with all kinds of culturally established ideologies and moral stands, I would like to quote what Dante Alighieri once wrote: "In the middle of the journey of my life, I came to myself within a dark wood where the straight way was lost. Ah, how hard it is to tell of that wood—savage and harsh and dense. The thought of it renews my fear; so bitter is it that death is hardly more."

NEW YEAR'S DAY

Readings: Num 6:22-27; Ps 67:2-3, 5, 6, 8; Gal 4:4-7; Lk 2:16-21

Solemnity of the Blessed Virgin Mary— Mother of God[4]

It seems like yesterday when we looked back in retrospection and reflected upon the year just coming to a close. It was New Year, too, when we came to ask ourselves about the goals we wanted to achieve, resolutions to make and those lessons we learned, along with knowledge we gained. It was an enduring year though, with hills and valleys to climb.

As we leaf through another year, our horizon of meanings explores the possibilities of renewal and assessment of where we have been, and await the unfolding of what life will bring about. It is reflecting on the past and looking forward with optimism at the potential of what the future has in store for us.

Perhaps some of us still have parties to attend with families and friends. Some may have gone to Times Square in Manhattan, New York City, where they saw the dropping of the crystal ball that was raised and then lowered to mark the coming of the New Year.[5] Traditionally, New Year is a time

---

4   cf. Pope John Paul II. *Mary is the Virgin Mother of God.* L'Osservatore Romano Weekly Edition in English. Sept. 20, 1995. p 7. The title "Mother of God" already attested by Matthew in the equivalent expression "Mother of Emmanuel", God with us (cf. Mt 1:23), was explicitly attributed to Mary only after a reflection that embraced about two centuries. It is third century Christians in Egypt who begin to invoke Mary as "*Theotokos*," Mother of God.

5   www.wikipedia, free encyclopedia online. The Ball descends 77 feet (23 m) over the course of a minute, coming to rest at the bottom of its pole at 12:00 a.m. Toshiba's Times Square billboard directly below the Ball counts down to midnight as well. Every year up to

for families to get together sharing food and relationships. While we traverse our busy lives or find within ourselves some worries and anxieties, we are still grateful for each moment that we show our humanness and vulnerability to make changes for the better.

The past year has been swamped with some disheartening reports about economic recession and its consequences, debates on health care reform and its filibuster, climate change, terrorist attacks and many episodes of tragedy. I remember the report of a woman (Banita M. Jacks, 35) who killed her four daughters, ages 5 to 16 in southeast Washington on Jan. 9, 2008 and lived for months with their decomposing bodies.[6] There was a train crash that occurred on the red line near Washington D.C. and Maryland border that killed 9 people and injured more than 70 in the deadliest accident in the 30-year history of the Metro.[7] The Justice Department filed numerous lawsuits against several state juvenile detention systems for subjecting children to neglect and abuse.[8] There was an uproar in Britain over the release of the only person convicted (Mr. Megrahi from Libya) in the 1988 Lockerbie bombing that killed 189 Americans in Scotland. Then we had the death of Sen Ted F Kennedy who is described as one of the greatest legislators of all time.[9]

---

one million people gather in Times Square to watch the Ball drop, and an estimated 1 billion watch video of the event, 100 million of them in the U.S.

[6] Ian Urbina. *Woman Who Killed her 4 Daughters Is Given 120 Years.* The New York Times. Vol. CLIX., No. 54, 894. December 19, 2009. p A16.

[7] Sarah Karush & Brian Westley. *Train crash probe focuses on computer flaw.* The Buffalo News. June 24, 2009. p A2.

[8] cf. Editorial. The New York Times. Vol. CLVIII, No. 54, 778. August 25, 2009. p A20.

[9] Sheryl Gay Stolberg. *For Better and for Worse, Senate has Seen Changes in Kennedy's Time.* The New York Times. Vol. CLVIII, No. 54, 781. August 28, 2009. p A15.

Those were like hills and valleys of hurt and pain, sorrow and affliction. And as we take the time to reflect upon these things, we keep a positive outlook on another threshold of coming in and going out in the future. Although we have had a plethora of hardships in this past year we still keep our perspective intact with a good attitude towards life. In spite of so many distractions we met along the way, we have that faith that something good will take place. This is our hope, the pillar of faith that propels us in the future.

In biblical reference to the ancient Israelites when they waited to enter the Promised Land, God promised them: "For the land which you are to enter and occupy is not like the land of Egypt from which you have come, where you would sow your seed and then water it by hand, as in a vegetable garden. No, the land into which you are crossing for conquest is a land of hills and valleys that drinks in rain from the heavens, a land which the Lord, your God, looks after; his eyes are upon it continually from the beginning of the year to the end" (Dt 11:10-12).

Today, too, as we celebrate the motherhood of Mary, we recapture her missionary vocation as a gift of sharing in the life and mission of Jesus. Her contemplative attitude towards God—her trust and humility to accept God's will is the best example of complete giving of oneself. It is a gift of unselfish love to fulfill a mission. We can look to Mary and reflect upon her deep faith as the foundation of her holiness. The fact that she is the Mother of God[10] is her primary gift and

---

[10]   Isaac of Stella, Sermon 51. (from which another excerpt is quoted by Lumen Gentium): PL 194, 1862-1865. This point of view summarizes and synthesizes St Augustine's opinions. "As there is one Son and many so Mary and the Church are only one Mother and many: both are mothers of Christ, but none of them can bring forth the total Christ without the other. The main objection proposed by

this makes her the most exalted human being that God ever created in this world.

Let us move forward to renewing and reflecting what we want to accomplish this year for ourselves, for our families, or for our communities. We have to get to the task at hand as we empower ourselves to make a difference for the better and to become better persons. Let us reflect upon our goals and priorities to work on for this new year of possibilities sharing with Mary's virtues of holiness, love, and faith commitment.

Irish playwright George Bernard Shaw once wrote: "I am of the opinion that my life belongs to the whole community, and as long as I live, it is my privilege to do it whatever I can. I want to be thoroughly used up when I die, for the harder I work, the more I live. I rejoice in life for its own sake. Life is no brief candle to me. It is a sort of splendid torch which I have got hold of for the moment, and I want to make it burn as brightly as possible before handling it on to future generations."

Best wishes for much joy, love, and health to everyone. May we all go forward in hope to learn, to experience, and reflect the challenges of our lives, the hills and valleys of where we may be going. Happy New Year!

---

adversaries against the title Mother of God is that the Second Person of the Blessed Trinity took only his human nature from Mary, but not his divine nature. Therefore, it is said, she is not the Mother of God but only the Mother of Jesus. The answer to this is that a mother conceives and gives birth not to a nature as such but to a person. Since Mary conceived and gave birth to the Word, the Logos, the Second Person of the Blessed Trinity, it follows that she is truly the Mother of God.

FEAST OF THE EPIPHANY

Readings: Is 60:1-6; Ps 72:1-2, 7-8, 10-11,
12-13, Eph 3:2-3a, 5-6; Matt 2:1-12

The Visit of the Magi marks the
Manifestation of Christ to the Gentiles

*"And behold, the star that they had seen at its rising preceded
them, until it came and stopped over the place where the child
was. They were overjoyed at seeing the star, and on entering
the house they saw the child with Mary his mother."*

Like the remarks of the late Gore Vidal about Tennessee
Williams who would incline himself if he had nothing better
to do—to rewrite something he had already published, I
think it is the same thing when our commitment to faith has
to be renewed. The need to rewrite those goals and priorities
in our hearts, though we may have already done these things
before may be true. But it makes sense to do it again as we
turn over a new leaf to enable us to understand what it really
means to be a follower or a disciple while giving an abiding
witness to people around us.

In this case we need to trace back the source of
revelation like these magi or wise men from the East in
today's celebration of the Epiphany[11] of our Lord. As men

---

[11]   It comes from the Greek word for "the showing," or "shining
forth," "manifestation", or "appearing". In Christian terms, it is the
manifestation to the world of Christ's divine wisdom and power—
"God in man made manifest" (Christopher Wordsworth). In the
same vein, it means "the manifestation of Christ to the Gentiles."
It is the first manifestation of the King of the Jews as the Savior of
the World. Story of all non-Jews are symbolized by the Magi. Both
Western and Eastern Christians describe the fundamental gospel
mystery of the Incarnation. On the other hand, during the middle

seeking wisdom (which denotes the word magi), they knew that the 'star of wonder' in the sky reveals the sign that the promised Messiah had been born. And his light was made known to the world as St John called it, "the true light which shines in the darkness," is the one we proclaim in the Nicene Creed—"Light from Light."

Matthew's writings tell us that they were non-Jews, foreigners or pagans, and that their visit significantly marked the first revelation of Jesus, the Messiah, to the world, particularly to the Gentiles as represented by them. Through them we find the pervading theme of God's revelation to a non-Jewish world. As it says in the NT quite often, the Gentiles would be favored over the Jews for reason of their faith in Jesus.

Speaking of the Gentiles, however, it became one of the most controversial issues within the first and second generation Christians as regards their admission to the gospel fellowship without first becoming Jewish. While God had indeed chosen the ancient Israelites, it does not follow that

---

Ages, Twelfth Day or Epiphany was celebrated by a play acted out in the services. For example, the "Preaching Friars" of Milan, in 1336, celebrated the Festival of the Three Kings through some portion of the city. A golden star was carried through Milan in front of three men dressed as kings, riding richly-dressed horses, surrounded by untold numbers of pages, bodyguards and followers. They proceeded to a point at which they met King Herod's representation, along with his scribes and wise men. The kings asked them to go to Bethlehem. They then proceeded to the church of St. Eustorgius, "with all their attendants, preceded by trumpets, horns, asses, baboons, and a great variety of animals." The custom of the Election of Kings by Beans may have derived from the Romans, whose children drew lots with beans at the end of Saturnalia to see who would be king. The custom developed of baking a cake, called Twelfth-Cake, which contained a bean. Whoever got the piece of cake containing the bean was declared king for a day, and called King of the Bean. This may be the origin of the Mardi Gras King Cake.

God had excluded the rest of humanity. Separation between Judaism and Christianity around the time of the destruction of the Jerusalem Temple in 70 A.D. should correct any biases, superiority complex or anti-Semitism among Christians because salvation revealed by Christ knows no distinction of races or cultures. Everyone is welcomed into the "people of God." No one is excluded from this invitation. It is meant to be universal.

As it says in Eph (2:11-19): "Therefore, remember that at one time you, Gentiles in the flesh, called the uncircumcised by those called the circumcision, which is done in the flesh by human hands, were at that time without Christ, alienated from the community of Israel and strangers to the covenants of promise, without hope and without God in the world. But now in Christ Jesus you who once were far off have become near by the blood of Christ . . . so then you are no longer strangers and sojourners, but you are fellow citizens with the holy ones and members of the household of God, built upon the foundation of the apostles and prophets, with Christ Jesus himself as the capstone."

As wise men that must have been gifted with the infusion of divine revelation, they used astrology to read beyond supernatural signs and phenomena. They were rich as shown by the gifts they brought to Christ-Child. They must have been well esteemed with their political importance in society as shown when King Herod received them in audience. Through the guidance of the Star, they came to see the Christ-Child to do him homage as it says more specifically in Latin, "we have come to adore him." This gave us some wisdom to reflect upon the fact that the promises made to Israel are geared towards the benefit of the whole world. Israel's Messiah is the longing of all races and cultures united in the same hope of redemption.

While I am always reticent to deal with those biblical interpretations or from someone who counters historical teaching and controversies about many Christian denominations swirling in today's culture of argument, I am convinced that as a church we should keep in mind that we are not a nation, not a body that comprises men and women like any other groups or corporations. Rather we are Christ's mystical body united with and to him through our sacrament of baptism. It is of his making. He is the author, the prime mover of all our missions in the church.

Vatican II teaches us that the Church founded by Christ "subsists in the Catholic Church"[12] but it acknowledges a relationship with other Christians "who do not profess the faith in its entirety or do not preserve unity of communion with the successor of Peter."[13] If our religion possesses divisive qualities or cultures breaking down, then evidently, we contradict the will of Christ that aims to unite us and thus far, it is not part of God's plan.

According to St Gregory the Great, the gifts that the three Magi offered to the Christ-Child can be equated with the richness of our spirituality as men and women of the gospel, namely, the gold of wisdom from on high, the incense of prayer, and the myrrh of self-denial (Gospel Homilies 8). We may look well externally, but there are deep shadows still being kept buried inside our hearts. And as committed Christians, we rise from our comfort zones though with difficulties, into the world where we share the light of Christ with a hidden strength of hope. Epiphany is God's revelation to all inviting us to sharpen our awareness of today's challenges and missionary urgencies. Our movement

---

[12]   Lumen Gentium, no. 8
[13]   ibid., no. 14.

is outward heading for a greater understanding of what it means to be a church, a people of God.

Whenever we see anybody being treated wrongly, it is implicit on our part to raise our voices and be involved to pass the act of justice and compassion; to share that light of Christ that transforms and takes the risk. This is the legacy of Christ's epiphany that we become caring people, united in him as a world-body in faith and ministry, the mystical body, his church. God bless you.

BAPTISM OF THE LORD[14]

The beginning of Jesus' public ministry

Readings: Is 42:1-4, 6-7; Ps 29:1-2, 3-4, 3, 9-10;
Acts 10:34-38; Lk 3:15-16, 21-22

While preparing to embark on a new promise of tomorrow after the bustling Christmas holidays, we are convinced that in our own way we have spent a good deal of time recapturing the meaning of our tradition with our families, friends and relatives. From the doldrums of our typically non-festive lifestyles, our deeply held conviction about a new springtime of hope or how to be born again emerges in one of the most important epiphanies of God—Jesus' baptism.

Year after year we celebrate the significance of Jesus' Baptism in the Jordan River[15]. If we recall, this is the same

---

[14]   cf. Catechism of the Catholic Church §1223—All the Old Covenant prefigurations find their fulfillment in Christ Jesus. He begins his public life after having himself baptized by Saint John the Baptist in the Jordan. After His resurrection Christ gives this mission to His apostles: "Go therefore and make disciples of all nations, baptizing them in the name of the Father and of the Son and of the Holy Spirit, teaching them to observe all that I have commanded you." §1224— Our Lord voluntarily submitted Himself to the baptism of Saint John, intended for sinners, in order to "fulfill all righteousness". Jesus' gesture is a manifestation of His self-emptying. The Spirit who had hovered over the waters of the first creation descended then on the Christ as a prelude of the new creation, and the Father revealed Jesus as His "beloved Son."

[15]   cf. Wikipedia, free encyclopedia online. The Jordan River (American English) or River Jordan (British English) is a river in Southwest Asia which flows into the Dead Sea. It is considered to be one of the world's most sacred rivers. In Jewish tradition, the river serves as a border of the "Promised Land." Jesus was baptized here by John the Baptist. The Jordan River is 252 kilometres (156 miles) long. In the Hebrew Bible the Jordan is referred to as the source of fertility

site where Elijah was last seen before he was taken up to heaven. 'He and Elisha, who was to succeed him as prophet, went on their way from Gilgal to the River Jordan.[16] And as they still went on, suddenly there appeared in the air a chariot of fire, with horses of fire, which, parting the two asunder, carried up Elijah in a whirlwind to heaven.'[17]

Liturgically, with this event we conclude the Christmas season, though it may continue on in spirit until Candlemas when we recall Mary's post-birth purification and Jesus' presentation in the Temple. After seventeen days to be exact we have celebrated the Infant Jesus. Now we celebrate Jesus as an adult in his decisive moment that marks the beginning of his public ministry, a change of direction in his life with a mission to fulfill: to redeem us from our sins and to restore us through his gift of eternal life.

---

to a large plain (Kikkar ha-Yarden), and it is said to be like "the garden of God" (Gen 13:100. There is no regular description of the Jordan in the Bible; only scattered and indefinite references to it are given. Jacob crossed it and its tributary, the Jabbok (the modern Al-Zarqa), in order to reach Haran (Gen 32:11, 32:23-24). It is noted as the line of demarcation between the "two tribes and the half tribe" settled to the east (Numbers 34:15) and the "nine tribes and the half tribe of Manasseh" that, led by Joshua, settled to the west (Joshua 13:7, passim). In biblical history, the Jordan appears as the scene of several miracles, the first taking place when the Jordan, near Jericho, was crossed by the Israelites under Joshua (Joshua 3:15-17). Later the two tribes and the half tribe that settled east of the Jordan built a large altar on its banks as "a witness" between them and the other tribes (Joshua 22:10, 22:26, et seq). The Jordan was crossed by Elijah and Elisha on dry ground (2 Kings 2:8, 2:14). Elisha performed two other miracles at the Jordan: he healed Naaman by having him bathe in its waters, and he made the axe head of one of the "children of the prophets" float, by throwing a piece of wood into the water (2 Kings 5:14; 6:6).

[16]   2 Kgs 2:7-8.
[17]   2 Kgs 2:11

With the prophetic call-vision of the theophany narratives in the feast of Pentecost, we recall the revelation of the Blessed Trinity. In the feast of the Transfiguration that took place on Mt Tabor, there is also an epiphany about the revelation of the Holy Trinity when Christ's divinity was evident in his resplendent light, when the bright cloud overshadowed him, and when the words of God the Father echoed what was heard at the Baptism of Jesus. The Father speaks declaring Jesus, the Son of God, and the Holy Spirit descends on Jesus in the form of a dove. It is a revelation that heaven is forever "opened to all humanity through the flesh of Christ by the Spirit of Christ."[18]

Jesus' Baptism in the Jordan[19] points ahead to what is in store for him—his baptism into death when he is going to be crucified on the cross. It has a close link between his death and resurrection. And as a consequence of his public ministry, i.e. his bloody baptism on the cross, Jesus becomes the new Passover Lamb of the New Covenant who shed his blood for us to redeem us from our sins. In the Jewish rituals, the Passover lambs were slaughtered in remembrance of the first Passover lambs whose blood was smeared on the

---

[18] Arthur A. Just, Jr. 1996. *Luke 1:1-9:50*, Concordia Commentary. St Louis: Concordia.

[19] cf. Wikipedia, free encyclopedia online. Jesus came to be baptized by John the Baptist (Matt 3:13; Mk 1:9; Lk 3:21, 4:1). The Jordan is also where John the Baptist bore record of Jesus as the Son of God and Lamb of God (Jn 1:29-36). The prophecy of Isaiah regarding the Messiah which names the Jordan (Isaiah 9:1-2) is recounted in Matthew. The NT speaks several times about Jesus crossing the Jordan during his ministry (Matthew 19:1; Mark 10:1), and of believers crossing the Jordan to come hear him preach and to be healed of their diseases (Matthew 4:25; Mark 3:7-8). When his enemies sought to capture him, Jesus took refuge at Jordan in the place John had first baptized (John 10:39-40).

doorposts the last night the Hebrews spent in Egypt to protect them from death.

Now as we commemorate the Baptism of Jesus, we also remember our own baptism. Different cultures have their own stories to tell about the rites of baptism; they have a variety of ways to do it and how they respond to the wisdom of their own customs and traditions. Like infants of believing parents, they deserve the sacrament of baptism because on the basis of God's covenant, any child of believing parents is a child of his covenant.[20]

It also reminds me of some superstitions connected with the rites of baptism. In other countries like Asia, South America and Africa, for instance, baptism is usually associated with a big reception where everybody will surely be served with rice. Hence, we can extract from that acronym of *rice* as follows: **R** stands for rebirth; **I** stands for initiation; **C** stands for consecration; and **E** stands for empowerment. [21]

Our whole life is a continuing process of baptismal life which calls us to live in the mission of Christ day by day. Every day is our baptismal covenant of sharing in the new life we receive from Jesus' death and resurrection. Following this our whole identity as Christians flows out of this Baptism of Jesus by John in the Jordan River.[22] We become united with Christ in his death and resurrection. It reminds us as Christians that we have to be men and women

---

[20] If the parents are believers, then their infant children are included in the covenant, and therefore they are to receive the sign of covenant relationship.

[21] www.homilies of Fr Munachi Ezeogu, cssp. Homily for Baptism of the Lord. The RICE for Baptism.

[22] David H. Petersen, sermon on the Baptism of our Lord, Matt 3:13-17, Jan. 11, 2004 (http://redeemer-fortwayne.org/displaySermon. php?Sermon=195)

of faith who constantly repent from our human weaknesses, faithful to the gospel values and empowered by the Holy Spirit. We belong to Christ. He loves us to the core; his gifts and blessings are freely given without strings.

When we receive the sacrament of Baptism we are called to live in a new way—to give an abiding witness to our neighbors. We are called to live by example and word with our family members or in the community. It thus connects us to something larger in context, i.e. moving away from our own selves to loving others through our attitude of service. In this case, we are interconnected and we are part of one web.

St Paul tells us that when we were baptized we spiritually entered the tomb with Jesus to leave a life of sin behind. When we were baptized we buried sin by spiritually entering the tomb with Jesus and we rose again with the new life of Jesus as Jesus rose to new life out of a tomb.[23] On the other hand, Luther writes in his Catechism: "To be baptized in God's name is to be baptized not by men but by God himself. Although it is performed by men's hands, it is nevertheless truly God's own act."[24]

Over the years in the ministry, I have spent a good deal of time reflecting on baptisms I have performed within the worship of the people of God—the Christian community. Infant baptisms, for instance, have enriched my spiritual foundation to share with others the gospel values in a way that is within their level, within their own experience as believers in faith. God's message about his redeeming love in the person of Christ has given me the opportunity to claim that we are a covenant community of God that is shaped by

---

[23]   cf. Rom 6:3-4.
[24]   Luther's Small Catechism. 1986. St Louis: Concordia. IV:10 (Tappert).

his promises that he is our God and we are his people. As it says in the first reading: ". . . I formed you, and set you as a covenant of the people, a light for the nations . . ." (Is 42:1-4, 6-7) God bless you.

ORDINARY TIME

Ordinary Time is a season of the Christian liturgical calendar. The name corresponds to the Latin term *Tempus per annum or "Tempus Annum"*, literally "time through the year". The Latin word *ordinalis*, which refers to numbers in a series, derives from the Latin word *ordo*, from which we get the English word order. Hence, Ordinary Time means the ordered life of the Church. It does not mean common or plain but is derived from the term ordinal or "numbered" since the Sundays of Ordinary Time are expressed numerically. It was used before the Second Vatican Council, but it was not until the council[25] that the term was officially applied to designate the period between Epiphany and Lent, and between Pentecost and Advent.

According to the General Norms for the Liturgical Year and the Calendar, the days of Ordinary Time, especially the Sundays, "are devoted to the mystery of Christ in all its aspects." They help us to meditate on the marvelous works

---

[25] It is the feature of the post-Vatican II liturgical calendar, before the start of the liturgical year of 1969, what is now known as Ordinary Time.

of God through the historical Jesus. It is an opportunity to grow in faith in response to God's invitation to follow his footsteps.

Ordinary Time comprises the two periods—one following Epiphany, the other following Pentecost—which do not fall under the "strong seasons" of Advent, Christmas, Lent, or Easter.[26] It is divided into two parts: the first and shorter part is between the end of the Christmas Season and the beginning of Lent; the second and longer part stretches between the end of the Easter Season and the start of Advent.

There are usually thirty-four Sundays. There is no "First Sunday of Ordinary Time" because of the celebration of the Baptism of the Lord. The last Sunday is the solemnity of Christ the King. In the United States, however, the first period begins after the Masses have been said on the evening of the Feast of the Baptism of the Lord (the Sunday after The Epiphany), meaning that the feast itself falls within Christmastide but the whole day does not.[27]

Ordinary Time denotes the "periods of the liturgical year which lie outside the principal seasons, a shorter span from the end of the Christmas or Epiphany season to the beginning of Lent and a considerably longer one from Pentecost to the beginning of Lent.[28] Sundays are described as the foundation of the Christian Year, the bedrock of the liturgical calendar. On them are built the special days and seasons that shape the liturgical pilgrimage of God's people.[29]

---

[26]   cf. http://en.wikipedia.org/wiki/Ordinary_Time
[27]   cf. ChurchYear.net (online) page written by David Bennett.
[28]   The New SCM Dictionary of Liturgy and Worship. Edited by Paul F. Bradshaw. SCM Press. 2002. p 342
[29]   Stake, Donald Wilson. *The ABC of Worship.* Louisville, KY: Westminster/John Knox Press, 1992. p 135.

Ordinary Time continues until Ash Wednesday, which marks the beginning of the Season of Lent. For Roman Catholics the period of Ordinary Time between Christmas and Lent may last from four to nine weeks, depending upon the dates of Epiphany (American Catholics) and Ash Wednesday. In the Roman Catholic Church, the actual number of weeks of Ordinary Time in any given year can total 33 or 34. In a year with only 33 weeks in Ordinary Time, if the Sunday before Ash Wednesday were the 6th Sunday in Ordinary Time, the day after Pentecost Sunday would begin the 8th Week in Ordinary Time.

Green is the liturgical color of Ordinary Time, a symbol for hope and the most ordinary color in our natural surrounding. Unlike in the other seasons of the liturgical year, funeral services are permitted on Sundays during Ordinary Time in the Catholic Church. Readings concentrate on sections of the Bible not read during other seasons. Themes on discipleship, the kingdom of God, or mission of the church in the world, usually focus their biblical connections to certain aspects of faith and the life experiences of the people.

The symbol for Ordinary Time is *Chi Rho* which dates from the early church. It is comprised of the first two letters of the Greek word for Messiah, *Christos*—the letter Chi looks like the letter "X," and the letter Rho looks like the letter "P". This symbol represents the Son of God, Jesus Christ.

SECOND SUNDAY IN ORDINARY TIME

Readings: Is 62:1-5; Ps 96:1-3, 7-10; 1 Cor 12:4-11; Jn 2:1-11

The Wedding at Cana[30]

There's a saying, "a traveler without observation is a bird without wings." I think it makes sense because one may learn something out of curiosity that could be interesting and significant. A traveler is not only confined to sightseeing; it is more than that, especially if he takes a chunk of time off from his busy schedule to live or interact with the locals and then reflect on their culture, history, their customs and traditions. It may generate a challenge to build bridges of opportunities but worth experiencing.

As a novice I remember when I was invited by my Italian teacher to visit their old house in the countryside where I had

---

[30]   Kay, Prag. *Blue Guide Israel and Palestinian Territories*. First Edition. pp 342-43. (Hebrew qanah "reed") appears in the gospel of John on three separate occasions, and each time it is followed by "of Galilee," to distinguish it from another Cana (NIV Kanah) on the border of Phoenicia, now Lebanon (see Joshua 19:23). It was at Cana of Galilee that Jesus performed his first recorded public miracle by changing water into wine at a wedding feast (John 2:1-11). Cana means "place of reeds" and that nearby are marshy stretches where reeds still abound, the name is entirely appropriate and the identification of the site with biblical Cana is certainly possible. (modern name kafr kanna; also known as Khirbet Cana) is a Galilean town 5 miles northeast of Nazareth. Its population of 8,500 includes Muslims and Christians. Following the destruction of Jerusalem by the Romans, the Eliashib family of priests settled at Cana. The Jerusalem Talmud mentions Cana as the origin of a famous 3rd century AD robber, Eli of Cana. The tradition of Jesus changing water to wine at this site may have continued when a Byzantine pilgrim church called the Church of the Master of the Feast was apparently located here. Ancient walls, pottery, glass and other artifacts litter the site.

the opportunity to adhere to the old tradition of crushing grapes by foot in granite *lagares* to make wine. With that we kept the temperature controlled for good fermentation. It was a big deal in the community as everybody drinks it during meals. For most Europeans and in Judaism wine was an essential part of the meal; part of their cuisine. In the current renaissance of wine culture, here in the U.S., for instance, attention to every taste, vintage or classification of wine has become a signifier of seriousness in quality of product.

What took place in the wedding banquet at Cana in today's gospel enables us to think about the creation of wine. This is the first miracle that Jesus did and his second appearance of glory fulfilled in the third moment where his disciples believed in him. And along this line, this episode has been an inspiration for so many writers, preachers, artists and poets.

Relying upon his first sign, Jesus' demonstration of power can be viewed from different emphases and meanings. Some biblical scholars identify the miracle as an act of caring for the needs of others especially at that moment of embarrassment when the wedding hosts ran out of wine. Wine in the bible is a gift of God that "gladdens the heart of man" (Ps 104:15). Jesus is not detached from the world where he is and this makes us think that he is people oriented. He is not an ascetic who lives a retired life in the desert like that of John the Baptist or the Essenes. Some of them say that this is a biblical thought on marriage[31] as one perspective in dialogue with today's context. While others say that it is a sign that the messianic age has come with the water of Old Law and that is now transformed into the new wine or "new

---

[31]   Gn 2:24; Matt 19:4-6

skins." In this case, it emphasizes that there is the need for a change of perspective about the Old Law.

However, if we look at the NT, allusions to wine have both positive and negative meaning. For instance, John the Baptist vowed not to drink wine as a sign of his mission being the last prophet in the OT tradition. While he was on the cross Jesus did not take wine because of his commitment to experience completely the so-called "cup of suffering." But in his public ministry while dealing with people like in today's gospel episode, he uses wine to introduce his teaching; his pedagogy about the gift of a new covenant—its symbolic content that has a deeper significance in the mystery of salvation, our redemption.

Perhaps some of us may have certain parts in the gospel that we want to highlight because of a significant connection to their relationship with their parents. For instance, how a son or daughter behaves towards their parents can be gleaned with relevance. I refer in particular to Mary's dialogue with her Son Jesus when she asks him to do something since the wedding hosts have run out of wine for their guests. Her immediate concern is to spare the young couple from embarrassment. At first though, Jesus seems to reject her request since his 'hour' has not yet come. But this gives us a further reflection on what is going to be revealed later on. Mary, being addressed as woman, brings us back to the first revelation when Adam and Eve were driven out from the Garden of Eden. That statement 'when that hour comes' refers to Jesus' death and resurrection—his glorious conquest of sin and death. There we see the role of Mary as our maternal intercessor who will always be the "woman" which means the 'mother of all the living, 'the new Eve of humanity.'

Through the centuries Jesus' first miracle in Cana reminds us that our faith must still grow to enable us to trust in him like what Mary did when she told the servants, 'do whatever he tells you.' It is interesting to know how that faith of his disciples has changed their relationship to their Master. It has become deeper and reflective of a new dawn of discipleship.

We may highlight the proof of this historical event as Jesus' first sign in the wedding at Cana. What remains is not the turning of water into wine which was consumed, but the faith of the disciples being rekindled with that encounter with Jesus. They have come to know who their Master really is to them. This is the main issue that makes a huge difference in the dawning of faith in Jesus. That experience of a Jewish rural wedding enables the disciples to connect those realities or revelations about their Master as an inspiration for keeping themselves aligned with Jesus' path—growth of faith in him.

At times we have difficulty to connect the dots and understand what the will of God is. With the recent catastrophic earthquake that struck Haiti, what message does it tell us? From today's perspective, this mass destruction is a worldwide concern that allows our faith to be strong and compassionate. As a nation we have a special responsibility to help our neighbor. It is implicit in our identity as Christians. What matters now is our action and prayer with faith that is tested in fire. To some people they ask: Is it a sign that the end of the world is near? Is it a confirmation of Christian prophecy that "God's instrument to shake us is to make us realize that we need conversion?

As St Paul puts it, it is the "twinkling of an eye"[32]—that a calamity might prove to be the longed-for transformation.[33] Like water that is transformed into wine, our sense of being the church of the poor will transform us to be real men and women committed to our Christian faith. God bless you.

---

[32] cf. 1 Cor 15:15. "Behold, I show you a mystery. Listen, I'm about to unveil a secret. I'm about to tell you something you never knew before. It is this, we shall not all sleep, but we shall all be changed. In a moment, in the twinkling of an eye, at the last trump, for the trump shall sound, and the dead shall be raised incorruptible and we shall be changed."

[33] Denis Dutton. *It's Always the End of the World as We Know It*. The New York Times. Vol. CLIX., No. 59, 907. Jan. 1, 2010. p A29.

THIRD SUNDAY IN ORDINARY TIME

Readings: **Neh** 8:2-4a, 5-6, 8-10; **Ps** 19_8-10, 15;
1 Cor 12:30; **Lk** 1:1-4; 4:14-21

Jesus' Saving Mission

*"The spirit of the Lord is upon me, because he has anointed me
to bring glad tidings to the poor. He has sent me to proclaim
liberty to captives and recovery of sight to the blind, to let the
oppressed go free, and to proclaim a year acceptable to the Lord."*

Over the years we have seen the United States and other
countries around the world doing their best to bring out
creative responses and initiatives as humanitarian efforts
to those nations afflicted with devastations. The aftermath
of a recent disaster, for instance, a major earthquake with a
magnitude of 7.0 that ravaged Haiti 10 miles from the capital
of Port-au-Prince, shifted our global focus to helping those
who are in need. Thousands of people have died and millions
need food, water, medicine and shelter. Government is in
ruins and the country's urban landscapes are shattered.

We may also recall the Oklahoma City bombings, 9/11,
Indian Ocean tsunami in South Asia, and hurricane Katrina.
All of these have provided us the opportunities to show our
unity and compassion to others. This has also defined our
nation that has been committed to helping others across the
globe.

In the darkest of moments as we walk now with the
Haitian people in their sufferings, the prophetic words of
Isaiah that Jesus read in the synagogue on the Sabbath day
may also be directed to us—to those who are victims of
disasters, oppressions and slavery. The Haitians, for instance,

who are now facing a set of challenges to rebuild their nation, have to turn stark devastation into the beginning of a new recovery.

"The spirit of the Lord is upon me, because the Lord has anointed me; because he has anointed me to bring glad tidings to the poor . . ." This is a passage of restoration profoundly rooted to the life and ministry of Jesus which defines his main goal as the Anointed One. And he sets the tone for being ready to fulfill his Messianic agenda or being called to his mission, i.e. to embrace the challenge of crucifixion, death and eventually his resurrection.

Isaiah, however, in his time when the Jews returned to Jerusalem from forced exile in the land of Babylon was commissioned to address his people who were devastated by the ruins of their city. He was commissioned to proclaim a message of hope to move on in spite of difficulties. It was indeed a tough time and a test of faith for them.

At the time of Jesus, the thorny issue was how to restore their Jewish freedom in their own lands under the oppressive government of the Roman Empire. Jews had a quest for freedom and inalienable rights of life. And Jesus pointed this passage, 'to bring good news to the poor . . . to release the captives, recovery of sight to the blind and to let the oppressed go free . . .' remind us of the non-Jewish widow from Zarepath in Sidon to whom the prophet Elijah was sent and to the non-Jewish leper named Naaman, the Syrian, whom Elisha healed. These are people who did not flow in the mainstream. They were poor, blind, and oppressed. Jesus applied it to the expansion of God's outreach to the Gentiles, to the non-Jews.

We see the radical meaning of this passage with the awe-inspiring power of the Holy Spirit that came upon Jesus being anointed and commissioned to bring good news to the poor. In the OT, however, anointing could be classified into three areas: 1). Anointing of the priests;[34] 2). Anointing of the kings;[35] 3). Anointing of the prophets.[36] And Jesus in this sense was anointed as a priest,[37] prophet, and king. On the other hand, according to the Jewish exegesis, allusions to the Spirit of the Messiah can be traced back from the OT when the Spirit came over chaos and brought order to the whole creation (Gen 1:2). In the NT, for instance, Luke says that the Holy Spirit came upon Mary and that the power of the Most High 'overshadowed her to give birth to an anointed child (Lk 1:35), whose name would be Jesus. His birth was the work of the Holy Spirit.

With our sense of restoration that has the potential to shape us from within, there is an implicit role to play on our part being commissioned to preach the good news of salvation. The ongoing conversation between faith and culture leads to restoring our relationship in light of

---

[34] cf. Lev 8:12. "And he poured of the anointing oil upon Aaron's head, and anointed him, to sanctify him." It took place once for every priest.

[35] cf. 1 Sam 16:13. "Then Samuel took the horn of oil, and anointed him in the midst of his brethren: and the Spirit of the Lord came upon David from that day forward. So Samuel rose up, and went to Ramah." This anointing happened once as a one-time religious ritual.

[36] cf. 1 Kgs 19:16. "And Jehu the son of Nimshi shalt thou anoint to be king over Israel: and Elisha the son of Shaphat of Abelmeholah shalt thou anoint to be prophet in thy room." Time and again, it happened once for each prophet.

[37] cf. Osborne, Kenan. 1988. *Priesthood.* New York: Paulist Press. In Hebrew, *'kohen'* is a person charged with religious functions. The term is derived from the Akkadian Kanu—"*bowing*" and *kun*—"to stand up." In Greek, the same person becomes *hiereus* from *hieros*—"sacred" (*sacerdos* in Latin). In the NT, the chief priests are called *archiereis* applied solely to Jewish priesthood. Today's priest comes from the Greek *presbyteros* "elder."

the gospel. Its vision evokes God's kingdom which is the central message of Jesus in the context of transformation of all human structures in favor of justice and the rights of the poor. The onslaught of cultural imperialism from outside, those pockets of violence and anarchy, slavery and invasion of foreign armies, and many others remind us that as a church we have a mission to fulfill, to restore peace and harmony in today's world.

In this case I am drawn to think of the 'priesthood of Jesus'[38] that we share with him as Christians. As developed with deep significance in the Letter to the Hebrews,[39] Jesus' priesthood is by virtue of being the Incarnate Son of God;

---

[38] James Mohler. 1970. *The Origin and Evolution of the Priesthood*. New York: Alba House. Biblical scholars claim that Jesus does not claim to be a priest because of the following reasons: 1). In Jesus' milieu, the title "priest" designates a definite function reserved to the members of the tribe of Levi. The Levitical priesthood is hereditary. Unlike John the Baptist, the son of the Aaronite priest Zechariah, Jesus is not from a priestly family. He is of the House of David belonging to the tribe of Judah. 2). Jesus desires not to reduce the disclosure of his personal identity to a linguistic transaction (cf Messianic Secret). He intends to leave the task of verbalizing what his disciples are able to grasp and what they believe in regard to his person and mission. 3). Jesus wants the title to be understood in the higher sense than the current understanding among the Jews.

[39] cf. Galot, Jean. 1984. *Theology of the Priesthood*. San Francisco, California: Ignatius Press. The exposition of the theme on "priesthood" can be found from Heb 4:14-10:18. The author sees Christ as the inaugurator of a new type of priesthood, not associated with Levi nor with Aaron but with Melchizedek. It is only in Hebrew that the term "priest" is applied to Christ. And its main teaching is that, true priesthood can only be found in Christ. That before Christ, the Jewish priesthood is but a shadow, a figure with no self-contained value. It is only in Christ that we can discover the genuine significance of the priesthood. In Heb 5:11, we are given a description that priests are appointed for people in things pertaining to God or acting on behalf of them in relation to God. In other words, he represents the people to God. And this essential idea of priesthood

it is linked to the mystery of redemption; it is because he brings a new covenant and he is our mediator (Heb 9:15; 8:6). In Heb 5:10 Jesus is considered as "high priest according to the order of Melchizedek. He is not a priest by reason of any of the OT Levitical or Aaronic family lineage of priesthood. His priesthood is not Jewish. Just as new wine is poured into new wine skin, Jesus refrains from letting his priesthood be poured into an old concept. To highlight this idea are examples in the gospel, e.g. the Parable of the Good Samaritan and the Cleansing of the Temple. In the parable there is a proof against the Jewish priest who fails to show to a wounded neighbor the love which he is supposed to manifest. In the Cleansing of the Temple, however, there is a symbolic attack against powers from those who profit for themselves, not the genuine service of God. Moreover, his priesthood is not even in the origin—for Melchizedek is a strange figure in Gen. 14:17-20; he has no origins, he is like the Son of God. He remains a priest forever (Heb 7:3). Hence the presentation of Melchizedek tells us that Jesus Christ is a priest from all eternity—having no beginning or end.

Our participation in the redemptive suffering of our brothers and sisters is the universal and ministerial priesthood[40] that we share with Jesus. Like him we are commissioned to live the life of service and be willing to sacrifice for the sake of the gospel—for the sake of restoring our relationship with God and one another. God bless you.

---

as a representative of man to God carries with it the right of access and of abiding in the presence of God.

[40] cf. Letter of Peter (1 Pt 2:5; 1 Pt 2:9), Paul's letter to the Romans (Rm 12:4) and in the Book of Revelation (1:5-6; 5:10; 20:6).

FOURTH SUNDAY IN ORDINARY TIME

Readings: Jer 1:4-5, 17-19; Ps 71:1-2, 3-4, 5-6, 15, 17: 1
Cor 12:31-13:13; Lk 4:21-30

The Cost of Being Called to Serve—a journey

The word of the Lord came to me, saying: "Before I formed
you in the womb I knew you, before you were born I
dedicated you, a prophet to the nations I appointed you."

When I first started my ministry as a missionary I braved the difficulties in coming to terms with culture, climate, food, and the like of foreign lands. Living in a community was another test that made me aware of my vulnerability being human and of the need to work together or help one another especially in times of need.

There's a saying that goes, 'for people of faith nothing happens by coincidence.' I think it makes sense when we look at our own experiences, our journey through memory lane, and our frequent references to what God has done for us especially when we struggle to achieve our goals or to decide which direction in life we should follow. In my mind though, there is the panoply of voices that tells me there are challenges to be addressed. They are meant to strengthen us and to realign us to the foundational gift of service. After all, this is our calling in whatever context or state of life we may have; we are all called to serve.

Jeremiah's prophetic call in the first reading allows us to reflect that God knows each of us. He knows our strengths and weaknesses, our abilities and limitations. As it says: "Before I formed you in the womb I knew you, before you were born, I dedicated you, a prophet to the nations I appointed you." Evidently, before Jeremiah was born, God had already a plan for him; he was called to a mission, i.e. as a prophet he was going to minister to the people of Judah and the other ancient Near Eastern nations during the time of crisis in Judah's history—the last days of monarchy and the early part of captivity. During his lifetime he saw the sufferings of his own people when Judah was held captive after her defeat under the armies of Babylon. He also witnessed the prophecies fulfilled with the destruction of Jerusalem.

Jeremiah challenged them to trust God and to repent from their sins. They had forsaken Yahweh and had worshipped pagan idols. He was faithful enough to warn them of God's judgment on Judah. He was almost on the brink of giving up as a prophet because they did not want to listen to him. He said, "Alas, Lord God! Behold, I do not know how to speak because I am a youth" (Jer 1:6). Like many other prophets of the OT they were not at all willing to submit to God as prophets. We recall Moses, for instance, when he confessed openly that he was not an eloquent speaker. He did not have that off-the-cuff style in public spotlight, so to speak. Isaiah, too, said that he was a man of unclean lips. Hence, he was not meant for that job. Jonah, too, as we all know ran away to avoid God's instruction to go to Nineveh. But God called him to preach to Ninevites.

It is interesting to imagine how these prophets made headway in their valiant efforts to assure their own people that God had a future for Israel and Judah. And they had to know that God remembers his covenant with Israel even when Israel, repeatedly, has rebelled against it.[41]

---

[41]   cf. Edited by Carolyn Osiek and Donald Senior. 1988. *Scripture and Prayer*. Michael Glazier, Inc. Wilmington, Delaware. (Frederick C. Holmgren. *Remember Me; Remember The*). pp 37-38

According to some scholars, Jeremiah's ministry as a prophet may have extended over 40 years.[42] His active ministry during the reigns of three Judean kings was filled with turbulence and opposition. He was branded and identified as a traitor by King Manasseh, Judah's most ungodly king (2 Chron 33:15-19), King Jehoiakim, the oldest son of King Josiah, who refused to follow his advice to accept the Babylonian rule. Hence he rebelled against Babylon in 601 B.C. Which is why, King Nebuchadnezzar attacked Jerusalem and occupied the whole city's population. Zedekiah, the youngest brother of Jehoahaz and Jehoiakim was captured by the Babylonians due to his rebellion against Nebuchadnezzar.

Reading Jeremiah's background—his life and ministry as prophet we see that he is the only prophet who has those remarkable similarities to the life and ministry of Jesus. He is the most Christ-like among the prophets of old. Both of them had a message for their own people; for Israel and the whole humanity. Both of them were so compassionate and loving that some Jewish scribes and Pharisees identified them with the Suffering Servant of Isaiah 53. Both endured the storms of contradictions as they stood against the barrage of attacks by the Jewish leaders. Both experienced condemnations, charged by their enemies with political treason and were

---

[42] Quoted from Dr. Constable's Notes on Jeremiah. Several reliable scholars believed that Jeremiah's ministry ended about 587 B.C. or a little later. See, for example, Peter C. Craigie, *Jeremiah 1-25*, p. xiv; Merrill, p. 467; and Thompson, p. 116. Charles H. Dyer, "Jeremiah," in *The Bible Knowledge Commentary: Old Testament*, p. 1123; and Leon J. Wood, *The Prophets of Israel*, p. 330, believed it continued to about 580 B.C. Craigie, by the way, wrote only the commentary on 1:1-8:3 and the Introduction in this volume. Dyer usually provided good explanations of time references that occur throughout Jeremiah.

eventually persecuted. Both of them prophesied the destruction of the temple (Jer 7:14; Mk 13:2). Both made use of human situations at the grassroots level using nature or figurative language to illustrate their purpose and relevance in their teaching. Both came from a high tradition: Jeremiah from a priestly and prophetic family whose father Hilkiah may have been the high priest who found the book of the Law in the temple during Josiah's reforms (2 Kgs 22:8-10)[43] and Jesus from a divine, royal background, lineage of David from the stump of Jessé. They both wept over Jerusalem (Jer 9:1; Lk 19:41), denounced those priests of their time, and went against the practice of commercialism in temple worship. They both experienced rejection by members of their own families (Jer 12:6; Jn 1:11).

While we bring to light our mission as committed Christians we share with others the common vision as living testimonies of God's word. We may not be accepted or welcomed by others for some reasons but we don't stop there. We keep going, keep in the race until we see what hope holds for us as we allow ourselves to be shaped by the wisdom of our experiences. Our journey may take a long litany of ups and downs with some scars and blisters, but let us continue to grow in appreciation for the wonder and mystery of God entering into our human conditions.

This time that so many around the world have been burdened by the massive catastrophe in Haiti, endless wars and tragedies like in Afghanistan, Syria, Baghdad and Yemen, we have all the reason to immerse ourselves in the same vision of connectedness where we live and the places we work. There are different seasons and yet there is for us

---

[43]   Roland Kenneth Harrison. 1969. *Introduction to the Old Testament.* William B. Eerdsmans Publishing Company. p 802.

all a process of letting go and taking on new things that life brings to us.

We have weathered many challenges that shaped our lives, our mission; and with the evolving character of our faith we come to grips with John Henry Newman's dictum that says: to live is to change and to be perfect is to have changed often. God bless you.

FIFTH SUNDAY IN ORDINARY TIME

Readings: Is 6:1-2a, 3-8; Ps 138:1-5, 7-8; 1 Cor 15:1-11; Lk 5:1-11[44]

Men and Women of Discipleship—A Biblical Perspective

Jesus said to Simon,
"Do not be afraid; from now on you will be catching men."

After four weeks when the eyes of the world turned to the Haitian people mourning the death of their loved ones and massive devastation in the capital city of Port-au-Prince caused by the earthquake, perhaps it is worth reflecting the words of St Benedict that he wrote at the beginning of his Rule of Life: "Listen, my son, to the precepts of the Master." In our prayer we bring before God the challenges that brace us for a concerted effort about going forward and re-living those experiences of compassion and care.

Listening to one another and watching those who struggle to survive or make ends meet, for instance, strengthen us to discover the spirituality of being on a pilgrimage of faith and being called to live our vocation as members of Christ's Body—his Church. We may come from different backgrounds and cultures with a myriad of priorities, goals,

---

[44] Scholars are divided over whether this incident is identical with Jesus' call of these fishermen as recorded in Matthew 4:18-22 and Mark 1:16-20. John 1:35-42 records the first meeting between Jesus and Peter. The incident here takes place about one year later. James and John, and perhaps some others, such as Peter's brother, Andrew (perhaps), were present, but the focus here is on Jesus and Peter. These men had already an encounter with Jesus and had started following him, but they were not yet completely committed to his mission and ministry. This incident realigned their focus and priority as called to serve.

skills and talents to, but our vision of connectedness reminds us always that we belong to one God, to one faith.

It is in today's gospel that Jesus tells his first disciples who were fishermen by profession that after having experienced the miracle of catching a multitude of fish, they will now be transformed to fishers of men. They become followers of Jesus who will challenge them to have a shift in focus where they will catch people for his purpose and be living witnesses for his mission.

The mission and ministry of Jesus always points to the vision of the kingdom of God. It is the truth of the gospel; God's word to us through his faithful witnesses. And his purpose involves taking simple people like these fishermen and turning them into his disciples for catching other people for God. This includes those who are lost, led astray and in the darkness of hunger, violence, homelessness, or fear.

In this episode we see that Peter gets more focus compared to James and John, and perhaps some others, such as Peter's brother, Andrew though he is unnamed in the story. It is probably because Peter will soon become the leader of faith community of the foundation stone of the Christian church (Matt 16:18). We see that Peter gets almost more fish than he could imagine for instance, on Pentecost as he preaches to 3,000 followers trusting in Christ. Then on another incident while he preaches at the house of Cornelius, before he finishes his sermon, the whole people in attendance respond positively. While we may think that not every Christian can be a potential preacher, nevertheless each one of us is a witness. We are called to be living witnesses to the Gospel. And we are always invited to reconnect with the Christian community to tell us that we are not in isolation; that we are always in the context of a community as Jesus himself emphasizes whenever he performs a miracle or preaches the kingdom of God.

One of the good qualities of Simon Peter that I see in this context is his sense of obedience. He obeys Jesus' command when he tells him put out into the deep water and let down the nets. This is important in the moral transformation that the gospel brings—purification of our hearts and our lives. Isaiah, in the first reading (6:1-2a, 3-8), says: "Woe is me, I am doomed! For I am a man of unclean lips living among a people of unclean lips . . . Here I am," I said; "send me!" Even Paul, for instance, in Rom 1:5 speaks of the Lord having given him a commission to "call people from among all the Gentiles to the obedience that comes from faith." According to him, faith produces obedience; obedience follows faith.

We may also recall Abraham, the father of all nations. "By faith Abraham obeyed when he was called to go out to a place which he was to receive as an inheritance; and he went out, not knowing where he was to go" (Heb 11:8). The strength of obedience produces a commitment to love and this is the path that leads us to focus on what is essential in God's teaching—to bear witness of the gospel.

I remember the Episcopal motto of Cardinal Martini of Milan that says: *Pro veritate adversa diligere.* It means that it is necessary to prepare oneself to love the obstacles which we will inevitably meet in the service of truth.[45] The implications of obedience within the flesh and blood of discipleship require each of us to face all forms of human deformities in terms of rejections, individual differences, brickbats and endless criticisms. These are all challenges that we have to face with faith foundation in our priestly or

---

[45] Carlo Cardinal Martini. 1991. *After Some Years—Reflections on the Ministry of the Priest.* Veritas Publications, 7-8 Lower Abbey Street, Dublin 1. ISBN 1 85390 038 9. p 69.

religious calling; in our vocation either as public servants or simply men and women with their family commitments.

Being aware of our own weaknesses and sinfulness makes us rely completely on God. His transforming grace shapes us from within like an inner echo that draws us to follow Christ with our way of life, simple and focused. Perhaps you may ask why Christ chose Simon Peter out of so many potential disciples in those times. Others may ask, too, why we have those leaders with great defiance on certain moral issues. God calls us by his grace. And Christ chose Peter by his divine plan: to become a leader and servant of the faith community—the first NT Church.

At the core of our witnessing in diverse situations through different lifestyles, there lies our priority in Jesus: to be a reflection of the reality that each of us is invited to take part in it—service in God's love and compassion. His word leads us to 'seek first his kingdom and his righteousness; for where our treasure is, there also will our heart be (Matt 6:19, 21). God bless you.

SIXTH SUNDAY IN ORDINARY TIME

Readings: Jer 17:5-8; Ps 1:1-4, 6; 1 Cor 15:12,
16-20; Lk 6:17, 20-26

The Lucan Beatitudes[46]

Many denominations, particularly the Pentecostal and charismatic churches, have the religious belief known as 'prosperity gospel theology'. It is the notion that God provides material prosperity for those he favors.[47] Proponents of this teaching believe that faith has a major role in human prosperity, i.e. the accumulation of wealth for those who trust in God. If one is generous, or godly in his Christian life, he will have the blessings of God in many ways.

While some critics argue that the ultimate goal of prosperity gospel theology leads to quality of life based on material prosperity, Christ, on the other hand, teaches us that we grow in his love and become rich with spiritual things, the values of the kingdom of God.

It is in this context that we read the Beatitudes[48] in today's gospel from a religious or spiritual perspective

---

[46] It originates from the Latin *beatus,* derived from the Hebrew ashre and the Greek makários. In selecting the Greek adjective makários to render the Hebrew ashre, the LXX translators intended to suggest a happiness that flows from justice, or having a right relationship with God.

[47] David Van Biema, Jeff Chu. *Does God want you to be Rich?* Time Magazine. Sept. 10, 2006. The Religion Pages.

[48] Carson, D.A. 1978. *The Expositors Bible Commentary: Matthew.* Grand Rapids Baker House. p 131. If Carson is correct, then makarios does not refer to simple "happiness." Zodhiates would agree: This book will point up the basic difference between the 2 words "blessed" (makarioi in Greek) and happy. To put it briefly here, "blessed refers to the one whose sufficiency is within him,

and from an economic or sociological point of view. They are difficult to take, however, as they possess irony in the spiritual reversal of life situations. Here Jesus speaks to a particular Jewish audience—to his disciples with emphasis upon following God, for those faithful Israelites, and for his disciples. There are also other curious groups of people who may be present listening to him. They want to find out what Jesus may have for them. Actually, his main focus here is not toward economic conditions of his time but rather a result or consequence of what he deeply regrets to convey—the rejection of his teaching and what he claims as the promised Messiah. Which is why, we can say that those who follow Jesus like his disciples, for instance, are the poor ones and those who reject his teachings and oppress those who follow him are the rich ones. The latter are evidently referred to as the religious leaders.

The whole passage with its brevity in the form of Luke's Sermon on the Plain, centers on the theme of conflict, rejection, and persecution. But along with that, there is also the theme of reversal that is pretty much dominant in putting side by side between the rich and poor, the wicked and righteous. Biblical literature is replete with the theme of reversal where there is no empathy to the rich but compassion to the poor. Let's take, for instance, the mission of Isaiah to the afflicted (61:1-3); Ps 37;[49] Ps 41 "Happy is he who has

---

while happy refers to the one whose sufficiency comes from outside sources. Happy comes from the word 'hap' meaning "chance." It is therefore incorrect to translate the word makarioi (which we find repeatedly in the Beatitudes) as happy. It means something far different, in its real sense; it means blessed.

[49] cf. New American Bible. It treats of the problem of evil: why the wicked seem to prosper while the good suffer. The answer of the psalmist is that this seeming injustice is short-lived. God will reward the good and punish the wicked even here on earth.

regard for the lowly and the poor; in the day of misfortune the Lord will deliver him." In the gospel of Luke we also find other incidents that embrace the theme of reversal such as: the Magnificat (1:46-56), in the first shall be last: "And behold, some are last who will be first and some are first who will be last" (13:30; Matt 20:16; Mk 10:31); and the parable of Lazarus and Dives (16:11; 18:14).

We can also recall what Jesus said, "I tell you the truth, it is hard for a rich man to enter the kingdom of heaven. Again I tell you, it is easier for a camel to go through the eye of a needle than for a rich man to enter the kingdom of God" (cf. Lk 18:24-25; Mk 10:24-25; Matt 19:23-24). Following this, Luke's beatitudes reference to rich and poor—'blessed are the poor but woe to you who are rich,'—are metaphorical expressions for those rejected and accepted because of their response to the prophet.[50] Jesus had some confrontation with his contemporary leaders of Judaism (Lk 6:11) and his contrastive language 'woe' refers to this particular group.

Perhaps when our wealth does not allow us to share with others or we consider it as the measure of self worth and success then Jesus could tell us, "woe to you who are rich, for you have received already your consolation."

With the values of the world on our Christian faith, we need to return to our biblical roots. We are called to share in the suffering of Christ by serving the poor, the powerless and the oppressed. This is the character trait of the Beatitudes. We need to cultivate those qualities of discipleship in a variety of contexts that will shape us to be examples of the life of faith.

---

[50]   Luke T. Johnson. 1977. *The Literary Function of Possessions in Luke-Acts*. Missoula: Scholars. p 140.

As we follow the steps with those who are poor, those who live the life of meekness, those whose relationships are exemplary to others, we can learn day-by-day that Christ's path to real happiness involves following his way of wisdom, his way of the cross, like a hidden treasure of the Beatitudes. Humility speaks to us how we are to walk with God and with one another. Which is why, we can say that the beatitudes can be a picture of life, an autobiography of Jesus whose life models what the values of the kingdom mean to us. God bless you.

LENT

According to the General Norms for the Liturgical Year and the Calendar, "Lent is a preparation for the celebration of Easter. For the Lenten liturgy disposes both catechumens and the faithful to celebrate the paschal mystery: catechumens, through the several stages of Christian initiation; the faithful through reminders of their own baptism and through penitential practices" (General Norms 27).

Lent is the Old English word of spring. In almost all other languages, Lent's name is a derivative of the Latin term *quadragesima* or "the forty days." It is the period of fasting, almsgiving, and prayer that leads up to the feast of Easter. It recalls Jesus' forty-day fast in the wilderness. Western Lent begins on Ash Wednesday and ends liturgically on the morning of Holy Thursday although Lenten penance continues through Holy Saturday.

Lent probably originated with the pre-Easter baptismal rituals of catechumens and the number of days set aside for fasting varied according to region. The number forty, hallowed by the fasts of Moses, Elijah, and especially Jesus, probably influenced the later fixed time of 40 days. The

Canons of Nicaea (AD 325) were the first to mention 40 days of fasting.

While Sundays are excluded from the Lenten fasting and abstinence restrictions, and are not numbered in the traditional forty days (40) of Lent, they are still a part of the Lenten season. The purpose of Lent is to be a season of fasting, self denial, Christian growth, penitence, conversion, and simplicity. The book of Daniel states, "In the third year of Cyrus king of Persia . . . 'I, Daniel mourned for three weeks. I ate no choice food; no meat or wine touched my lips; and I used no lotions at all until the three weeks were over" (Dan. 10:1-3). Lent, which comes from the Teutonic word for springtime, can be viewed as a spiritual spring cleaning: a time for taking spiritual inventory and then cleaning out those things which hinder our community and personal relationships with Christ and our service to our brothers and sisters.[51]

The Western Rite of Catholic Church requires its members age 18 and 59 to fast on Ash Wednesday and Good Friday, unless a physical condition prevents otherwise. This means only one full meal is permitted. The Fridays of Lent are days of required abstinence. It means to say meat is not permitted. Abstinence is required of those ages 14 and older.

---

[51]   cf. CatholicYear.net (online) written by David Bennett.

ASH WEDNESDAY

Readings: Joel 2:12-18; Ps 51:3-4, 5-6ab, 12-14
& 17; 2 Cor 5:20-6:2; Matt 6:1-6, 16-18

Our Journey of Conversion

*"Yet even now, says the Lord, return to me with your whole heart,
with fasting, and weeping, and mourning; Rend your hearts,
not your garments, and return to the Lord, your God . . ."*

At no time in memory have we thought of nailing ourselves to
the regimented do's and don'ts of our religion—Catholicism.
Rather we opt to take a journey both inward and outward as
we focus on worship and good works.

Some years past I was asked by a certain lady about my
own opinion regarding the celebration of Ash Wednesday
where there is a ritual for smudging our foreheads with
ashes.[52] I told her that as members of the Body of Christ we
all share the need for continued conversion. Which is why,
our Judeo-Christian values, the greatest gift that we can pass
on to the next generation, keep us faithful in a direction that
leads us all to God—to his kingdom.

Today is the beginning of Lent. It is a time for a
restoration project that deals with relationships to God and
to one another. At the core, it reflects our major turn around
the three main disciplines of the season: giving alms, praying
and fasting.

---

[52]   cf. Jer 6:26; Is 58:5; Dn 9:3; Jdt 4:11; 4:15 & 9:1; 1 Mc 3:47; see also
4:39; Matt 11:21, Lk 10:13 (Gen 3:19: Remember, O man, that you are
dust . . . ; Mk 1:15: Turn away from sin & be faithful to the Gospel;
Mk 1:15: Repent and hear the good news.

This symbolic occasion of wearing that smudge on our foreheads reminds us of our mortality—that we are sons and daughters of God; that we are baptized and that we are called to a conversion journey so that we may grow closer to God through our repentance and renewal.

While we may owe an extraordinary tradition to biblical people both in the Old and New Testaments who have brought us to acts of repentance with these signs of ashes, we are convinced that we are a community of sinners. Hence, we need to return to God so that we become a reflection of what we are called for—to be living witnesses to the gospel values. After all, that's what our religion is all about. It's about cultivating those virtues that shape us from within and nourish the best version of ourselves before God.

FIRST SUNDAY OF LENT

Readings: Dt 26:4-10; Ps 91:1-2, 10-15; Rom 10:8-13; Lk 4:1-13

The Temptations of Jesus

*". . . and was led by the Spirit into the desert for
forty days, to be tempted by the devil."*

Last January 2010 we were swamped with voluminous media coverage of the quake in Haiti and its aftermath. Reports by journalists and commentators gave weight to what the bible says about compassion towards the poor and disadvantaged. But there was one observation that came out as a source of discourses on Haiti's history, religion and destiny. It was the practice of voodoo. It is one of the official religions of Haiti[53] which could be traced back for 2 centuries from their ancestral African faiths. Studies show that 50 to 95 percent of Haitians practice at least elements of voodoo.[54]

Catholicism in Haiti coexists with voodoo where saints are blending with African deities and those who have already died are invoked upon to act as interlocutors between God and humanity. As one author says, Catholicism in Haiti is not like Catholicism in a Polish parish in Chicago or Milwaukee or an Irish one in Boston. Because Catholic faith in Haiti coexists with voodoo and its religious texture, it has this sinister sorcery and diabolical rituals about which we know little.

I am saying this because Jesus in today's gospel allowed himself to coexist with the devil by being tempted when the

---

53 Samuel G. Freedman. *Voodoo, a Comfort in Haiti, Remains Misunderstood.* The New York Times. February 20, 2010. p A14.
54 ibid.

Spirit led him into the desert known as Jeshimon (Matt 4:1-11; Lk 4:1-13; Mk 1:9-13), which means devastation. There he ate nothing for forty days and forty nights. In this case, if we come to think about the two greatest challenges in Scriptures that show the devil in his quest for power, authority, and worldly glory, this is one of them. The other is the temptation of Adam and Eve (Gen 3:1-6). Both were approached by the devil by means of these three categories of temptation: the lust of the flesh (letting the angels save him—fear of death), lust of the eyes (turning stones to bread—material hunger), and the pride of life (to worship the devil).[55] Adam and Eve were persuaded, however, in Jesus' case the devil failed.

I remember one particular narrative poem written in late 14th-century Middle English—Sir Gawain and the Green Knight.[56] It is an important poem in the romance genre because of its sophisticated use of medieval symbolism. Perhaps the term 'romance' implies differently in today's context as we may focus on love relationship and sentiments. But medieval romances should be viewed more on the level of chivalry and heroism where the main character goes on a quest that tests his ability; he takes a journey.

With a Christian understanding and reference to Christ's crown of thorns at the concluding part, the story itself is replete with temptation and testing, drawing parallels between Gawain and Lady Bertilak and the story of Adam and Eve. There is a series of tests and individual's failures,

---

55   cf. 1 Jn 2:16. "For all that is in the world, the lust of the flesh, and the lust of the eyes, and the pride of life, is not of the Father, but is of the world."

56   Stephen Greenblatt (Ed). 2006. *The Norton Anthology of English Literature*. 8th Edition. Vol. B. New York, London: W.W. Norton and Co. 19-21 and 160-161. ISBN 0393928330.

and eventually, Gawain's ability to pass many trials and mistakes testing his devotion and Christian faith.

Like Jesus' journey in his mission to fulfill the will of his Father, he also underwent many tests and trials. One of them is his own experience to be tempted by the devil. His temptation would be rather unique since he was tempted in defiance to his mission that would chain his higher purpose of saving humanity to the devil's deceit and worldly plan. His purpose is to avoid the way of the cross which involves suffering and tribulation, rejection and humiliation.

Perhaps some of us may ask why Jesus being the sinless Son of God was also subject to temptation. This perspective allows us to reflect that his temptation was an attempt to gain a foothold on him, to avoid the cross and as pedagogy of discipleship. It aims to teach his disciples how to resist temptations themselves.

Over the course of his forty days and forty nights in the desert[57] without eating, we could imagine Jesus' hunger. The devil came to him and said, "If you are the Son of God, command this stone to become bread." But Jesus said, "It is written: "One does not live on bread alone." Evidently, it was a temptation for Jesus to use his divine origin as the Son of God which is outside of God's will. But later, he would feed five thousand people with five loaves of bread and two fishes—feeding *others* (Mat 14:19). Just as God gave the Israelites bread from heaven, Jesus was the true bread from heaven (John 6:32-35).

---

[57] The desert is the abode of demons and where Israel was tested for forty years. Forty days is the longest man can fast without permanent injury. He had water (Lk 4:2). The forty days in the desert parallels the forty years wandering in the desert of the Israelites where they ate manna (Ex 16:35) to test you in order to know what was in your heart, whether or not you would keep his commands (Dt 8:2).

Then the second temptation was about authority, power, and worldly glory when the devil took him up and showed him all the kingdoms of the world in a moment of time. This was like a vision. And the devil asked Jesus: "If you worship me, it will all be yours." Jesus answered with Scripture he had learned as a child: "It is written, 'worship the Lord your God and him alone shall you serve." Jesus knew that power was the hard way to glory—the power of the cross and resurrection.

The third temptation was when the devil led him to Jerusalem and told him, "If you are the Son of God, throw yourself down from here and command your angels to catch you." But Jesus answered him, "Do not put the Lord your God to the test" (Dt 6:16). We may call to mind the Israelites forcing God to act when they were thirsty at Massah in the desert. They had tested God by saying, "Is the Lord among us or not?" If so, then prove it to us by providing us with water." This was the case even for the doubting Thomas when he made the statement that he would not believe "unless he sees the nail marks in his hands and put his finger where the nails were, and put his hand into his side . . ." (Jn 20:25b).

According to St Luke, Jesus continued to be tempted throughout his public ministry. There are a number of incidents recorded in the gospel that he was indeed tempted. Some of them are through demon-possessed people (Mk 1:22-24); his own family (Mk 3:31-35; Jn 7:5); his own disciples (Mk 8:31-32); leadership (Mk 2:6-7) and also when he was praying in Gethsemane (Jn 14:30-31).Thus, the temptations must be interpreted as the constant struggle or conflict between God's reign and the reign of Satan.

As humans we continue to be tempted and that's for sure. We will always be lured by countless temptations. These are temptations to lie, steal, manipulate others, or crave for power and use it to abuse and oppress others.

St Paul in his letter to the Ephesians says, 'the sword of the Spirit is the word of God and Jesus' temptations show us how he used the word of God (6:10-17). In every circumstance of our lives, there is meaning that gives weight to what the Bible says about our commitment and fidelity to God. And it always leads us to make Jesus' response our own, his own example our own, his goal our own, especially when we are confronted with the allurements and enticements of our everyday lives. God bless you.

SECOND SUNDAY OF LENT

Readings: Gen 15:5-12, 17-18; Ps 27:7-8, 8-8,
13-14; Phil 3:17-4:1; Lk 9:28b-36

Jesus' Transfiguration[58]

*"While he was praying his face changed in appearance
and his clothing became dazzling white. And behold,
two men were conversing with him, Moses and Elijah,
who appeared in glory and spoke of his exodus that
he was going to accomplish in Jerusalem."*

In our ministry like in teaching, there is always a challenge
of connecting faith experiences from the bits and bytes of
information that we impart with the present situation. As we
try to figure out how to demonstrate or transmit a certain
issue that would bring new insights and facilitate a change
in behavior, one recurring message from scripture that is
pretty much enduring and primarily God's main concern
with us is the nature of our relationships. With apologies to
St Ireneaus of Lyons who once wrote, "The glory of God is
a human being fully alive." Perhaps in this context we can
argue that we are most 'fully alive' when we are in right
relationship with ourselves, with our companions in the
community, and with God himself.

---

[58]   It is Mark 9:2-13, Matthew 17:1-13 and Luke 9:28-36. It is a miraculous
event in the Synoptic Gospel accounts. Taken as a whole, the
Transfiguration at its generative moment attests Jesus' introduction
of his *talmidim* to a vision of the divine throne comparable to his
own at his baptism. Luke's account points Moses and Elijah who
spoke about his departure. Glory and exodus emerge as key themes
in the interpretation of the transfiguration.

The Transfiguration of Jesus[59] in today's gospel is described as the foretaste of the glorious epiphany of the Son; the culminating point of his life that prefigures his suffering, death, and resurrection. And this belongs to the most profound dimension of his significance and his ever-increasing glory. Just as his Baptism initiates the opening disclosure of his public ministry and his Ascension as his concluding part, his Transfiguration, however, has these dramatic features which are visually spectacular as an historical event in terms of God's revelation in Jesus with his glory and holy divinity. That vision conveys the actuality of his Messianic Sonship,[60] his Divinity; and the embodiment of Law and Prophecy in his life and ministry.

---

[59] Arthur Michael Ramsey. 1966. *The Glory of God and the Transfiguration of Christ*. Longmons, Publisher: London p. 144. He says that "the transfiguration stands as a gateway to the saving events of the gospel, and is a mirror in which the Christian mystery is seen in its unity. Here we perceive that the living and the dead are one with Christ, that the old covenant and the new are inseparable, that the Cross and the glory are of one, that the age to come is already here, that our human nature has a destiny of glory, that in Christ the final word is uttered and in him alone the Father is well pleased. Here, the diverse elements in the theology of the NT meet."

[60] cf. Josh. 1-3. It is worth noting that attention has been drawn to some sort of connection between a subsequent story in Joshua and the Transfiguration: see Richard Hess. 1996. *Joshua*. Leicester: IVP. p 127. Before we interpret Moses and Elijah, whatever our theology of Sonship and Servanthood 'listen to him.' It is placed in the context of the summons to humble and obedient listening, the acknowledgment of the lordship of Jesus. Israel was trained to obey as a basis for comprehension. In the opening chapters of Joshua, for example, with its thematic wealth—conquest after Exodus; Jordan after the Red Sea; the produce of Canaan after the manna, above all, God, the great deliverer, there is a remarkable focus on the person of Joshua.

Over the years our understanding of the historical Jesus and the Christ of faith has been articulated in the context of theology and its ongoing conversation with significant issues of human experience. Perhaps in our commitment to the heart of Jesus' purpose to enter our lives, it is worth reflecting a little further on the theology of glory as this is what the gospel is all about with its biblical traditions and images of grandeur, grace and gratitude. Most of our theological reflections on being human with an implicit mission to serve begin and end by emphasizing the value of justice like the prophet Micah's (6:8) immortal words to "Do justly, love mercy, and walk humbly with your God,"[61] in situations of poverty, discrimination, and unjust structures. But I think God's glory is revealed when we are 'fully alive.' And to be fully alive means: 'to be in good relationship with ourselves, others, and God as we move forward in our exodus experience.'

Luke heavily accents the word 'glory' in the Transfiguration account. He says, 'and behold, two men were conversing with him, Moses and Elijah, who appeared in *glory* and spoke of his exodus . . .' Then in another instance he says, 'but becoming fully awake, they saw his *glory* and the two men standing with him.' He is the only one who tells us that Jesus was praying when his face changed in appearance, just as he alone records that Jesus prayed at his baptism (3:21) and just as before this incident happened, earlier in the chapter while he was also praying in solitude he asked his disciples, "Who do the crowds say that I am" (9:18).

If we think about some biblical traditions and images of glory, it is Luke who uses more in his selection of stories taken

---

[61]   See also Amos 5:24, ". . . . let justice flow like water, and uprightness like a never-failing stream."

as a whole and that shows God's preferential concern for the poor, marginalized women and children, the outcast and the afflicted. He is the author of two of Jesus' famous stories— the Good Samaritan and his best-seller and masterpiece, The Prodigal Son. Because of his non-Jewish audience his goal was focused more on equality, without being discriminated against God's love, grace and compassion; and that being in right relationship made more sense than obeying rules with rigor and rigidity.[62]

We recall some events from the Book of Exodus when God delivered the Israelites from Egyptian slavery through cloud and fire, his *glory* could be revealed in terms of strength, destroying Pharaoh and his hordes at the Red Sea (Ex 14:4-31). Then when the Israelites got to Sinai and God called on Moses to go up the mountain to receive the Ten Commandments, the cloud covered it for six days and 'the *glory* of the Lord settled on Mount Sinai' (Ex 24:6). When he came down from Sinai, his face was radiant; whenever he entered the presence of the Lord in the Dwelling, his face shone (Ex 34:29-35). Then Moses ordered his people to make a golden altar or dwelling in the meeting tent and the *glory* of the Lord filled the place (Ex 40:26-34 ff).

In our everyday conversation the idea of glory has been associated with so many events. We think about the Olympics, 2010 in Vancouver, the Oscar Award, Pulitzer Award, Nobel Prize, World Cup, Men and Women of the Year and many others. To the winners, certainly, the theme of glory accompanies their triumphs and successes in life. In our religious celebration, for instance, it is like a familiar cadence in giving worship to God. At Christmas time, feast

---

[62]   cf. Marcus, Borg. 1995. Meeting *Jesus Again for the First Time: The Historical Jesus and the Heart of Contemporary Faith*. San Francisco: Harper San Francisco.

days, and other big celebrations, our liturgy is replete with glory as our sacred hymns and songs express that faith, hope, and joy to God and to one another. They reflect our gift of relationships and define our unity in faith.

Seeing Moses[63] and Elijah[64] in splendid vision and the disciples being fully awakened upon seeing Jesus' glory, we take up this challenge to continue living the life according to what God intends for us all—to reflect his glory in our ministry, in the religious community or in other life situations where we are called to heal broken relationships as a cause and consequence of pride and poverty. Our theology of glory will be based on our response as believers and doers of the Christ of faith in our quest to get our relationship right with ourselves, with our companions, and God himself. God bless you.

---

[63]   According to the OT accounts, Moses had died though his burial-place could not be located. Like Elijah he was a great contender against idolatry; he stands for the Law; a great man of prayer. He was a lawgiver and Jesus was accused of transgressing the law.

[64]   cf. Jeremias' article on Elijah in G. Kittel and G. Friedrich eds. Theological Dictionary of the New Testament, II. Eerdmans, 1964. He was one of the biblical characters who had a book written about him under the title of "Apocalypse", a book which spoke of things 'which the eye has not seen nor the ear heard. His confrontation with the priests of Baal, in the name of Yahweh, is one of the most dramatic tales in the historical books of the OT. His departure from the world was as startling as his arrival on the narrative scene for, according to 2 Kings 2, he did not die but was taken up into heaven. Jesus spoke of those who would not taste death: Elijah was an example par excellence. His role is to restore community order within the context of restoration of covenant relationships, with its trans-generational significance. He was the great opponent of idolatry and Jesus' enemies were troubled by the excessively close proximity to God in which he placed himself. His function is covenantal like that of John the Baptist.

THIRD SUNDAY OF LENT

Readings: Ex 3:1-8a, 13-15; Ps 103:1-4, 6-8,
11; 1 Cor 10:1-6, 10-12; Lk 13:1-9

The Parable of the Fig Tree

*"But I tell you, if you do not repent, you
will all perish as they did."*

At a moment of global hardships when we are faced with a period of grim disasters and tragedies like what happened in the Philippines, Japan, or Chile, strident voices reflected the concern of many people asking for help and human support. For decades we have been plagued by conflicting issues that run wide and deep shedding light on the plight of the poor and disenfranchised. And our moral response gets to the mainstream with deeper insights.

Perhaps a more coherent view of the gospel today can be taken from its background when two major horrors of murder and disaster created a climate of anger among the Jews and a landmark decision that deals with the call of repentance.

At that time, the leadership of Pilate[65] could be gleaned with cruel capacity and abuse of power. He had a number of projects that aimed at developing the civilization, the quality work force and stability of Jerusalem. One of them was to build a water system but that would require a great contribution of the Jews through taxes to pay off the labor and other expenses. This brought massive protest and backlash

---

[65] He was governor of Judea almost 10 years, and about the 4th year of his government, which might be about the 15th year of Tiberius' reign.

among the Jews and Galileans denouncing the increase of taxes to the Roman government.

There was a radical group of Galileans known as 'anti-taxation movement' headed by Judas of Galilee[66] (or Gaulonites) that was placed on a heightened state of alert to seize control of Roman domination in Israel through a coup d'état, to overthrow the Roman occupation. With strongest disapproval for such a rebellion, some scholars believe that Pilate might have had them killed while they were giving worship in the synagogue and made their blood mix with those animals sacrificed as part of their rituals.

Then the tragic news that brought the death of 18 people who were killed in an accident when the tower near the Pool of Siloam collapsed. They might have been construction workers who were doing some repairs and renovations to the tower which some scholars claim was part of defensive works like a citadel around the city walls of Jerusalem.

Following the consequences of these tragedies people conjured up social categories of those Galileans who sinned and reflected on the broad stereotypical reaction that they deserved what they got. As John Milton once said, 'they met their rendezvous with death.' But Jesus rectified their understanding conditioned by core beliefs about the fruit of the act; that their spiritual condition had nothing to do with the tragedies that happen in their lives.

Jesus, however, stressed the fact that all of us are sinners and those disasters are not the aftermath of sin, but they can be the occasions to reflect upon faults and misgivings. He argued that this is closely tied to all humans, not only a few people. Which is why his pedagogy on the meaning of his

---

[66]   Acts 5:37

coming redemption and on certain questions and concerns of his disciples, highlights his patience.

With insecurity in the world, with its journey from budding to fruition, from fear to assurance, and hidden secrets of the end of time to revelation about the return of the Son of God, Jesus made it clear with his disciples that those who live out their lives as his true followers should not worry about missing God's kingdom since it is already revealed in their life's journey today and tomorrow. He told them that the experience of God's love is not only after death but rather, in the present time, today—in this generation.

The whole discourse of the parable teaches the symbolic meaning of a fig tree[67] that had its purpose to bear fruit but failed. It refers to Israel because of her unbelief and rebellion. Jews rejected Christ as the promised Messiah, and they are symbolized by the withered tree that shows God's favor and prerogative was turned away from them. Like any other tree in the vineyard, the fig tree had the same sustenance from mother nature as regards the soil, rain, sun, wind and of course, the caring presence of the gardener. And yet it

---

[67] Figs are considered characteristic fruit for the land of Palestine. The best loved and most nutritious were the spring fruits, which ripened in May and referred to as figs in the fig tree of the first time (Hos 9:10). It is one of the more frequently mentioned trees in the bible. It was from its leaves that Adam and Eve made their first covering (Gen 3:7). It was also a symbol of prosperity and security as it says in 1 Kgs 4:25. It was used as a picture of Israel not without a cause. As early as in the OT, figs were identified with the nation of Israel by the prophets. Jer. 24:5 is a parable of the fig tree and is one of the prime roots for the parable. He received the vision of two baskets of figs, which represented Israel. Hosea, too, in chapter 9:10 says: 'I found Israel like grapes in the wilderness, I saw your fathers as the first ripe in the fig tree in her first time.' When Jesus told his disciples in Matt 24, Mk 13, and Lk 13 of how it would be in the time of the end, in the last days, this parable of the fig tree was referred to.

did not bear fruit and the owner decided to cut it down. However, the gardener asked the owner of the orchard to give it another chance for a year to see if it would bear fruit.

Just as the fig tree was given another opportunity to bear fruit in the future, so God gives us another chance to make amends, to repent, to change for the better, and become a living witness of the gospel. Repentance is the key-issue in this parable giving us a picture of God's patience in our lives. Sometimes they may be better seen in our struggle to relate with others that has a familiar tone of transparency and humility.

Circumstances determine which of our conflicts provide direction to embrace the flaming fire of God's love and forgiveness in our hearts like the burning bush in the first reading. If Moses[68] was commissioned to rescue his own people from the hands of the Egyptians, we in today's generation, are given the tasks to help one another in our quest for conversion, e.g. new attitudes of the heart. Our concrete experience of loving enables us to transcend our limitations and the rough edges of our personalities. We have much to learn in our lives and at the same time we have much to share especially in the context of relationship.

---

[68] After fleeing Egypt when he intervenes on behalf of a fellow Israelite, he tends the flocks of his father-in-law Jethro in the wilderness of Midian. It is here, at Mount Horeb, that he comes face to face with the manifestation of God's presence. The wilderness and the mountain themes run through the Jewish experience of God, as places where, removed from the easy material pleasures of life, the people are thrown back to their search for God. The burning bush, symbolic of the presence of God, reminds us of the tongues of fire that descended on the disciples in the Upper Room. Moses is given to know the mystery of the Name. 'YHWH' is so sacred to Jewish tradition that it must not be pronounced. It is translated as 'I AM'. Perhaps it is best understood as 'The Real, The Authentic, The True'.

In closing I would like to echo the words of St John: "You did not choose me, but I chose you and appointed you that you should go and bear fruit, and that your fruit should remain, that whatever you ask the Father in my name he may give you" (Jn 15:16).

FOURTH SUNDAY OF LENT

Readings: Jos 5:9a, 10-12; Ps 34:2-7; 2
Cor 5:17-21; Lk 15:1-3, 11-32

The Parable of the Prodigal Son

*"Father, I have sinned against heaven and against
you. I no longer deserve to be called your son; treat me
as you would treat one of your hired workers."*

For centuries countless writers and artists such as Rembrandt
van Rijn, Jacopo Bassano (16th), Antonio Montauti (1720),
Bartolomé Esteban Murillo (1617-1682) and many others,
have explored the startling mystery of the father's love and
forgiveness in Jesus' story of the Prodigal Son. They have shed
light on the moral values of forgiveness as a focal mystery
and spirituality for all seasons.

This great masterpiece of Luke's gospel has a powerful
theology and insight that demonstrates God's love for each of
us—the whole humanity. In the story Jesus identifies himself
with the father in his loving attitude to the lost son.

We have seen in various pieces of literature the many
faces of forgiveness particularly in Scripture. They pose
important questions and challenge us to respond with
our Christian values. The biblical narrative of Joseph, for
instance, when he was sold into slavery by his own brothers,
begins with betrayal and ends with forgiveness. Miriam,
along with Aaron,[69] at the time when she criticized Moses

---

[69] Why was Miriam punished, and not Aaron? According to Lev 13,
anyone with a skin disease was disqualified from the high priesthood.
The Talmud notes that if Aaron had been punished as well as his
sister, he would no longer have been able to perform his duties.

for marrying a black woman,[70] was punished by God with a disease that made her skin white and putrid. Moses prayed that God would heal her and her sin was forgiven; she was healed (cf. Num 12). When David, for instance, ignored the law that says 'only the Levites could carry the ark of God to bring it back to Jerusalem,'[71] he was shaken with fear when Uzzah dropped dead after he had touched the Ark. He realized that it was all his fault; he disobeyed the word of God. He repented and God forgave him (cf. 1 Chron 13)

In 2 Kgs 18:5, we find that Hezekiah trusted the Lord more than any other king of Judah. He brought up his son Manasseh according to ideals of his faith in God. However, when Manasseh became king at the age of 12, he immediately turned against God and "did evil in the sight of the Lord" (2 Chr 33:2). Manasseh was truly wicked, committing all sorts of idolatry, sorcery and immorality, including the sacrifice of his own sons to pagan gods. Later, after Manasseh and the people of Judah had been taken in chains to Babylon, he finally turned back to the one true God that his father had taught him about. God heard Manasseh's cry and brought him back to Jerusalem. After years of rebellion, God was still loving and merciful to Manasseh, when he finally recognized that God alone was Lord.

Evidently the history of forgiveness lies in the bible. It is even recurrent in talmudic and midrashic literature. The ancient Israelites used three main words to express its

---

[70]   Richard E. Friedman. 1997. *Who Wrote the Bible?* New York: Harper Publications. pp 76-78, 92. Zipporah is identified as the wife of Moses, so the traditional Jewish and Christian view is that Zipporah is the wife in question. Other modern scholars described Zipporah as being a Midianite ('J'). Cush, however, refers to Ethiopia from the Elohist.

[71]   1 Chron 13: David went down to the Philistine city where the ark was being held captive and took it upon a cart and tried to bring it back to Jerusalem.

meaning. Kippur (atone) and shalach (let go) speak of God's forgiveness alone, never humankind's way of forgiving. Nasá (lift up, bear, dismiss, send away) is the word that refers to forgiveness most often used in the OT, and this may refer to either human or divine forgiveness. However, in the NT three Greek words to refer to forgiveness are Apoluo (let go, loose) and charizomai (be gracious) appear far less frequently than aphiemi (let go, send away, pardon, forgive) which is parallel in meaning to nasá, the OT term.

Like in this parable, Jesus shows us who God is—his perspective of God's image particularly in the context of forgiveness. While the theme of the story may convey the conversion of the sinner, as narrated in the previous incidents about the parables of the lost sheep and lost coin, apparently, it is more on the restoration of a believer into fellowship with the Father. His homecoming echoes the excitement of discovery; a healing quality that reveals the father's unconditional love; a kind of jubilation as the father waits and watches eagerly for his son's return. There is a joyful reunion. The beautiful robe,—a sign of dignity and honor as well as a proof of acceptance back into his own family; the shoes,—a sign of not being a servant anymore; the ring,—a sign of authority and sonship; and the festive meal describe the symbolic meaning of new life, a return to God. It is like resurrection from spiritual death.

However, the older son, the real heir, cannot accept it. His argument is justice and fairness for he has been faithful to serve his own father. But he fails to see the other side of his brother's life—he has repented and returned. He is angry,[72] disgusted, and jealous. He is not able to forgive and show his

---

[72] This is the Greek word *orgizo,* which means "passionate rage." It comes from the root word *orgao,* which referred to plants and fruits swelling with juice to the point of bursting. The elder brother in this

compassion toward his own brother. He sees his brother's return as if it were a threat to his own inheritance.

Given the main highlight in the story, the father himself initiates his gift of restoring his younger son back to whole again—to his full privilege of being his father's son. This provides us with a picture of hope and a sense of what it is like to be reconciled with one that you have been estranged. It also helps us see the psychology of God's salvation different from ours as we look at the son's sense of loss after he has squandered his inheritance and has become destitute.

Towards the end, we do not know what happens to the older son but following Jesus' adversaries in the temple, the Pharisees continue to oppose him and his teachings. They discriminate against his followers. It is in this language of Jesus' parable that we find the metaphorical allusions to the reality of his own context with these people. Like the father in this story who pleads his older son to join with them but is refused, the scribes and Pharisees, too, are the ones who don't want to believe in him; to accept him as their Messiah. As a result, they instigate his arrest and his rendezvous with crucifixion (Matt 26:59).

As we now bring back to our senses the picture of a merciful Father who forgives his son, these familiar words of William Cowper (1731-1800) may be appropriate to bring to the fore: "God moves in a mysterious way; his wonders to perform." It tells us that God has his own way in dealing with our life's issues different than we have. Through Jesus Christ, God forgives our transgression. Because of Christ, God forgets our sin. The psalm says beautifully: "As a father

---

parable was so filled with rage that he was ready to burst! He was "so mad he could have exploded!"

has compassion on his children, so the Lord has compassion on those who fear him." (Psalm 103:10-13).

When we understand how God holds us in our struggles especially in our quest for healing of relationship, then we can extend to others that kind of proximity and attention that shape the true mark of authentic discipleship—love (Jn 13:34-35). It is not only in the nature of or understanding our service but it is more in the act of loving.

Our moral responsibility when confronted with perspectives, (e.g., justice must be tempered with love), is our sensibility that comes from within and enables us to respond to the needs of others. This is the language conceivable for the core values of caring and sharing as our Christian principles. This shows our attitude, too, as we respond to those who need help[73] like the lives of warring spouses, friends in conflict, or a community with a running sore of division

I am reminded of The Brothers Karamazov by Fyodor Doestoevsky. It is a story of a Russian family that reflects the real life of the author himself. The three sons in the story are: Dmitir, Ivan, and Alexey (Alyosha). One of them is the prodigal son of sorts—Dmitri, who has received much of his inheritance but realizes that his own father has cheated him out of the rest. The father gets killed and Dmitri is accused of the murder and is set on a trial as the epilogue winds down. He is found guilty. He is sentenced to 20 years of hard labor in Siberia. While he is recovering in the hospital before he is due to be taken to the jail, it is striking that he promises to Katerina that they will love each other forever and with his 2 brothers to love each other, too, and to keep each other in their memories forever.

---

[73]   1 John 4:20-21, Luke 17:3, Galatians 6:1, James 5:19-20.

Following this, Jesus said, "A new commandment I give to you, that you love another, even as I have loved you, that you also love one another. By this all men will know that you are my disciples, if you have love for one another" (Jn 13:34-35).

FIFTH SUNDAY OF LENT

Readings: Is 43:16-21; Ps 126:1-6; Phil 3:8-14; Jn 8:1-11

Jesus and a Woman Taken in Adultery[74]

"Let the one among you who is without sin
be the first to throw a stone at her."

There is a famous saying in French that goes, "Tout comprendre, c'est tout pardonner"[75] (To understand all is to forgive all). That sounds difficult, doesn't it? But in many events of our lives the tension between understanding and judging belongs to the discipline of justice and history. And justice has to be tempered with mercy.

I cannot count the number of times I have been barraged with problems. But one thing is certain: If we look at them as opportunities to grow in the wisdom of experience not with a chip on our shoulders but with a right attitude, they help us develop our own skills of handling those problems in our lives. We follow that path of healing and reconciliation apart

---

[74] It is "cheating on one's lawful mate; sexual misconduct with another." Under the law of Moses the penalty for adultery was death. Leviticus 20:10 declares that when an adulterous situation occurs, both "the adulterer and the adulteress (i.e., both the man the woman) shall surely be put to death" (Dt 22:22-24). The familiar definition of "adultery" is certainly a biblical one. Its Greek word is *moicheia*. It appears in its various forms, just under 30 times in the NT documents. Like a great many English words, it can have several meanings and applications and these should not be lightly discounted in anyone's interpretation of those passages in which the term *moicheia* appears.

[75] This precise formulation is used by Tolstoy in War and Peace (1868), vol. 1, part 1, chap. 28. It means understanding everything is forgiving everything.

from holding grudges and anger. After all, because of Christ, God forgets our sins.

Considered one of the most controversial stories, today's gospel speaks about Jesus and the woman taken in adultery.[76] It is another biblical narrative of repentance and its moral challenge to live a new life. It also gives us a sense of meaning and purpose that shows in a beautiful encounter the forgiving quality of Jesus' teaching.

We know that Jesus' presence in the Temple is evidently in light of his pedagogy, his commitment to teach, along with his appetite for stories that generate lessons about a good Christian life. He is given a place reserved only for the Sanhedrin. They are the only council in Israel that allows rendering legal (*halakhik*) sessions.

While still in the course of discussion, the scribes and Pharisees bring in the woman caught in adultery.[77] She is

---

[76] Verse 53 is included in chapter 7. Verses 53 to 11 are enclosed within single brackets. There is a footnote following the section title "A Woman Caught in Adultery." "The story of the woman caught in adultery is a later insertion here, missing from all early Greek manuscripts. A Western text-type insertion, attested mainly in Old Latin translations, it is found in different places in different manuscripts; here, or after 7:36, or at the end of this gospel, or after Luke 21:38, or at the end of that gospel. There are many non-Johannine features in the language, and there are also many doubtful readings within the passage. The style and the motifs are similar to those of Luke, and it fits better with the general situation at the end of Luke 21, but it was probably inserted here because of the allusion to Jeremiah 17:13 (cf. the note on 8:6) and the statement, 'I do not judge anyone,' in 8:15. The Catholic Church accepts this passage as canonical scripture."

[77] Gerhard Kittel. *Theological Dictionary of the New Testament*. Vol. 4. pp 733-734. Perhaps the following insightful quote from a classic Greek reference work makes the point best: "From the religious standpoint adultery does not consist merely in physical intercourse with a strange woman; it is present already in the desire which negates fidelity." Yes, adultery can occur only and entirely, within

caught red-handed. That somehow upsets the whole mood and for one thing—it is a sign of irreverence and disrespect toward a teacher of disciples—Jesus. As a confrontation that deals with the subject of morality over whether a woman, caught in an act of adultery ought to be stoned, Jesus, however, is able to shame the crowd into dispersing with the famous principle: 'let the one without sin be the first to throw a stone at her.'

It is actually the plan of Jesus' opponents in the temple to bring charges against him, if by some chance he makes misjudgment over this scenario. It is to test him and whether he upholds the Law of Moses that requires a public sinner to be stoned. This puts him in a difficult situation as far as the Roman authorities are concerned. The latter don't allow the Jews to inflict the death penalty without the approval of a Roman tribunal. The case is that if he forbids stoning the woman, they would accuse him before the Sanhedrin that he is making his own law which is above Moses and the Jewish law. Then if he remains silent without saying anything about it, they would allegedly accuse him of cowardice. But Jesus is able to manage a trap that aims to test his legal knowledge about the Law of Moses. He stands up and says to them: "Anyone who is sinless be the first to throw a stone at her."

Immediately after that intense and verbal challenge with them, Jesus bends down and writes in the dirt. According to Rabbinic culture, this strange gesture that Jesus makes is

---

one's heart, with no other person actually, physically involved. It is unfaithfulness to a covenant relationship; an unfaithfulness that may manifest itself in any number of ways, but which inevitably leads, if not corrected, to the breakdown of that relationship. The Jews, for example, regarded the intermingling of Jews with those of other races to be "adultery" and from our study of the OT Scriptures we know for a fact that part of the covenant God made with his people was that they were not to mingle with the nations about them.

offensive and disrespectful to the Scribes and Pharisees. To write (or scribble), for instance, as one awaits a verdict in a Jewish court setting is a sign of disrespect. The finger is a symbol of authority in the bible. It symbolizes the finger of God which has to do with his kingdom and his dominion over his creation.

Biblical scholars believe that Jesus was writing one of the commandments. Some think that he was pointing at the trial of jealousy for women (Num 5:17). But one thing is certain: out of his generous heart he was writing the sins of every one of them because when he arose he spoke of it.[78] "Anyone who is sinless be the first to throw a stone at her."

Today's public talk about moral scandal in society is usually framed within the explosion of revelations in various media networks. They bleed in the mainstream. It is like nailing the person in his moral shame. And we have seen the so-called 'infotainment' culture that has evolved into a series of tawdry episodes and has democratized the distribution of information by leaps and bounds.

Our society continues to grow and yet our history continues to repeat itself. I am reminded of Nathaniel Hawthorne's The Scarlet Letter' where the main character Hester Prynne is publicly shamed as an adulteress and forced by the people of Boston during the time of the Puritans to wear a badge of disgrace—her humiliation that nailed her to be ostracized from society. Her shame is attached to her scarlet letter.

Some of our brothers and sisters may have been caught in a deplorable situation or in a tragic series of circumstances. Hostility towards them does not explain the religious vision

---

[78] Bruce M. Metzger. 1998. *Textual Commentary of the Greek New Testament.* 2nd Revised Edition of the United Bible Societies' Greek New Testament. New York, NY 10023.

that is rooted in the reality of God. Like Jesus' teaching redolent of language about forgiveness and compassion to this woman in the gospel, our religious principles are placed on equal footing with inclusion rather than exclusion or condemnation. We believe each person still has his redeeming qualities. He may have some rough edges but with a promise or with a remarkable sense of God's presence in his life. And above all, he still has the future that God would like him to have.

In our time though, being a public sinner is equated with a moral weight of crime. One becomes a disease, a moral disorder, a disgrace. Let us be reminded against too much legalism of our norms or the 'easy-way-out' mindset we employ because one is only a part of the whole. We commit to what we believe in, a value that is rooted in the person. God bless you.

HOLY WEEK

According to the General Norms,[79] Holy Week is the opportune time to remember Christ's passion, beginning with his triumphant entry into Jerusalem. This marks the meaning of his paschal mystery that is implicit in his passion, death and resurrection. The memorial of this event is included in every Mass with the procession or solemn entrance.[80] The solemn entrance (but not the procession) may be repeated before other Masses that are usually well attended.[81] Red chasuble is worn or with red cope for the main celebrant and dalmatic for the deacon.

On Palm Sunday the gospel of the passion of the Lord is read without candles or incense and with no greeting or signing of the book by a deacon or another priest.[82] A lay member of the parish may be involved to take part in proclaiming the gospel. At the end of the reading, the book

---

[79]   31
[80]   cf. The Order of Prayer in the Liturgy of the Hours and Celebration of the Eucharist. 2007. Archdiocese of New York and Diocese of Albany.
[81]   ibid. p 81.
[82]   ibid.

is not kissed, but "The gospel of the Lord" is said with its response.[83]

As stated in the Constitution on the Sacred Liturgy,[84] Catholics have to be mindful of the paschal fast which "should be observed everywhere on Good Friday and continued, where possible, on Holy Saturday. In this way, the people of God will receive the joys of the Lord's resurrection with uplifted and responsive hearts."

On Holy Thursday[85] and Good Friday, the Eucharist may be brought to the sick at any convenient time. However, on Holy Saturday,[86] the Eucharist is not given before the Easter Vigil celebration; it may be given only as a viaticum.[87]

It is common knowledge that Holy Thursday commemorates the day Jesus instituted the Eucharist while Good Friday[88] is the day when Christ died on the cross. The

---

[83] ibid.

[84] 110

[85] Maundy Thursday or Holy Thursday commemorates the washing of the feet, the Lord's supper, and the prayer of Jesus in the Garden of Gethsemane. The word "Maundy" comes from the Latin for "command" *(mandatum)*. It refers to the command given by Jesus at the Last Supper, that his disciples should love one another.

[86] Stake, Donald Wilson. 1992. *ABC's of worship.* Louisville, KY: Westminster/John Knox Press. pp 90-91es the day that Jesus lay in his tomb. In the Philippines it is known as Black Saturday. The day is observed in silence by many Christians since there is nothing said about it in scripture. It was, of course, the Sabbath for the followers of Jesus, a time for them to abstain from all work and to reflect on God's grace and mighty deliverance. Christian observance of Holy Saturday often takes the same course, a quiet reflection on the paradox of Good Friday and the wondrous grace of God's act of redemption in Jesus Christ.

[87] The Order of Prayer in the Liturgy of the Hours and Celebration of the Eucharist. 2007. p 83.

[88] It recalls the death of Jesus on the cross. It is Good Friday because of the good that Jesus did by purchasing redemption for us by his blood.

Easter Vigil,[89] however, commemorates his emergence from the tomb.[90]

What happens now deep within one's heart takes the centerpiece in celebrating the Easter Triduum.[91] It is not so much about what happened in the past as with Christ but, more importantly, in the inner conversion of a person.

Before the mass of the Lord's Supper the tabernacle should be entirely empty; a sufficient amount of bread should be consecrated at this Mass for the communion of the clergy and laity today and tomorrow.[92] After communion, a ciborium with hosts for Good Friday is left on the altar. Then it will be carried in procession to the place of reposition. The altar will be stripped privately. Any crosses displayed in church especially in the sanctuary should be covered with a red or purple veil. Lamps should not be lit before images of saints.[93] The faithful should be encouraged to make adoration to the Blessed Sacrament for a suitable period of time after the procession with the Holy Eucharist.

The Liturgy of this day frequently takes place at the traditional death time of Jesus at 3:00 p.m.

[89] Stake, Donald Wilson, p 70. Easter Vigil is a time of waiting for God once again to come for our redemption. It is a time of anticipating the Easter joy by remembering the wonders of God's grace and God's love for all people.

[90] The Order of Prayer in the Liturgy of the Hours and Celebration of the Eucharist. 2007. p 84

[91] cf. Celebrating the Eucharist. February 25, 2009-May 2, 2009. A publication of Liturgical Press, Collegeville, Minnesota 56321. p 130. During the Triduum we celebrate the core mystery of our Christian faith: we ritualize Jesus' transition from life to death to risen life, and our own participation in that timeless mystery. Rather than "transition," however, we tend to use another word: "Passover." This is the context for what we celebrate throughout the Triduum: "It is the Passover of the Lord." It is our own Passover, as well.

[92] ibid. p 87

[93] ibid p 87

On Good Friday the paschal fast is observed in solidarity with the suffering and death of Christ and to prepare oneself to share with his resurrection. The celebration of the Lord's Passion takes place about three o'clock unless pastoral reasons suggest a later hour.[94] Those parts of the liturgy which should always be sung are: the general intercessions (the deacon's invitation and the acclamation of the people) and the chants for the showing and veneration of the cross.[95] Only one cross should be used for the veneration, as this contributes to the full symbolism of the rite.[96] Following the formula for veneration, the cross may be veiled or unveiled. After the celebration, the altar is stripped. However, the cross with 4 candles, remain.

Nine readings are assigned to the Easter Vigil: seven from the Hebrew Scriptures, two from the New Testament.[97] If necessary, they may be reduced accordingly. But three selections from the Hebrew Scriptures should be read before the Epistle and the Gospel although, when necessary, two may be read.[98] Keep in mind that the reading from Exodus (no. 3) should be included.

On Easter Sunday the rite of renewal of baptismal promises is repeated after the homily (USA).[99] Throughout the Easter Season, it is a practice that in lieu of the Angelus, the *Regina coeli* is chanted or said. The paschal candle, a symbol of the presence of the risen Christ among the people of God, remains in the sanctuary near the altar or ambo through Vespers on Pentecost Sunday.[100]

---

[94]   ibid p 89
[95]   ibid
[96]   ibid
[97]   ibid p 93
[98]   ibid
[99]   ibid
[100]   ibid p 95

PALM SUNDAY OF THE LORD'S PASSION

The Suffering Servant of Israel—Christ

Readings: Is 50:4-7; Ps 22:8-9, 17-20,
23-24; Phil 2:6-11; Lk 22:14-23:56

For centuries this sacred time of the year in our faith tradition has been a great deal about what we have been preparing for—as we enter the holiest week in our Church calendar, the Palm Sunday of the Lord's Passion. Jesus enters Jerusalem as the Messiah with an ultimate goal to redeem humanity. This marks the final battle, his final showdown with authorities around as he enters the solemn drama of human darkness which will later on become the story of our own redemption. Following this, his entrance into the city of Jerusalem and the proclamation of the passion are two places that we focus on as we allow them to speak to our hearts.

There is much pomp and spectacle. There are details about the darkest depths of human nature as shown in the attitude of betrayal and denial, retaliation and arrogance. In a similar vein, there is a struggle between earthly power and selfless love. These are sources of the so-called 'darkness' that characterize the somber story of Jesus' passion. They are filled with tension but rich and powerful

As a long narrative with peculiarities of Luke's emphasis on prayer, the love of a suffering Messiah which is full of mercy and hope, with interest in the wider Roman Empire, with much geographical detail, and with the presence of women in the crowd, indeed teaches us that we are part of God's story.[101] They face us squarely with who Jesus is

---

[101]   cf. Joel B. Green. 1997. *The Gospel of Luke*. The New International Commentary on the New Testament. Ww. B. Eerdmans Publishing.

in our lives; his significance in regard to the movement of redemption. His mission and our mission are the same since we are all called to be obedient to the implications of God's love for us and for one another.

It is interesting to imagine those people singing praises to Jesus while riding on a donkey and proclaim hosanna for the fulfillment of God's promises—the coming of God's kingdom. But these are the same people who would later shout "Crucify him!" The crowds exhibit noise and pandemonium as Jesus enters the city of Jerusalem. There are shouts of joy—proclaiming him their own king—the king of the Jews. But when he goes before the Sanhedrin and to Pilate, to Herod, and back to Pilate who finds him not guilty of anything, the crowd presses for the release of Barabbas and for Jesus—crucifixion.

With these events at great length because of their importance in the life and ministry of Jesus, we are challenged to open our hearts to the sacredness of our story of redemption. Time and again, we are reminded of what this whole season means as we re-establish our proper priorities that lead us to follow Jesus in love and service. His embrace of suffering speaks to us, too, as we humble ourselves for an act of love[102] and with the reality that is deeply rooted in God's grace.

I remember an incident when a certain mother came to me and asked me to pray for her son who had turned out to be a non-believer—an atheist. Being a devoted Catholic she could not accept that her son had given up his faith and had completely left the church. I told her not to be discouraged and not to be hard on him because like in any relationship,

---

p 21. ISBN: 0-8028-2315-7

[102] cf. Raymond E. Brown. 1997. *Introduction to the New Testament*. New York: Anchor Bible. pp 267-268. ISBN: 0-385-24767-2

it is best to strike when the iron is cold, figuratively. I asked her to allow a space for a journey with God that may require a sense of being almost beyond time. Like the words of the two disciples on the way to Emmaus who urged the stranger who had accompanied them along the way to join them for a meal in that evening: "Stay with us Lord" (Mane nobiscum Domine), is also our constant prayer to God; our mantra to the Lord.

After three years I got a phone call from her. At first I did not recognize her voice but eventually I was able to find out that she was the one who I talked with regarding her son. She told me that her son is now back to the fold. He volunteers as a catechist on weekends in the parish. But what happened was a miracle because when he became very ill and was almost close to death, he turned to God for help. The whole family prayed for him. And God listened to their prayer.

I think one of the reasons we never give up in life is prayer. Throughout Jesus' ministry he always has moments to pray to his Father. It is a holy moment in the passion narrative when Jesus prays: "Father forgive them; for they do not know what they are doing." I find it perhaps one of my favorite moments in the passion story and a source of inspiration for our own relationships with friends, family and the community. While being crucified, one of the condemned criminals said in prayer, "Jesus, remember me when you come into your kingdom." Jesus answers: "Amen I tell you, today you will be with me in Paradise."

Let us now accompany Jesus on the way of the cross and be firm to follow him. God bless you.

HOLY THURSDAY
Evening of the Lord's Supper

Readings: Ex 12:1-8, 11-14; Ps 116:12-13, 15-16bc,
17-18; 1 Cor 11:23-26; Jn[103] 13:1-15

The Symbolic Act of Foot Washing

*"Now that I, your Lord and Master, have washed your
feet, you also should wash one another's feet."*

The legendary principle that brings light to our seasons of
awareness tells us that when we begin to recognize that our
life is about God, not about us—that is the beginning of
wisdom. Perhaps you remember that incident in the life of St
Thérèse of Lisieux when she was confined in the infirmary.
She could no longer join in the choral recitation of the
Divine Office but her three blood sisters—Mother Agnes,
Sister Genevieve, and Sister Céline were given permission
to stay with her as much as possible. Mother Agnes was the
one who kept record of her sister's sharing[104] about her own
experiences in the monastery, her insights, anecdotes, and
even her humor.

---

[103] Robert Kysar. 1992. *John, The Gospel of.* ABD III: 912-931. Generally,
it is agreed by scholars that the written Gospel form began to take
shape between 80-95 C.E. from the area of Ephesus. (cf. Robert
Kysar. 1976. *John the Maverick Gospel.* Atlanta, GA: John Knox
Press. p 12. It is almost certain that the author of the Gospel had
access to an oral tradition of the life of Jesus associated with the
Synoptic traditions. That may account for the similarities in John
and the earlier Synoptic traditions. However, one cannot emphasize
enough the unique style, theology and narrative which John offers
in comparison to the Synoptic traditions).

[104] St Thérèse of Lisieux. 1975. *Story of a Soul.* Translated by John
Clarke. Washington, D.C. ICS Publications. p 105.

One time while the other sisters were having their recreation, one of her blood sisters asked her: "Thérèse, what are you doing? It's better for you to sleep now." She replied, "I'm praying Sister." Quite curious, she asked Thérèse, "What are you saying when you pray?" "Nothing," she said, "I'm just loving him."[105]

This is an example of wisdom that has power and significance to understand life's essence in the context of loving. Because God has loved us so much that he gave his only Son to save us.

Tonight as we begin the Sacred Triduum—the three-part drama of Christ's redemption, Jesus' symbolic action in the Last Supper with his disciples speaks powerfully to us about the significance of what he will do by laying down his life for others through his passion and death on the cross. Here Jesus acts out the role of a servant or slave that communicates the wisdom of God's love for us. It tells us his ministry and mission are his main focus where unity is to be preserved but on the same ground of mutual respect, service and dignity.

His disciples have been bickering over who is the greatest (Lk 12:24-30). But his hour has come—his departure from this world and his return to the Father. This heightened sense of drama and suspense is spelled out in the symbolic and prophetic act which Jesus is about to demonstrate.[106] Jesus now deals on humility and servanthood. He may not reject

---

[105]   Quoted from Gerard McGinnity. *Christmen. Experience of Priesthood Today.* Christian Classics. Westminster. MD. p 48. ISBN: 0-87061-124-0

[106]   Sandra M. Schneiders. 1981. *The Foot Washing* (13:1-20): An Experiment in Hermeneutics. <u>Catholic Biblical Quarterly</u> 43. p 81. Schneiders defines a prophetic action as one which is divinely inspired, revelatory in content, prophetic in structure, symbolic in form, and pedagogical in intent.

his power or authority as their Master (Jn 13:13) but in this case, he radically redefines his leadership and relationship to his followers through a symbolic and profound act of service and love.[107] And he shows it through an act of foot washing.

Following this, in John's gospel,[108] one striking observation about Christ's final meal with his disciples is that, it does not feature the institution of the Lord's Supper as the Eucharist unlike in the gospels of Mark, Matthew, and Luke. It is narrated differently where there is the omission of Jesus' anamnesis, e.g. his last will and testament over bread and wine 'to do this is memory of me.' Instead, we find the radical act of foot washing, a narrative which no other gospels contain. But the context of a meal at the time of the

---

[107]   Alan Culpepper. 1991. *The Johannine Hypodeigma: A Reading of John 13*. Semeia 138. 1133-152.

[108]   Robert Brown. 1979. *The Community of the Beloved Disciple*. New York: Paulist Press. One reputable scholar of Johannine literature who has done extensive study into the life of the Johannine community or the community of the Fourth Gospel is Raymond E. Brown. One marked area of difference between the Synoptic and Johannine traditions which Brown observes has to do with the role of the apostle Peter in relation to the Beloved Disciple of the Fourth Gospel: Jn 13:23-26; 18:15-16; 20:2-10; 21:7. Peter is clearly depicted as the spokesperson and significant leader of the early apostolic community, according to the Synoptic tradition, e.g., Mk 8:27-29, Matt 16:13-20, Lk 9:18-21. p 31. In the Gospel of John, the hero of the community is the Beloved Disciple who is never named. The apostolic leadership role of Peter is not rejected but reinterpreted in the Fourth Gospel, though some scholars would maintain otherwise (cf. See for example Arthur H. Maynard. 1984. "The Role of Peter in the Fourth Gospel," NTS 30: 531-548. I am inclined to agree with Brown who maintains that though the Beloved Disciple may have had special importance to the Johannine community, the preeminence of Peter is nevertheless recognized by the Gospel, but on the Gospel's term of service and love

last supper can surely refer to the Eucharist and to events that are to follow.

Jesus calls for conversion shown in the symbol of water as a reminder of one's discipleship through baptism. His followers must continually undergo the process of purification and conversion to enable them to follow the radical way of love and service even to the point of laying down one's life for the other (Jn 13:15; 15:13). He says very clearly: 'What I have done for you, so you are to do it for others.'

The symbolic act of foot washing helps bring us into a deeper knowledge and relationship with Christ and in turn with each other.[109] According to some scholars, they can be interpreted in a number of ways. But seen in the context of the community of believers, the symbol of foot washing is a powerful expression of service, love, hospitality and equality. Others, however, describe it as a gesture of extraordinary intimacy with our brothers and sisters in faith.

Some scholars say that the act of foot washing is exclusively an example of humility; an example of purification of believers (through baptism, the word of Jesus, or believing in Jesus); a sacramental meaning; an end-time signifying Jesus' submission to death on the cross; an act which functions as a sign of hospitality and a background in the Old Testament.[110] But I am convinced that it is not only isolated within that perspective that it is seen as an exclusive instance of humility. Certainly Jesus humbles himself, but we cannot ignore the dynamics of giving and receiving (Jn 13:5, 20), of knowing and doing (Jn 13:17), and of loving and

---

[109]   Koester, Craig R. 1995. *Symbolism in the Fourth Gospel.* Minneapolis, MN: Fortress. p 230.

[110]   Arland Hultgren J. 1982. *The Johannine Footwashing* (13:1-11) *As Symbol of Eschatological Hospitality.* <u>NTS</u> 28. p 539.

serving (Jn 13:1). This is a language event that evokes a new covenant, a new direction as we look at the grassroots level or simply in the context of Johannine community where there were tensions, problems and obstacles inside and outside.

In biblical times foot traffic was on dusty roads in open sandals. It was a custom of hospitality for a host to wash a guest's feet, or to provide him with water to wash his own feet, or perhaps a servant to do it for him (Gen. 18:4; 19:1-2; 24:31-32; 43:24; Jdgs 19:16-21; 1 Sam 25:40-41; Lk 7:36-38). We may recall Abraham when he told his guests the three angels that he would get some water so they could wash their feet (Gen 18:4). When Joseph welcomed his brothers to a banquet, the steward provided water for them to wash their feet before supper was served (Gen 43:24). There is also the story of the old man from Ephraim who housed the traveling Levite and his concubine (see Jdgs 19:16). They also washed their own feet before they ate (Jdgs 19:21). Ruth, however, laid down her life for another as she lay at Boaz's feet—symbolic of the foot washing attitude.

Perhaps in Western culture foot washing is extremely foreign. But as we allow symbols like this to speak to us on a number of levels especially in our spiritual and ministerial life, we bring the two worlds of our Christian life today and of the Johannine community into dialogue. There is respect and understanding and our task is to accept them.

Jesus offers himself as a paragon of humility and service that his disciples ought to follow. Among ourselves it is more than a call to 'humble service' but we are invited to break through barriers to intimacy, to accept and serve one another. As a post Vatican II Church, we have seemed to reverse some of the changes and perhaps we have gone far enough and some of us are anxious to move forward. The tension continues. The challenge is not easy.

But I love what St Thérèse wrote on June 9, 1897 to Fr Belliere while she was in the infirmary: "I am not dying; I am entering into life." Like her, I think, in spite of her physical pains, along with the pain of being misunderstood in the monastery, we can think positive and keep going[111] as we take to heart the example which Jesus leaves us: love others to the end. Though it may be painful it is worth taking as Jesus tells us: "If you understand this, blessed are you if you do it" (Jn 13:17). God bless you.

---

[111]   Frederick Buechner. 1973. *Wishful Thinking: A Theological ABC*. New York: Harper and Row. p 27. Novelist Frederick Buechner spoke truly when he observed, "Generally speaking, if you want to know who you really are as distinct from who you like to think you are, keep an eye on where your feet take you."

GOOD FRIDAY
Celebration of the Lord's Passion

Christ in His Redeeming Mystery of the Cross

Readings: Is 52:13-53:12; Ps 31:2, 6, 12-13, 15-17,
25; Heb 4:14-16; 5:7-9; Jn 18:1-19:42

At the opening mass of the 49th International Congress in Quebéc City, Canada in 2008, Slovakian Cardinal Josef Tomko[112] said that when people pause and question the purpose of their lives, they 'yearn for a spiritual answer.' In the aftermath of tragic loss, for instance, it takes enormous strength to go on with life and even more to rediscover faith in quest of a spiritual answer. The memory lane is our keepsake and we hold it close to our hearts.

We are in the season where we are reminded of the Paschal mystery, particularly today as the entire church is in mourning. It is the downward mobility of God in Christ's passion, on the way of the Cross, which is the central element of this liturgy. Though we may see the cross as a symbol of paradox and contradiction, our faith tells us that what looks like defeat is indeed success and what looks like the end is indeed the beginning and that we have the future to

---

[112]   cf. Wikipedia.com. Jozef Tomko (born 11 March 1924) is a Slovak Cardinal of the Roman Catholic Church. He served as Prefect of the Congregation for the Evangelization of Peoples from 1985 to 2001, and was elevated to the cardinalate in 1985. He was born in Udavské, near Humenné, in Czechoslovakia (now part of the Republic of Slovakia). He studied at the Theological Faculty of Bratislava, and then traveled to Rome to study at the Pontifical Lateran Athenaeum and Pontifical Gregorian University, from where he obtained his doctorates in theology, canon law, and social sciences. Tomko was ordained to the priesthood by Archbishop Luigi Traglia on March 12, 1949.

look forward to—the promise of eternal life. The power of Christ's suffering, crucifixion and death is the tremendous gift of love for us. The redeeming mystery of the Cross is the unconditional love of God that has its own parallel to our spiritual lives. Its essence makes us see beyond and allow ourselves to trust in God.

I remember Mark Twain who, on two occasions, was mistakenly feared dead. People thought he was near death as published in the New York Times of 2 June 1897. Indeed, it was a premature obituary. In fact it was his cousin who was very ill. Which is why, he said, "The reports of my death are greatly exaggerated."[113]

For centuries, reports of Jesus' death have been described in many facets of our Christian life that generated a treasure trove of spirituality and other subjects of countless writers. One of them as you well know is the criticism against the Johannine passion narrative that for some are anti-Jewish because it is believed for some reasons that Jews were responsible for the death of Jesus. But in spite of that, one thing is certain as a common path that leads to God—there is hope for us believers.

Our experiences of pain, turmoil, or death in itself are not the final end. The blessing is hidden that awaits each struggle to deal with. This is the cycle of life replete with trials and tests; with passing sorrow and joy; with new life and growth. And these form the connection of Christ's suffering in our lives. We identify our own journey with the image of the cross written in our hearts. What matters to God is that we endeavor to deepen more our faith, to believe instead of rationalizing and be loving persons more than intelligent human beings.

---

[113] Ron Powers. 2005. *Mark Twain: A Life*. Free Press: New York.

71

With this sad and desolate quality of our liturgy, we fix our gaze on the Cross with faith and hope that holds a gift of Christ's redeeming mystery—his gift of eternity.

EASTER SEASON

E aster, also called "Pascha", is the feast of Christ's resurrection from death. It is celebrated on the Sunday following Holy Week. According to St Augustine, "Easter was the season of the Alleluia, a hopeful sign of the time when 'we shall do nothing but praise God." Easter is also a fifty-day season, often called Eastertide. This is the greatest and oldest feast of the Church. The term "Pascha" is borrowed from the Jewish word for "Passover," and Easter is calculated based on the lunar calendar (all other feasts are on the solar calendar). These facts show the ancient, probably Apostolic, origins of Easter. We even have a baptismal liturgy of Easter dating to the mid-third century.

The word "Easter" might come from an Anglo-Saxon spring goddess. This is probably because the festival of Easter overlapped some pagan holiday in ancient England.

Traditionally, our Easter Vigil begins with a lengthy celebration. St Augustine called it the "mother of all vigils". The whole story of salvation is retold during the vigil, through scripture and liturgy. At the Easter Vigil in the West three traditions developed: the baptism of new converts, lighting of the paschal candle, and the blessing of the new fire taken from the Jewish blessing of the lamp on the eve of the Sabbath. This is often taken by procession into the Church to light the Paschal candle. Eucharist is then celebrated in the morning hours, being also the first Eucharist of new converts.

The Roman Catholics (West) celebrate the octave of Easter. Usually Orthodox and Western Christians celebrate Easter on two different Sundays. The reason is that Orthodox churches still base their calculation of Easter's day on the Julian calendar whereas Western churches follow the Gregorian calendar. In order to keep the date of Easter on a Sunday, the date changes yearly based on the Paschal full moon. The possible date range for Western Easter day is March 21st-April 25th. Keep in mind that Easter is observed on the first Sunday after the first full moon on or after the day of the vernal equinox. The vernal equinox is the beginning of astronomical spring. However, ecclesiastical rules are slightly more complicated than this formula.

According to history, different Church regions celebrate Easter at different times. It's controversial and they called it Quartodecima (Latin for "fourteenism"). In Asia Minor, many churches, including the church of Smyrna under the pastoral care of St Polycarp, they celebrate Easter on the 14th of Nissan, following Jewish Passover customs. However, Church historian Eusebius tells us that the Church in Rome and most other Catholic dioceses always celebrated Easter on a Sunday. Also, differences emerged between the Churches of Antioch and Alexandria as to the computation of the Paschal Moon. The Council of Nicaea settled the date of Easter, in favor of the Alexandrians, putting Easter on the Sunday after the vernal equinox. However, Eastern

Orthodox and Western/Eastern Catholic Easter celebration falls on different dates because of discrepancy in their calendars.[114]

---

[114] cf. ChurchYear.net (online) written by David Bennett and Jonathan Bennett.

EASTER VIGIL

He is not here, but he has been raised.

Readings: Gn 1:1, 26-31; Ps 104; Gn 22:1-18; Ps 16: Ex 14:15-15:1;
Ex 15: Is 54:5-14; Ps 30: Is 55:1-11; Is 12: Bar 3:9-15, 32-4:4; Ps
19: Ex 36:16-28; Ps 42, 43; Rom 6:3-11; Ps 118: **Lk 24:1-12**

We can say with a great deal of certainty that indeed this evening celebration has much to tell us in the fullness of our Easter experience seen in the light of Jesus' life, ministry and death. The depth and power of Christ's resurrection remains central to our faith. As St Paul says, "And if Christ has not been raised, then empty, [too] is our preaching; empty, too, your faith."[115] . . . Your faith is vain; you're still in your sins."[116]

It is true with our young generation today who has been raised with a global worldview. With internet and cell phone technology, with ipod to listen to and cable television with hundreds of channels to watch, I wonder if they would agree right away to their religion teacher telling them about the reliability of the empty tomb story. They may disagree and ask for reasons or proofs as they say, "show me." Others may probably go online and Google the answer. But most likely the difficulty for many of us would be an attempt to give highlight to the core of its meaning—'what does it mean?' 'What does my faith tell me?' What about the inner transformation that took place in Jesus' earliest followers who believed that he is risen? Rather than to deal with that question: 'did it really happen?'

---

[115] 1 Cor 15:14
[116] ibid. verse 17

The historical accuracy of the empty tomb tradition has been challenged by so many scholars and critics. It has been debated due to lack of witnesses at the very moment when Jesus resurrected. They deny the historical basis behind the empty tomb. They say that it never happened. In this case, they refuse to believe that such an empty tomb is the answer for Jesus' resurrection. Claims suggest grave robbery by Jesus' disciples, removal of the body by a local gardener as mentioned by Tertullian in his third century work de Spectaculis.[117] Others suggest that Joseph of Arimathea shifted the body to a more convenient tomb without the disciples' knowledge, or that other grave robbers took the body.[118] One early twentieth century writer suggests that the women went to the wrong tomb.[119] Others suggest that Jesus did not die on the cross, but recovered in the tomb before making his way out.[120]

However, historical basis for the empty tomb should not trigger and condition our faith because Jesus' resurrection belongs to the category of faith. The empty tomb tradition does not explain itself. Its core is understood in light of its meaning and interpretation by the revelation through an angel, or simply through an encounter with the risen Christ. The tomb was empty and he rose to bring new life to all. He appears at his own time, to a number of his disciples.[121]

---

[117] Gerald O'Collins. 1987. Jesus *Risen. An historical, fundamental and systematic examination of Christ's resurrection.* New York: Paulist Press, p 9.

[118] ____ p 125

[119] ____ p 124.

[120] H. Schonfield, referred to in Roch Kereszty. 2002. *Jesus Christ: fundamentals of Christology.* Revised and updated edition. (New York: St. Paul's), 50. Also B. Thierring.

[121] Rowan Williams. 2000. *On Christian theology.* Oxford: Blackwell. p 194.

What happened to the disciples, to Mary Magdalene and some other women reflected the kind of inner change and new awareness of their Master. They were brought to believe. The risen Christ has gone ahead on the road;[122] he has gone to assure us of his promise to bring us all to new life.

It is essential to our Christian faith that at the resurrection, Jesus entered in the threshold of another life—a new form of life. It is not resuscitation from the dead like what happened to Lazarus or Jairus' daughter when they returned to their old life. Jesus, the risen one, enters a new kind of life which he is going to share with us at the end of time. At our resurrection, our whole body, including our physical bodies will be transformed and raised. Unlike the Greeks in their sense of dualism, Jews see a person more as 'body and soul' together. This is our living hope, too, when God's time calls us for the ultimate redeeming value of our own resurrection.

As we celebrate the meaning of our Easter faith in the Risen Christ, we come to believe and commit ourselves to the movements of our shared heritage as men and women of the gospel. Like Peter, Mary Magdalene, Joanna, Mary the mother of James, and many others mentioned in this narrative, our mission is to be living witnesses in our efforts to live out this Easter conviction—hope and renewal for all seasons.

While the history of our past may have been burdened by a multitude of challenges and conflicting issues, what is most important about the Easter experience is, of course, our movement toward the future. In a fundamental sense, we are called to share with others the central message of a new

---

[122]   Elizabeth Schüssler Fiorenza. 1995. *Jesus: Miriam's child, Sophia's prophet. Critical issues in feminist Christology.* Continuum New York. p 126.

birth—our effort for true biblical love in our relationships with others and God.

Much has been spoken and written about the resurrection of Jesus like a happy ending to a sad story of his crucifixion and death. But resurrection is not like that. It is the opposite; the beginning of a new story, a new chapter to begin with, as we have seen among the first disciples' mission to preach the gospel. Hence, for us, too, we are given the opportunity to start anew by reaching out to others with that love shared with them.

We may have a traffic memory of experiences that happened in the past when we struggled to get on our feet, but as Easter people we have that so-called glowing torch in our hearts for a continuing mission. And that is the mission to love others to the end like that of Christ's redeeming value of great love for all of us. Happy Easter!

EASTER SUNDAY

Readings: Acts 10:34a, 37-43; Ps 118:1-2, 16-17, 22-23;
or 1 Cor 5:6b-8; Jn 20:1-9; or Lk 24:1-12[123]

The Resurrection of the Lord

*"They have taken the Lord from the tomb, and
we don't know where they put him."*

We have reached the climax of our intense encounter with
the power of the Easter experience in the liturgy. Last night
our Easter Vigil was indeed a great biblical journey and
solemnity reflecting the fullness of our redemption in light
of Jesus' paschal mystery. I would say it was suffused with
richness and meaning as it evoked the triumph of the Risen
Christ over death—the promise fulfilled in human history.

Today, however, I am delighted to see everyone here
with a sense of worship and abiding faith in the sacredness
of Jesus' gift of redemption for us. We take to heart the
meaning of each symbol and the language it conveys within
the movements of our liturgical celebration. It is our shared
experience with a deeply united community that celebrates
and commits herself to the sanctity of giving and restoring
relationships.

The resurrection of Jesus forms two fundamental
themes: proclamation and witness. It is the foundation of our
Christian faith; the mighty deed of God as Paul once said.[124]
In Paul's theology, Jesus has been from all eternity, the Son

---

[123]   Norman Perrin. 1977. *The Resurrection Narratives: A New Approach.*
London: SCM Press. p 76. Luke understands the resurrection of
Jesus as Jesus' entering into his glory after suffering (24:26).
[124]   Ulrich Wilkens. 1979. *Resurrection.* Edinburg: St Andrew Press. p 16.

of God and as sent by God down to human existence.[125] He explicitly pointed this out in 1 Cor 15:12 ff and 1 Thess 4. For him, all will indeed be raised and resurrection is God's way of facilitating the continuation of life eternal.[126] The earliest formula is the one-member clause "God has raised Jesus from the dead" which is found eight times in the NT (Rom 4:25b, 8:11a, 8:11b, 2 Cor 4:14, Gal 1:1, Eph 1:20; Col 2:12; 1 Pet 1:21).

As Christians, the human element of being united in faith claims that without resurrection, Jesus' life, teaching, and ministry would be useless. As St Paul says, "And if Christ has not been raised, then empty, [too] is our preaching; empty, too, your faith."[127]

A famous Protestant theologian, Rudolf Bultmann, said that, "Jesus was risen in the kerygma. He encounters us not as objective, historical phenomenon but in our faith to the preaching that his death brings salvation for us.[128] In other words, resurrection belongs to the category of faith. It is trans-historical since its journey from death can no longer be identified with history. It transcends history, thus Christ belongs to the present and to all times.[129]

Models of new experiences, vision, and insight give rise to the disciples' encounter—their own personal experience of Jesus moves to their priority of proclamation. It is their encounter with the Risen Jesus in a very human way. He can be touched (Lk 24:36-43), and he was recognized by them

---

[125] ibid. p 14.
[126] The Anchor Bible Dictionary. Vol V. 1992. Ed. David Noel Freeman. New York: Doubleday Press. p 691.
[127] 1 Cor 15:4
[128] Gerald O'Collins. 1987. *Jesus Risen*. London: Anchor Brendan Ltd Publications. p 195.
[129] Herbert Richards. 1986. *The First Easter: What Really Happened?* Mystic Twenty-Third Publications. p 66.

as the risen one in sharing their meal at table (Lk 24:30). We can say here the appearance of Jesus as emphasized by Luke is well present in the Eucharist.[130]

While we link the resurrection of Jesus[131] with our own experience, it is pretty much evident in our Christian lives. It is participating in the ups and downs of life, the wefts and warps, the act of dying and rising again from our mistakes and shortcomings. As a journey, our quest for an authentic Christian life comes to grips with the pains, hardships and sufferings. It is horizontal mobility where it always puts others in priority and opens the horizons for a life-giving quality of life.

As Christians in today's world, what we need is not to focus more on the resurrection in the future or in the past but rather, to commit ourselves, first and foremost in living out the values of love, peace, and justice as the basic, fundamental elements of life. Our experiences of resurrection, i.e. from sorrow to joy, failure to success, resentment to forgiveness, illness to healing bring us to be people of hope. We have reason to articulate that resurrection in the course of life makes us whole again; brings us back to rejoice in the Lord

---

[130] Perrin. *Resurrection Narratives*, p 68.
[131] Gerald O'Collins. 1988. *Interpreting the Resurrection*. New York: Paulist Press. p 9. At the time of Jesus, a Jewish tradition existed, of the martyrdom and resurrection (vindication) of eschatological figures like Enoch and Elijah. This widespread belief provided the conceptual horizon for the emergence of belief in Jesus' resurrection. Although opinions vary regarding the reception of the disciples of Jesus' self-understanding, still it is a consensus among scholars that the life, ministry and self-understanding of Jesus provided the foundation for faith in his resurrection. This contrasts the modern apologetic approach to base the belief in the resurrection upon a historical demonstration of veracity of the empty tomb and the appearances.

and even trust him and bear within us the promise of the future that Christ has won for our sake.

Our experience of death in a multitude of life's struggles makes us aware of the meaning of resurrection in a language that is within us and beyond. The same spirit dwells in us (Rom 8:11) and we come to believe and commit ourselves to the covenant of life and love. Like Peter, Mary Magdalene, and other disciples, we have this Easter conviction to be people with a heart of love and sacrifice for the others. Our shared meaning and purpose is to reach out to others with biblical love as Jesus did for our salvation. Our present movement prepares us for the future. And that's our redeeming value of resurrection. God bless you.

SECOND SUNDAY OF EASTER

Readings: Acts 5:12-16; Ps 118: 2-4, 13-15,
22-24; Rev 1:9-13, 17-19; Jn 20:19-31

Divine Mercy Sunday

*"Jesus said to them again, "Peace be with you. As the
Father has sent me, so I send you. And when he had
said this, he breathed on them and said to them, Receive
the Holy Spirit. Whose sins you forgive you are forgiven
them, and whose sins you retain are retained."*

Perhaps in some churches today the feast of the Divine Mercy
is celebrated with a great deal of devotion and spiritual
reflections depicted in the diary of Sister Maria Faustina,
the saintly Polish visionary. She promoted the message of
Divine Mercy giving highlights to trust God completely and
to repent from all transgressions. In her Diary, she shared
her visions and inner locutions that Divine Mercy is in her
soul—the mystery of mercy revealed in Christ.

However, in today's narrative taken from the gospel of
John, I would like to focus our reflection on the giving of
God's Holy Spirit to the disciples the morning after Easter
Sunday,[132] especially Thomas, who expressed his reservation

---

[132] Johannine Pentecost. This is something different from what we all
know based on the gospel of Luke who wrote the Pentecost account
in Acts 2:1-13 where he separated the Christological moments of
redemption. In his account, there is a day for the resurrection of
Jesus, another for his ascension, and still another for Pentecost. John,
however, has a different way of looking at these moments. For him,
Jesus' resurrection is bound up with his exaltation and the giving of the
Holy Spirit. When he rose from the dead, Jesus at the same time was
exalted and bestowed the Spirit on the faith community gathered to
worship him. It is not surprising, therefore, that when Jesus appeared

and doubt about the resurrected Christ. In this case, we are called to believe that God in his own way sustains us in our breath of life through faith and his Spirit. We know that the disciples first received the Holy Spirit when Jesus first appears to them as a group. Then at Pentecost according to the Acts of the Apostles (1:1-5), the disciples received the baptism of the Holy Spirit that made them recreated with power.

The power of God's Holy Spirit is identified with God's breath as 'a creative power of life' (Ps 33:6). In Hebrew it means spirit 'ruah'[133] or wind 'pneuma' in Greek. Though the Bible[134] does not tell us much about God's breath, yet some have said that it is one of the personalities of God as a Blessed

---

to his disciples, he breathed on them and said, "Receive the Holy Spirit" (John 20:22). John does not use words and images that evoke the giving of the Law at Sinai, as Luke does in Acts. It is instructive that in describing the giving of the Holy Spirit, John uses the words "breathed on them" (John 20:22). Since the term "to breathe on" or "to blow in" is linked with Gen 2:7, there is no doubt that he made an allusion to the creation narrative when God breathed into the nostril of Adam who became a living being. That is to say, just as God gave life to Adam by blowing into his nostrils, so Jesus was giving a new life to the faith community by giving them life.

[133] Baker's Evangelical Dictionary of Biblical Theology. 1996. Edited by Walter A. Elwell. Baker Book House Company, Grand Rapids, Michigan. *Ruah* can also refer to feelings. The queen of Sheba was left breathless when she saw the wisdom and wealth of Solomon (1 Kings 10:5). She was overcome by astonishment. Eliphaz accuses Job of venting his anger on God (Job 15:13). Ahab was dispirited and sullen because of Naboth's unwillingness to sell his vineyard (1 Kings 21:4). "Shortness" of spirit is impatience, whereas "longness" of spirit is patience (Prov 14:29). To be proud in spirit is to be arrogant (Eccl 7:8). The suspicious husband is said to have a (fit) spirit of jealousy (Numbers 5:14 Numbers 5:30).

[134] In Greek: pasa graphé theopneustos "All Scripture [is] God-breathed." It does not only contain the Word of God but it is the Word of God.

Trinity. There are, however, many biblical incidents where God's breath is mentioned. According to some scholars, God's breath appears 389 times in the OT. One particular incident was when God created Adam. It was the same thing that God breathed into his nostrils, the breath of life, and he became a living soul (Gen 2:7). When God was talking about the unrighteous people who lived before the Downpour, he said: 'I won't allow them to keep my breath throughout the rest of the age' (Gen 6:3).

God gives breath to people (Is 42:5) and even to lifeless bodies like in Ezek 37:9-10—when God commissions Ezekiel to prophesy to the spirit. Thus says the Lord God: 'From the four winds come, O spirit, and breathe into these slain that they may come to life . . . and the spirit came into them; they came alive and stood upright, a vast army.'

Many of the ancient Hebrew Judges and Prophets were gifted with God's breath. They were able to perform wondrous things. One of them was Joseph, the son of Jacob. He had that ability to interpret dreams as described in what he did for the Pharaoh of Egypt. He had that Breath of God (Gen 41:38). It was a drink that caused the spirit or strength of Samson to return and revive him (Jdgs 15:18-19). And it was the coming of the wagons from Egypt that revived Jacob's numb heart (Gen 45:26-27). Other men who had God's breath with special powers were Gideon and Jephthah. Even some faithful kings received special powers by God's breath. It was God himself who said that he had filled the men who took the lead in building his tent in the desert, along with all its clothing and utensils, with his breath (Ex 31:3).

It is good to remember that the apostles themselves had already demonstrated their having God's breath in miraculous ways even before the events of Pentecost. They had the power to cast out demons and to perform healing.

At Pentecost, however, they were given the added gift of prophesying and they were able to speak in tongues. As we can see, for instance, in Matthew's gospel: 'Then he called his twelve disciples to him and gave them the power to dominate and throw out unclean spirits, and to cure every sort of disease and infirmity' (Matt 10:1).

And the reason why Christ breathed on them was to give them spiritual life, new birth, and to prepare them to receive the gift of the Spirit[135] who would make them stronger and more persevering in their mission. Hence, it is the purpose of God's breath to be of service to others, not for one's self-glorification or prestige. It is always seen in the context of sharing for the sake of others.

It is the same thing in the presence of God's breath in our world today. Our faith keeps challenging us in our quest to become truly authentic Christian individuals. Like Thomas in the gospel, we, too, have doubts and reservations. We, too, want evidences and possible signs to see before we are able to believe. We may have a lot of problems to deal with, but with God's breath in our lives, we could still see a glass half full, not half empty. To keep the centerpiece promise of our faithfulness to God is to rediscover his presence in us through our prayer life where at the core lies hope in the Risen Christ.

---

[135] It was Mary's spirit that rejoiced (Luke 1:47). Jesus "grew and became strong; he was filled with wisdom" (Luke 2:40). He was "deeply moved in spirit" when he saw Mary weeping over the death of Lazarus (John 11:33). Apollos was characterized as speaking with "great fervor" (Acts 18:25) and Paul "had no peace of mind" when Titus did not meet him at Troas (2 Cor 2:13). Jesus pronounced a blessing on the "poor in spirit" (Matt 5:3). In the letters of St Paul, indeed, "the Spirit reaches the depths of everything, even the depths of God . . . . And the depths of God can only be known by the Spirit of God" (1 Cor 2:10-11).

God's breath is sacred. When we read his Word and pray to him, we are challenged to breathe new life into a significant path of our calling. As Christ gives Thomas a convincing message that he is truly risen, in our calling, there is also a message that draws us to live the values of the gospel with a risk involved—a risk of being rejected or despised. Let our doubts or disbeliefs especially in our journey of relationship be transformed into a new vision with God's breath to bring his love to all people. There is much to say for those who are wounded in their lives and in our world today, but the wounds of Jesus' suffering are wounds that turn into spiritual healing and salvation. It is the power of God's breath that enables us to believe and see beyond the marks of Jesus' passion. God bless you.

THIRD SUNDAY OF EASTER

Readings: Acts 9:1-6, 7-20; Ps 30; Rev 5:11-14; Jn 21:1-19

Dynamic Relationship with God

Jesus said, "Simon, son of John, do you love me? . . . . Feed
my sheep! . . . . Tend my sheep! . . . . Peter felt hurt because
he said to him the third time, "Do you love me?" And
he said to him, "Lord, you know everything; you know
that I love you." Jesus said to him, "Feed my sheep."

Perhaps in the world of superstitions each culture has something to tell us. There are certain values and wisdom like in fishing that have been passed on from generation to generation. In Judaism, for instance, there are many superstitions related to life cycle events and some of them are connected to the evil eye *'ayin ha rah.'*

Among fishermen we find their sense of reliance upon the changes of the moon side by side with the weather. Many of them believe that children are always born when the tide is full and die when it is ebbing. Countless tales and superstitions about fishing have been told. Ernest Hemingway's The Old Man and the Sea, for instance, recounts Santiago's struggle for 84 days without catching any fish at all. He is so unlucky but eventually on the eighty-fifth day, he's able to catch a big 'marlin.' One superstition says that to bring a banana or a black suitcase on a crab fishing boat is a bad sign. One cannot catch fish. I am not sure about the popular reason for that but as far as I know, banana peels could cause crew members to slip and fall on deck. Then a black suitcase, as they say, is a harbinger of death or illness.

I am saying this because in today's gospel we find the seven disciples fishing all night and catching nothing. Some Jewish superstitions give rise to their belief that they probably have travel bags with them or they miss the direction of shooting stars. But the Risen Jesus on the shore tells them to try again. And they catch plentiful fish. That's the beginning when one of the disciples, John the Beloved, recognizes him. And the other disciples like Peter, for instance, join Jesus for breakfast in the shore.

We could probably imagine places like Cancun in Mexico and many other Caribbean beaches that are popular these days for summer holidays. Beds and breakfast, for instance, are pretty common in various cities. And in Jesus' time we could also imagine the disciples with the Risen Jesus near the Sea of Galilee as they are bound for home to continue their occupation of fishing.

This time though, they are invited by Jesus for breakfast in the seashore. Like all the gospel meals there are eucharistic actions reflected in his hospitality. As it says in the gospel, 'Jesus came and took the bread and gave it to them.' Allusions to his other meals with the sinners and tax collectors, the Beatitudes, feeding the multitudes of 5,000 people, and his Supper in Emmaus, bring to mind similar eucharistic overtones and the common element of the celebration of the mass today: 'Go in peace to love and serve the Lord.'

This is a gospel of relationship that restores, transforms and heals any wounds of betrayal and abandonment as shown by the disciples at the height of Jesus' passion and death on the cross. They all have left Jerusalem for Galilee and have returned to their major occupation as fishermen.

Jesus' invitation to come and eat is the engine room of nourishment. It restores opportunities to enter into God's future for us and challenges us to move forward with that missionary task as Jesus tells Peter: 'Feed my lambs, tend and feed my sheep.' It speaks to what is needed to know clearly in that perspective of proclamation and profession of faith in the Risen Christ.

Peter this time gets reconciled with Jesus as he is asked if he really loves him. It must be a humiliating experience for him being guilty of the betrayal he commits. But Jesus has waited for the right time and that's after they have eaten breakfast together. He asks him if he really loves him. Jesus' psychology is well enough to guide Peter into a deeper knowledge of his faith in him. To love him means to be willing to sacrifice himself for his sake; for his kingdom and for his church.

Like Peter each of us is called to this kind of relationship that we can commit to loving and sharing our lives with others through sacrifice and compassion. I remember what the American novelist Mary Flannery O'Connor[136] taught us in her writings regarding the value of reading great literature. The most important challenge is not developing a style but developing the ability to see, to be receptive to the wonders in the created world, the mysteries present in the lives of people.[137]

---

[136] cf. Wikipedia, free encyclopedia online. Born on March 25, 1925-August 3, 1964. She was an American novelist, short-story writer and essayist. An important voice in American literature, O'Connor wrote two novels and 32 short stories, as well as a number of reviews and commentaries. She was a Southern writer who often wrote in a Southern Gothic style and relied heavily on regional settings and grotesque characters. O'Connor's writing also reflected her own Roman Catholic faith, and frequently examined questions of morality and ethics.

[137] Quoted from *Good Literature unveils God's Creation*. Fr Robert Lander. The Tablet. Vol. 99, No. 1. April 1, 2006.

We are called to develop our dynamic relationship with God centered on Jesus and his mission to love without limits. He sets us on the road where we are now—to keep those values alive, our Judeo-Christian values, which I think are the greatest gift we can pass on to this generation. We don't lose our focus as we remember those generations who have brought us to where we are now.

As we find meaning, both personal and communal, in our sense of witnessing as followers of Christ, we experience his presence in our lives. Each time we celebrate the eucharist we touch upon the paschal mysteries—his passion, death and resurrection and we are drawn or challenged to respond to his offer of life and love through our brothers and sisters in faith. God bless you.

FOURTH SUNDAY OF EASTER

Readings: Acts 13:14, 43-52; Rev 7:9, 14-17; Jn 10:27-30

Jesus, the Good Shepherd

Nowadays, movements across the world seem to be clouded with fear, skepticism and moral degeneration especially in family structure or faith formation. The erosion of public confidence in institutions as well as individual leaders in many countries makes us think that there is tension, along with a multitude of voices asking that their demands be addressed. They are pretty strong as we brace for a kind of culture that has been a challenging experience—the culture of argument.

The Irish-born British literary writer, Clive Staples Lewis,[138] also known as C.S. Lewis, once made a remark about blending two virtues as a key to understanding the meaning of our faith in God. He said that if we ask twenty good men of this present time what they consider as the supreme Christian virtue, most of them would likely say it is unselfishness.[139] However, if we ask the Christians of old about it, most of them would tell you, it is love.

As a normative pattern in our quest to become truly Christian in today's world, love and our sense of otherness are inextricably linked with one another. There is a connection

---

[138] cf. Wikipedia, free encyclopedia online. Lewis was a close friend of J. R. R. Tolkien, and both authors were leading figures in the English faculty at Oxford University and in the informal Oxford literary group known as the "Inklings". According to his memoir Surprised by Joy, Lewis had been baptized in the Church of Ireland at birth, but fell away from his faith during his adolescence.

[139] cf. C. S. Lewis. *The Weight of Glory*. 1980 (Revised). Harper Collins Publisher. New York, NY. p 25.

when we deal with human relationship. As we seek to live the gospel there is a basic principle that is implicit in our lives—to love and be willing to sacrifice.

In today's liturgy of Good Shepherd Sunday, we see the Christ-like leadership who cares for his sheep. In this way, we see the intimate union with great richness of shepherding and witnessing to the covenant of God's love for his sheep—his people. Jesus invites us to use our imagination as we take to heart the essentials of being called to serve either as a leader or a follower. Jesus is not a literal shepherd. We are not literal sheep. He is not talking about literal thieves and bandits. He uses a figure of speech that has a whole spiritual meaning in the context of service and commitment to church, to our continuing ministry or vocation as inspired by the love of God. The spirituality draws us to unite ourselves with Christ as we become dedicated servants of our brothers and sisters. All these comprise our response to the great mystery of God.

We could imagine here that Jesus is comparing himself to the scribes and Pharisees, the religious leaders and teachers of the law who, instead of setting good examples to others, are making themselves look foolish and even discriminated against. The imagery of a 'thief' or a 'bandit' takes the forces or attitudes that make it difficult for someone to engage life according to the ideals of his faith. It could be some form of greed or addiction to power, alcohol, gambling. It could also be a form of excessive emphasis on oneself as regards his needs and desires.

A shepherd *knows*[140] his sheep. He loves them and is willing to risk his own life to protect the sheep. He is familiar

---

[140] The word "know" *ginosko* means to know experientially. Very often in the Bible it is used in terms of a love relationship.

with their behavioral patterns or tendencies. He knows which one likes to wander; he knows which ones are most inclined to eating and those who are slow. Sheep, however, dislike wind blowing in their face. You notice that they always turn their backs to the wind. But with a shepherd they follow without any problem because they know that following him is the way to get home.

Shepherds are known for leading the flock to green pastures and quiet water—feeding them and protecting them too (see Jer 31:10). Their biblical image of leadership has a lot to say as spiritual guides. They have a great sense of generosity and service to others. It is what Peter says in his letter: "Do not lord it over those in your charge, but are examples to the flock" (1 Peter 5:2-3). Even Paul's letters to Timothy and Titus, say that it is their responsibility as pastors[141] of God's people for the care of Christ's people, leading them to holy life.

I remember an article about Archbishop Timothy Dolan that was published in the New York Times recently. It was a good reflection of shepherding as he has earned the affection of many priests and lay people. He is always moving around, visiting parishes where 'parishioners stood in line for hours to shake his hand and say that he—a bearish warm-blooded, tough-talking Midwesterner—was "a breath of fresh air."[142] He's theologically a conservative leader with his loyalty to

---

[141] The term 'pastor' is used only one time in the Bible to explain the role of the spiritual leader of a local church: "it was he who gave some to be apostles, some to be prophets, some to be evangelists, and some to be pastors and teachers" (Eph 4:11) The concept, however, is found throughout the bible. "Pastor" is another word for shepherd. Jesus himself declared, "I am the good shepherd" (Jn 10:11).

[142] Paul Vitello. *Archbishop Earns Praise In First Year, As Tests Await.* The New York Times. Vol. CLIX, No. 55, 011. April 15, 2010. pp A20 & A24.

the pope, an outward-looking leader with a vision as he revitalizes the morale of parishioners and priests during this difficult time.

He is an example of a shepherd who knows his flock; one who calls his people to holy life; and one who really loves them. His sense of management and pastoral ministry are combined with intellect and a Christ-like leadership.

As we struggle these days to respond to the signs of the times, we turn our gaze to Christ as our high priest and Good Shepherd. We never lose sight of the center whose great mystery sustains us with his grace and allows us to develop more in our faith that we are indeed men and women of the Gospel.

Our priestly life that we share with Christ by virtue of our baptism reminds us of our role as bearers of the good news to others and this is one of the best expressions of our spiritual identity as Christians. We strive to live out our sense of belonging to Christ in unity and hope as we echo his words on the night of his betrayal: "I ask not only on behalf of these, but also on behalf of those who will believe in me through their word, that they may all be one. As you, Father, are in me and I am in you, may they also be in us, so that the world may believe that you have sent me" (John 17: 20-21). God bless you.

FIFTH SUNDAY OF EASTER

Readings: Acts 14:21-27; Ps 145:8-13;
Rev 21:1-5a; Jn 13:31-33a, 34-35

Love One Another

*"My children, I will be with you only a little while longer. I give
you a new commandment: love one another. As I have loved you,
so you also should love one another. This is how all will know
that you are my disciples, if you have love for one another."*

In the heart of any form of literature either biblical or
literary representation of the heroic figure, the concept of
love is largely identified within a relationship that copes
with life's tests and struggles. While there is virtually
unanimous accountability and interpersonal involvement,
human love is certainly the voice so powerful that can make
a huge difference in this world. It is a response to the ongoing
challenge that allows God to evangelize our hearts or shape
us from within as we stand in relationship with others.

The love command of Jesus in John's gospel helps us
focus on God's purpose and why he sends his only Son to
the world, i.e. to give eternal life to all of us as we bring
ourselves in fellowship with him through unity and mutual
love. This is the touchstone of all subsequent reflections in
Christian life.

It might be better to say that life and love can be
summed up in one word: "you never know." Befitting the
life we lead, we are confident that everything will be fine. But
when problems begin to afflict us, then we start to doubt and
question our human nature. We begin to fight, inflame our
passions for something that at times goes beyond proportion.

Difficult times require strong disposition to act with courage and conviction that we are faithful to the covenant of love. Evidently, this is what Jesus tells his disciples as he uses his final hours preparing them for the future when he is no longer with them. He explains to them what they must do in his absence in order to fulfill his legacy.

Perhaps it is good to keep in mind that many of the commands of Jesus connect revelation with obedience. Some of them, for instance, "If you obey my commands, you will remain in my love" (Jn 15:10); "If you hold to my teaching, you are really my disciples (Jn 8:31); "If anyone keeps my word, he will never see death (Jn 8:51). Sometimes Jesus invites people 'to believe' with obedient action which is peculiar to John's gospel.

However, looking in today's world some people find it difficult to believe that God is love. They keep saying that 'if God is a God of love, how can he allow so much injustice, tragedy and misery in the world?' Although God may not always reveal to us the reason why he allows suffering and injustice to continue, at least we know that he is willing to take it on himself. We know that from the beginning there was perfect harmony between God and our first parents. But in Gen 3, we see that they rebelled against God and sin and evil entered the world. Which is why, all the suffering and injustice we experience in this world is a consequence of human sin.

Each time I deal with the issue of why God allows suffering and injustice, I think of Job. He is like an OT theologian who would say 'I firmly believe in God' and who would care for God's concerns in daily life. He is a stunning example of suffering or orthopathy. His school of formation was his own life experiences. As he went through trials and tests, he began to long for God's mercy and compassion. Job never asked for healing. He just asked for friendship with God (Job 29:4). Most of his discourses are directed to God inquiring of God's goodness, challenging God, demanding of God, and confronting him with holy persistence (cf Jas 5:11).

If we look at history in Europe there is a long story of man's inhumanity to one another.[143] There's greed, power, fear, and the running sore of racial tension. We speak of the Spanish Inquisition in the 15th century at the time of Ferdinand and Isabella when they enforced the policy of converting Spanish Jews and Muslims to Christianity. This is known as *'limpieza de sangre'* (cleanliness of blood) against descendants of converted Jews or Muslims.[144] The Atlantic slave trade primarily of African people to the New World by the British, French, and Dutch;[145] the large-scale gas chambers used for killing by Nazi Germany's bureaucracy as part of their genocide program during the Holocaust;[146] Imperial Russia use of the remote Siberian forced labor camps.[147] What's the bottom line of all these? Power and greed.

As a young generation inclined to discover anew the springs of faith in our human perspective, there is always meaning and significance when the work of love takes the centerpiece—the linchpin to our Christian lives. Our

---

[143] cf. John Wenham. 1974. *The Goodness of God*. London: Intervarsity Press.

[144] Henry Kamen. 1999. *The Spanish Inquisition: A Historical Revision*. Yale University Press. ISBN 0300078803. The slave trade is sometimes called the Maafa by African and African-American scholars, meaning "holocaust" or "great disaster" in Swahili. Some scholars use the terms African Holocaust.

[145] cf. Roger Anstey. 1975. *The Atlantic Slave Trade and British abolition, 1760-1810*. London: Macmillan. p 5.

[146] Michael Berenbaum. 2006. *The World Must Know*. United States Holocaust Museum. p 103.

[147] cf. wikipedia, free encyclopedia online.

common reason for being in this world is to share God's love for one another. That's the main essence of being created. In his last will and testament to his disciples, Jesus emphasizes that they should love one another. No matter how difficult or painful it may be, in relation with God means to be men and women rooted in their loving actions where the mystery of God's presence reflects his true identity—the God of love. God bless you.

SIXTH SUNDAY OF EASTER

Readings: Acts 15:1-2, 22-29; Ps 67:2-3, 5-6,
8; Rev 21:10-14, 22-23; Jn 14:23-29

Obedience to God's Commands

*"The Advocate, the Holy Spirit, whom the Father
will send in my name, will teach you everything
and remind you of all that I told you."*

If we look back at the time during the collapse of the Western
Roman Empire in the fifth century which also marked the
beginning of the Dark Ages, Europe became feudalistic
with the construction of many castles and walled cities for
protection against barbaric raids and invaders, especially
the Vikings, the Normans. It was a time so replete with
war, plague, sorrow, torture, and invasions that Christianity
became stronger and spread bringing the promise of eternal
life to all believers.

However, there was one famous scholar in the later
8th century who is known in history as the ear of Europe's
intellectual elite, tutor and adviser to Charlemagne the Great
on religious and educational matters. He was known as
Alcuin of York. It was a difficult time when the Church was
constantly attacked by those who opposed her orthodoxy.
There was widespread illiteracy and schools of learning
were only concentrated in monasteries and cathedrals. But
Alcuin helped Charlemagne achieve the renaissance of
learning and reform of the Church. He set up schools for
quality instructions and one of the things they established,
still in use today, was writing standards.[148] He and other

---

[148]   Online: http://www.jaars.org/museum/alphabet/people/alcuin.htm

monks inculcated the value of patience, discipline, practice and obedience. It was obedience to the prescribed format, rules like in the alignment of each letter, and consistency in style.

I think it is the same in any discipline where there is a need to apply these values. Even in today's gospel Jesus tells his disciples, 'whoever loves me will keep my word, and whoever does not love me does not keep my word.' Evidently, it also reminds us of his own perfect obedience to the will of his Father when he poured out his very lifeblood for our salvation. It is the key to achieve the goal; the secret of success. And many texts in the bible provide us with obedience to commands heard. Some of them are: But this I commanded them, saying: 'Listen to and obey my voice, and I will be your God, and you shall be my people; and walk completely in the ways that I command you, so that it may be well to you' (Jer 7:23). 'Blessed are those who hear the word of God [within your heart] and keep it [practice, obey]' (Lk 11:28). 'He [Jesus] became the Author and Source of eternal salvation to all those who give heed and obey Him (Heb 5:9).'

There are times when our temptation to defy or negate the rules and regulations triumphs over us. By nature, we are indeed free spirited people. We want to do it in our own way; we want to be different or unique the way we interpret certain things like in liturgy, for instance. We want to be free and make our own choice without bothering anybody. But I think we also need structure. To ensure peace, justice, and harmony, we need to establish laws in our land. This is part of any institution either family or government or church. Abraham Lincoln best captured this spirit by describing the spirit of democracy in a form of government: 'government of the people, by the people, for the people.'

Jesus assures us with his promise that if we obey his teaching, the Father will love us and will send the Holy Spirit. In a world where our lives at times may seem unbearably difficult, leaving us vulnerable in many circumstances, I feel that the challenge for our Christian obedience allows us to rediscover in depth the dimensions of hope in our genuine growth as people called to holiness. Public negativity on several cases rises as regards past failures, lost of moral credibility, hostility to religion animated by a religious vision no longer rooted in the reality of God, or religion that is exclusive that makes distinctions between believers and unbelievers.

To say 'where there is much historical smoke, there must have been a fire' reminds us of our roles to play as we respond to new challenges. We believe something must have happened that reflects the image of our history. But equal opportunity to move from the bottom of the ladder to enable ourselves to participate in human mobility, would fire the engines of achievement.

Like Jesus' instruction to his disciples, our Christian life will be shaped by God's love for us, his abiding presence in us will bring to fruition in many ways, and his Spirit will remind us of all that he taught and bring us peace. Peace that is built on communion with God; peace that is essentially at the core of our sanctuary—in our hearts and in our minds.

The angst of the Dark Ages[149] may now provide us the gateway to other healing crusades with our virtue of hope for the true quest of who Jesus really is in today's world. Perhaps

---

[149] "The Dark Ages" because they were in fact full of grief, sorrow, torture, invasions and plague. This went through for a full millennium until the XV century when Constantinople finally fell and the Renaissance emerged bringing new ways of thinking along with more rights for people

our faith in God, with all of our historical differences and perspectives, is now superseded by faith in the delicate distinction of every human being. We carry within ourselves the genetic blueprints and versions of the past that seem to be the same pattern, a consequence of moral transgressions that replicate human history.

As we live out the meaning of obedience in our Christian lives and the gift of the Spirit that will guide us in this world, we keep hope alive that life can be what we make it and with a remarkable sense of God's presence in our lives. We can truly say what Pope Benedict XVI wrote to his brother-priests during the proclamation of the Year for Priests in June 2009: "to welcome the new springtime which the Spirit is now bringing about in the Church, not least through the ecclesial movements and the new communities."[150] God bless you.

---

[150] cf. Faith and Statistics. <u>The Tablet</u>. Vol. 103, No. 4. May 1, 2010. p 11.

ASCENSION OF THE LORD

Readings: Acts 1:1-11; Ps 47:2-3, 6-7, 8-9; Eph 1:17-
23/Heb 9:24-28; 19:19-23; Lk 24:46-53

A New Kind of Presence—Our Commissioning
to Preach the Good News

*"Then he led them out as far as Bethany, raised his
hands, and blessed them. As he blessed them he
parted from them and was taken up to heaven."*

There are times that we all need to step back—a time for
reflection. We can take heart in the recognition that God's
action often happens in moments of our human frailties;
when we experience sufferings or failures. I sometimes insist
that we need the experience of listening to the wisdom of
others. We need to see in the perspective of what our lives
tell us as we endeavor to make amends for and rectify certain
issues that have to do with our relationships.

I remember when I grieved at the thought of leaving the
parish where I started knowing the people and my ministry
was just beginning to take shape. Part of my prayer at that
time was a deeper understanding of our mission and in my
own little way I welcomed it as a challenge where some of
my wounds became locations of God's grace. I embarked on
another path not with a chip on my shoulder, figuratively
speaking, but with obedience and trust in the Lord.

Today as we celebrate the feast of the Ascension
of our Lord, we rediscover in depth the solemn event of
commissioning anchored in the mission of charity and
commitment to the moral vision of the Church. The call we
have been given has a colossal meaning larger than we are.

We embrace it with awareness of the world within us and around us. We explore it with an attitude of sharing and a welcoming culture.

Literally, Jesus returns to his Father in heaven. But he does not leave us orphans. He sends us the Holy Spirit to clothe us with courage and guide us in our way. He provides us with his legacy—leaving us with his mission to preach the good news of salvation. He shows us the way to evangelize our hearts through his teachings of loving one another either in parables, metaphors, allegories, or his beatitudes. His mantra of love transfigures our mortality, our vulnerability in diverse movements of our humanity.

What our future holds in regard to our destiny in the life hereafter is like that of Jesus in his triumphant glory that is no longer conditioned by time and space. Just one snapshot of that vision or foresight perhaps, a new springtime of hope allows us to shape more from within our love relationship with God. It is like a bridge across the gulf of separation which is being inhuman to others. His challenge follows a path of imitation with the inner voice of Christ in many circumstances. The words of the apostle Paul urge us to give ourselves preferentially to our brothers and sisters who are most in need.[151]

In biblical literature we find, for instance, Jacob when he is about to die Immediately, he calls all of his sons and gives his blessings over them. But these blessings also serve to some degree as predictions about what's going to happen to them in the future (cf Gen 49). Moses, however, when God commissions him to interpret the law for the leaders of the community, has a prediction, too, that the people will

---

[151] Quoted from Pope Benedict XVI. Message for World Day of Migrants and Refugees. Theme focuses on the Family. Vatican City, Nov. 14, 2006. "Caritas Christi urget nos" (1 Cor 5:14).

worship other gods. It is why Moses commands Eleazar the priest, son of Aaron, and Joshua, son of Nun, to speak the words of the law. And he goes on to ask the people to choose their own leader who can interpret the law for them and can dedicate their lives to this mission. He cautions them to be very careful in obeying the law, along with the precepts. The Book of Deuteronomy echoes the long speech of Moses to the people of Israel before they enter the Promised Land.

At the time when Cardinal Karol Wojtyla became pope on Oct. 16, 1978, Cardinal Stefan Wyszynski told him that his duty as the new pope would be to introduce the Church into the Third Millennium—the 21st century. He did it with so much difficulty similar to what Pope Emeritus Benedict XVI had experienced. Several themes of his papacy: the threat posed by secularism in Europe, the tension between faith and reason, and the role of ethics in economics.[152] Whether one agrees or not we believe he fulfilled his Petrine service. We recall when he reached 80 years of age and asked himself if the time had come for him to say the prayer of that biblical Simeone we usually pray at night: 'nunc dimittis' which means 'now Master you may let your servant go.'

His last will and testament evoked his complete trust in the Lord with a grateful heart for that gift of vocation to serve him and for countless people who had been part of his life since the beginning. His 'totus tuus ego sum' (Latin for "I am completely in Your hands") inspires us to keep going with our role to play either in the family, church, or society. Each of us has his own mission to fulfill; a mission with which to be held accountable. As Frederick Buechner once said, "To find your mission in life is to discover the

---

[152]   Rachel Donadio. *Pope Issues Forceful Statement on Sexual Abuse Crisis*. The New York Times. Vol. CLIX., No. 55, 038. May 12, 2010. p A4.

intersection between your heart's deep gladness and the world's deep hunger." Where our heart goes for people who hunger for God's word, there lies the depth of joy in our heart. God bless you.

SEVENTH SUNDAY OF EASTER

Readings: Acts 7:55-60; Ps 97:1-2, 6-7, 9;
Rev 22:12-14, 16-17, 20; Jn 17:20-26

The Testament of Jesus (Jesus' High Priestly Prayer)

Lifting up his eyes to heaven, Jesus prayed, saying *"Holy
Father, I pray not only for them, but also for those who will
believe in me through their word, so that they may all be one,
as you, Father, are in me and I in you, that they also may
be in us, that the world may believe that you sent me."*

A sociologist of American society stated that "all American
values point to a central constellation: the value of the
individual personality."[153] I think it makes sense since
we're all different, we're all individuals. We can be known
and labeled as such through our own identity, personality,
uniqueness, gifts and talents, etc. Our relationships through
the daily affairs of our life determine who we are especially
in the hustle and bustle of the lives we lead these days. Our
commitment defines us as we continue to get involved in the
challenges of being ethical human beings in our daily lives.

I was reading a section from the New York Times
about a famous Russian cellist—Mr. Rostropovich who
was remembered by the music performers in a concert held
recently. I think it is a common expression if not universally
acknowledged by many students in the conservatory of music
that pianists are neurotic, violinists vain and cellists are nice.
They are sociable, friendly, and straightforward. I don't know

---

[153] Robin Williams, *American Society: A Sociological Interpretation*.
Second Edition (New York: Knoph, 1960), reprinted in William
Dryness, *How Does America Hear the Gospel?* (Grand Rapids, MI:
Eerdmans, 1989), p. 97.

if it's true but again, it all depends on the personality of the individual person. According to the writer, all students of Mr Rostropovich talked of being required to learn a concerto in two days or to come back and play the Bach cello suites from memory in a week.[154] No one is excused. He said he could not forget him saying when he played Brahms, 'You haven't cried enough tears in your life to play this music.'[155]

Comparatively, today's gospel reminds me of this: what life means. Its continuing conversation with the world—its ups and downs, joys and sorrows, successes and failures, etc. As death draws closer, Jesus speaks well to his disciples of what his life and ministry/mission really mean and what awaits them when he returns to his Father in heaven. This is like a solemn prayer that Jesus utters in this particular chapter of John's gospel (17:20-26). It is called "Jesus' High Priestly or Intercessory Prayer." Like those farewell discourses of Moses in the book of Deuteronomy and the Testaments of the Twelve Patriarchs,[156] there are elements of what life of discipleship is and parting advice to loved ones.

This episode in today's gospel is a solemn prayer of Jesus to his Father. He prays for his glorification, for Christian unity and protection against the evils of society. He prays not only for his community of disciples but also for those who will believe in him through their preaching (Jn. 17:20). Love appears five times in three short sentences.[157] He prays that unity among the members of the Christian community be

---

154   Michael White. *Remembering Rostropovich, The Master Teacher.* The New York Times, Sunday, May 13, 2007. Section 2 Arts and Leisure, p. 22.
155   ibid.
156   cf. Fr John R. Donahue, S.J. *Reading the Will.* America, Vol. 184 No. 17, May 21, 2001.
157   ibid.

a sign of God's love so that all may come to know who Jesus is. His prayer towards the end reminds us of the incident in the Last Supper with his disciples when he tells them about his new commandment that they love one another as he has loved them.

Jesus follows the road to crucifixion. It is how he makes us realize what life of discipleship means in the context of love. His death on the cross becomes a model for us—a compendium of his love for us. It is not, as they say, one of the issues that becomes the straw to break the camel's back. Rather, it stands at the heart of Christ's mission: total giving of oneself for the sake of others.

Jesus' prayer for love and unity inspired many of us, like those saints, leaders, and proponents of peace and justice in this world. Our calling as teachers, musicians, priests, religious, etc is associated with the quality of love and sacrifice and our primary mission is to care for our brothers and sisters, especially for those that the Lord places in our care. As a leader, for instance, his/her primary mission is to care for the vulnerable lambs and sheep in a world so harsh that fidelity to this mission may lead to martyrdom.[158]

I'd like to close with a story you have probably heard already. It's about a young mother whose eight-year-old daughter came to her one day and said, "Mommy, if you've done something bad and say you're sorry and you really do mean it, can it be okay? Well, the mother might not know exactly what her daughter really meant about it and said to her, "Yes, of course, if you really mean you're sorry about it things can be okay." And her daughter said, "Well, mom, you know that piece of furniture that you really love? "Yes, honey,

---

[158]   John R. Donahue, S.J. *The Word*. <u>America</u>, Vol. 184 No. 14, April 23, 2001.

that's a family heirloom—a sofa which I inherited from your great grandma—Margaret." "What about that?" asked the mother. "Well, you know, mom, yesterday I was so mad at you. I took my crayons and I wrote, "Stupid mommy, stupid mommy," all over that sofa. The mother groaned inside. That was a family heirloom, but she loved her daughter and so she just said, "Because you're very sorry about it, it can be okay." And they went and got a bucket of water and some rags and they gently scrubbed the sofa and restored it to the way that it should be. And the mother said. "You know, I think that's a metaphor for how God treats us. Because he loves us, in grace he cleans us so that we become whole again, renewed, and at peace with ourselves and others.

Mr. Rostropovich's statement: You haven't cried enough tears in your life to play this music is a continuing parallel which addresses us to live in love and seek unity through our living sacrifice. God bless you.

PENTECOST SUNDAY

Readings: Acts 2:1-11; Ps 104; 1 Cor 12:3-7, 12-13;
or Rom 8:8-17; Jn 20:19-23/Jn 14:15-16, 23-26

The Pentecost Moment in the Life of the Church

*"Peace be with you. As the Father has sent me, so I send you."
And when he had said this, he breathed on them and said to
them, "Receive the Holy Spirit. Whose sins you forgive are
forgiven them, and whose sins you retain are retained."*

Perhaps you remember the story of Prometheus[159] in Greek
mythology where he stole fire from Zeus and gave it to human
beings. With that he awakened in humans a consciousness of
the gift and power of knowledge. But Zeus was enraged by
what he did and punished him for that crime. He chained
him to a rock in the Caucus mountains while a great eagle
ate his liver every day only to have it grow back to be eaten
again the next day.[160]

In a world wounded by many conflicts it is necessary for
humanity to commit to the fire of knowledge and love within
us: our Prometheus bound relationship to the institutions—
family, church and society. Today, as we celebrate Pentecost
Sunday, we are challenged to respond to different voices
as we continue to face in church circles the crisis in moral
credibility and leadership. Even in civil affairs as regards
our government, health care, education, and many others,
we are challenged to take part in establishing a voice for the
good of all.

---

[159] Whose name means "forethought" or "he who thinks ahead."
[160] cf. M.L. West Commentaries on Hesiod, W.J. Werdenins
commentaries on Hesiod and R. Lamberton's Hesiod, pp 95-100.

In biblical literature there is something different from what we all know based on the Pentecost account written by Luke in Acts 2:1-13 where he separated the day for the Resurrection of Jesus, another for his Ascension, and still another for Pentecost event. John's gospel, however, has a different way of looking at these moments when the Holy Spirit descends upon the first community of disciples. For him, Jesus' resurrection is bound up with his triumph and the giving of the Holy Spirit. It is his Johannine Pentecost and for him, when he resurrected, Jesus at the same time was exalted and gifted the Spirit to the faith community gathered in worship. It is why, Jesus breathed on them and said, "Receive the Holy Spirit" (Jn 20:22).[161]

Questions that arise while we espouse great tolerance for other disciplines and faith traditions tell us: how do we respond to the signs of the times and what is the Pentecost meaning in all of these things? In many ways we have seen a lot of changes during the past four decades after Vatican II. We also have witnessed waves of indifference along with the culture of arguments that have been plunged well into the fabric of our everyday life.

These are the challenges we face; issues we deal with in human history. The powerful gift of Pentecost entails a mission that shapes the inner life of the church. We are the church! And we are called to work together using our gifts and talents that have to be shared with others so that we become one Body of Christ.

---

[161] John does not use words and images that evoke the giving of the Law at Sinai, as Luke does in Acts. It is instructive that in describing the giving of the Holy Spirit, John uses the words "breathed on them" (Jn 20:22). Since the term "to breathe on" or "to blow in" is linked with Gen 2:7. John made an allusion to the creation narrative when God breathed into the nostril of Adam and became a living being.

A large part of the call is the attitude of sharing. It is going an extra mile to reach out to those who are in need. We may recall moments when much of our communication continues to plague the family or church with a number of misdeeds and tragedies. As a church we continue to deal with legal and financial problems from crises in authority and leadership.

This is what we argue and disagree over, discuss lengthily and defend with commitment to faith like those of Jesus' disciples, as our institution is in deep crisis. The shortage of priests in parishes and communities is also one of the challenges we face. According to reports in the Catholic Reporter, more than 3, 300 U.S. parishes are led by pastoral administrators, of whom nearly half are lay, a third women religious and nearly twenty percent permanent deacons.

As a church, we are urged to pray for more vocations in the priesthood and religious life. We pray for those who will dedicate their lives to God and continue the work of Christ. This is one voice that this Pentecost moment is telling us and continuously inviting us not to be afraid to find a new voice that will unite us to hope across the divides of our perspectives and ideas of church. God bless you.

TRINITY SUNDAY

Readings: Prov 8:22-31; Ps 8; Rom 5:1-5; Jn 16:12-15

The Threefold Nature of God—A Deeper
Understanding of our Own Nature

I still remember as a newly ordained priest when I first embarked on a parish setting as an assistant to the pastor. Being 'fresh from the oven' as my senior confreres used to call me, it became well known to me as a challenge to my theological struggle for the social and political transformation in the context of inequality and oppression. It also involved me with exploration into the grassroots level of parishioners who come from different cultures. In my ministry, however, I learned to integrate my theological studies in situations where every Christian desires to understand and apply God's message for life in relation to others.

If ministry is about relationships where the heart of the gospel gets incarnated in the flesh and blood of witnessing, I think in dealing with our understanding of the triune life of God—the Blessed Trinity, the concept of relations is pretty much intertwined within their identity and role as Trinitarian. Because the Spirit is sent, the Father and Son stand into loving unity. It is the Divine unity which is actively unifying in the one Divine life the lives of the three Divine persons.[162] The triune God is the God who is open to man, open to the world, and open to time.[163]

Today's feast of the Blessed Trinity allows us to be reminded once again of God's internal relations as essentially

---

[162]   L. Hodgson. 1943. *The Doctrine of the Trinity*. London. p 95.
[163]   J. Moltmann. 1977. *The Church in the Power of the Spirit*. ET. London. p 56.

spiritual and eternal. They give us a glimpse of their closeness, intimacy and communion.[164]They embrace a very significant mystery in our mission and worship. Gregory Nazianzen, the great Cappadocian Father of the fourth century who contributed immensely to the formation of the doctrine of the Trinity wrote that when he says "God," he means Father, Son, and the Holy Spirit.[165] It is the name of the relation in which the Father stands to the Son, and the Son to the Father.[166] Today, for most of us Christians, our usual way of referring to God is 'God' or, at a popular level, 'our Lord.'

A clear outlook on the Trinity brings us to turn our attention more inward as we live in a relationship of love and communion. Their relationship to one another in planning and securing our salvation flows from their unity as three Divine persons. In connection with our lives, it makes us deeply aware of our relationship with others; how we treat others or respond to their needs. Our horizontal level of relating with them and a vertical level that leads to God is the flesh and blood of what the Blessed Trinity reveals to us. It is simple and yet their sublime image is meant to be extended to others. In our prayer, worship or communion with God, there is a Trinitarian meaning where our Christian experience focuses on loving being the concern of every human person.

In biblical literature there are so many passages in the life and history of Israel that refer to Yahweh as Creator. One of them is the Genesis story where God is referred to as

---

[164] cf. 365 Days with the Lord—Liturgical Bible Diary. 1998. St Paul's Publishing, Philippines. p June 7, 1998.
[165] Gregory Nazianzen, *Oration*. 38:8.
[166] Gregory Nanzianzen. Loc. cit. cf. T.F. Torrance. 1994. *The Trinitarian Faith*. op. cit. pp 239 f., 320 ff,: 'Idem Trinitarian Perspectives. Edinburgh: T & T. Clark.

Creator. If we look at the exodus experience of the Israelites from the bondage of Egypt, we find that the God of history reveals himself as Savior. What is only foreshadowed in the OT becomes clear in the NT.[167] Through the coming of Christ he makes the mystery of God's innermost life present in us and it is through the Cross that the life of the Trinity becomes a revelation of God's unconditional love for us. His legacy implies a commitment to loving which speaks volumes about willingness to sacrifice for the sake of others. Without it one cannot claim that his Christian experience is Trinitarian. There is always an element of love that evidently describes who God is in our lives. God is love (1 Jn 4:8). And when we address him as our God and Lord, we simply refer to God the Father, God the Son, and God the Holy Spirit.

Frederick Buechner, an American writer and theologian, wrote: 'to find your mission in life is to discover the intersection between your heart's deep gladness and the world's deep hunger.' It is our task of sharing our faith, love and service to others. As a church we see ourselves more in a mission as we make the Gospel and its values the center of our lives. Our unity in diversity and our diversity in unity of the world, for instance, enable us to widen our perspective in a Trinitarian way where we are challenged on how we treat others and one another.

Perhaps you have heard about what is going on in Arizona in regard to their stringent immigration enforcement bill. The estimated 460,000 undocumented immigrants living in this state are now facing the possibility to be deported or lose their jobs. Just as the country has become a mix of cultures, a blend of legal and illegal immigrants, the mystery of the

---

[167] cf. 365 Days with the Lord—Liturgical Biblical Diary. 1999. St Paul's Publishing, Philippines. p May 30, 1999.

Blessed Trinity helps us to more fully commit ourselves to become oriented to others instead of being self-centered. We need a new humanism which focuses on the vision of Christ in his Trinitarian meaning. In a similar vein, the world now abounds with that tendency to make personal choice rather than the common good the end-all of morality.[168]

Let us always endeavor to be a reflection of the Holy Trinity by being authentic Christians, faithful and committed to living God's love through our neighbors. On the strength of this testimony, the more we practice love the more we reflect the Trinity in our lives. God bless you.

---

[168] Fr Allan Figueroa Deck, S.J. *You Can't Ignore the Mandate to Evangelize*. The Tablet. Vol 103, No 2. April 17, 2010.

THE MOST HOLY BODY AND BLOOD OF CHRIST

Readings: Gen 14:18-20; Ps 110:1-4; 1 Cor 11:23-26; Lk 9:11b-17

Eucharist—A Whole Series of Signs

"Then taking the five loaves and the two fish, and looking up to heaven, he said the blessing over them, broke them, and gave them to the disciples to set before the crowd."

One of my favorite classical sources of myths in European literature is Ovid's Metamorphoses. It is like an encyclopedia of mythology where the divine power determines all— especially those stories of personalities in conflict. Aside from that, it provides an opportunity for the revelation of the victim's true identity[169] and most of all, the common theme on transformation usually accompanied by violence.

As I was trying to understand the magical world of fiction of yesteryear and today's generation, the legendary principle that stands to reason is, evidently, the continuing struggle between good and evil. It is like the mantra of human pride in Ovid's episodes that start at the very beginning of creation and eventually, the imperial greatness of Rome with the death of Julius Caesar in 44 BC.

In today's feast of the Most Holy Body and Blood of Christ, there is a fundamental principle that provides a perspective of opening ourselves to others through our act of giving. Though we may always be confronted with personalities in conflict or situations replete with struggles of human pride, the challenge involved is pretty much in

---

[169] Karl G. Galinsky. 1975. *Ovid's Metamorphoses: An Introduction to the Basic Aspects*. Berkeley & Los Angeles.

line with the vision of Christ—to love, serve and care for our brothers and sisters. Indeed, it is our own self-gift of life.[170]

As a faith community that celebrates and worships God in the context of a sacred meal, our actions and reactions are embedded in the meaning and spirituality of the Eucharist. According to Second Vatican Council, the Eucharistic celebration is the "source and summit of the Christian life"[171] and "the center and culmination of the entire life of the Christian community."[172] With faith in Christ as our sacramental mediator with the Father, we believe that Christ is present on the altar keeping in mind his 'work of redemption through sacramental signs.'[173]

Many times interpretations of the Eucharist are intertwined with a joyful spirit as a community that celebrates the gift of ourselves to one another for the sake of Christ's love for us. We live a life of continued growth in our journey of relationship. The Lord Jesus himself, told us, "By this all men will know that you are my disciples, if you have love for one another" (Jn 13:35).

There are times that our communion with one another is obscured by our secular lives or overshadowed by countless other distractions. We need to bring ourselves in contact with Christ through our inward access to the power beyond where the core of our sanctuary unites with 'the reality of his bodily presence as bread and wine.'[174]

---

[170]   cf. Celebrating the Eucharist. April 25, 2010-August 21, 2010. Liturgical Press. St John's Abbey—Collegeville, Minnesota 56321. p 127. or www.litpress.org
[171]   cf. Lumen Gentium, 11.
[172]   cf. Christus Dominus, 30.
[173]   cf. Luis Bermejo M. S.J. 1986. *Body Broken and Blood Shed*. Gujarat Sahitya Prakas, India.
[174]   Quoted from *On Bits and Pieces.—Along with Crooked Lines*. 2007. Mark A. Escobar. Xlibris Publications. p 116.

I remember one of the stories of Cardinal Bernardin when he first traveled with his mother and sister to his parents' homeland in northern Italy. He said he felt as if he had already been there after years of looking through his parents' photo albums. He recognized the countryside landscape, the trees planted in each side of the road, the Alps, the antiquated houses, the people at large. He said, "My God, I know this place. I am home."[175]

Following this, I think we are also home with God each time we celebrate the Eucharist with the eyes of faith that focuses us on the life of endless loving and giving of ourselves as a gift to others. A nun who used to tell us stories about heaven and the life hereafter said that whenever we celebrate mass, the canopy of heaven opens its vision, immortal ones worship in awe, sing joyful songs as they also take part in the celebration. It's just a story to little children but I think there is wisdom in it as we come to think of ourselves, the community that reflects the spirit of being Eucharistic people who are open to be wounded, broken and shared for the sake of the kingdom of God.

There are countless implications of the Eucharist as we share our faith experiences. But one thing is certain as a key point for any possible challenge it may entail: to live the words of the Gospel in ways of thinking and acting, of loving and serving, in spite of uncertainty, disillusionment and negativity in our encounter with others.

In a world wounded by so many human conflicts and tensions, we are all challenged to give witness to the spirituality of the Eucharist while we shape or reform our humanness in us with the language of discipleship. Ovid's

---

[175] Joseph Cardinal Bernardin. 1997. *The Gift of Peace*. Loyola Press. Chicago. p 152.

Metamorphoses may be just a collection of Greco-Roman narratives in medieval times, nevertheless, it makes sense to connect different personalities in conflict that always seek to commit to a life of love with a wounded identity. God bless you.

ELEVENTH SUNDAY IN ORDINARY TIME

Readings: 2 Sam 12:7-10, 13; Ps 32:1-2, 5,
7, 11; Gal 2:16, 19-21; Lk 7:36-8:3

A Common Scope on Healing and Forgiveness—
A Horizontal Movement

"So I tell you, her many sins have been forgiven because she has
shown great love . . . Your faith has saved you;
go in peace."

In retrospect, I never thought I could be more outraged by an
incident in the novitiate when my companions left me alone
working in the field for two hours. It was a commitment with
obedience to the structures of religious formation. Though
some inner complaints and anger engulfed me in the course
of that incident, what came out as a challenge was to liberate
my heart and mind from thoughts that we are still human.
It was, however, the crucial issue of my inward experience
that identifies where I was coming from.

The theme of today's gospel is forgiveness. For us, this
embraces a very significant reality in most of the teachings of
Jesus. It is the hallmark or essential feature of the Christian
religion; a choice that brings healing of hearts. It is a gift, too,
that liberates one from guilt for sins committed.

Perhaps you remember the ancient Sanskrit word or
the Hindu salutation that says: 'the divine in me honors
and acknowledges the divine in you.' It is recognizing the
presence of God in each of us that enables us to understand
and apply his love and forgiveness. The concept of relation
is essentially the seed of being human and how we treat
one another. We see ourselves drawn more to highlight that

we are part of something that God has created for us—our interconnectedness.

It is why in many of Jesus' encounters with people in the gospels, the issue of relationship is articulated in a variety of settings particularly in the context of hospitality. Let's say when there is a gathering or a feast organized by the family—it is a cultural thing for the Jewish host to show his welcoming kiss, to have a bucket of water ready for the guests to wash their dusty feet, and the oil to anoint their forehead as a kind of aromatic perfume.

And here we see Jesus being invited into the house of Simon, the Pharisee, for dinner, along with other invited guests. While everybody enjoys the pleasure of being together, an unexpected woman comes like a gatecrasher. She shows her great faith in Jesus by wiping his feet with her hair as a sign of humility. She kisses his feet as a gesture of respect and honor and she anoints them as a sign of gratitude for what he has done for her. But for Simon, the Pharisee, these actions are inappropriate, bizarre.

Jesus knows what's going on in the mind of Simon and so he tells him a short story to make him understand that it doesn't matter how much one has done sinful things. What matters is how deeply one feels a desire or quest for healing. He says, "The greater you sense your own need for forgiveness, the greater will be your love when you are forgiven." Jesus knows that this woman also has a future to look forward to.

At critical junctures in our journey of relationship, I think we now live both in the best of times and in the worst of times, with apologies to Charles Dickens' opening line in his masterpiece 'A Tale of Two Cities.' Why? Evidently, globalization has contributed immensely to our technology today while at the same time cause us to experience devastations in different forms. We see the running sore of hatred and injustice, violence and death, suffering and resentment, and so many others that afflict human relationship especially in families. And we all need to step back, to re-align ourselves to what is essential and fundamental.

Our response to today's gospel shares a common scope on healing and forgiveness accompanied by caring a presence that pursues the interests of others. It is always in that direction—in a horizontal or outward movement where the context of relationship reveals its purpose. And that defines our identity about who we are before God and others.

Victor Hugo's Les Miserables makes me reflect on many Christian values especially forgiveness. Early in the story, we are shown the act of forgiveness to Jean Valjean by the abbé (abbot) for stealing silver candlesticks while he is given hospitality in the chancery. When the gendarmes come to report to the abbé about what he stole, the abbé says to the gendarmes, "I gave him the candlesticks, you can let him go." He is given another chance to turn over a new leaf. He never forgets it and he has become a new Jean Valjean, suffused with a forgiving spirit.

With this incident I think healing brings hope back in life. One becomes whole again. God bless you.

TWELFTH SUNDAY IN ORDINARY TIME

Readings: Zech 12:10-11; 13:1; Ps 63:2, 3-4,
5-6; Gal 3:26-29; Lk [176]9:18-24

Confession of Peter

"If anyone wishes to come after me, he must deny himself and take up his cross daily and follow me. For whoever wishes to save his life will lose it but whoever loses his life for my sake will save it."

Through the centuries Peter's confession in today's gospel, the proclamation of Jesus' identity as 'The Christ,' has engendered a great deal of theological study and reflections on the issue of identity, discipleship, or mission that embody cultural and religious perspectives. An abundance of literature focuses on the implications of discipleship as a key-word to identify one's dying to himself.

I am convinced that it has many points of relevance and application to our lives today. I am tempted to say it is like a litmus test of spiritual genuineness as we echo this question 'Who do you say I am?' The wealth of intimacy and knowledge may go together in the foundation of living a life with Christ. And this is by creating relationships with others on the basis of true loving and giving. As I always say: 'you can give even without loving, but you cannot love without giving.' It is a life-time investment; a commitment that requires one to work from where he is back to the beginning without counting the cost.

---

[176]   The Gospel of Luke and the Acts of the Apostles are part one and part two of the same book, written by the same author. Both books are written to a Roman of some nobility named Theophilus (see Luke 1:1-4; Acts 1:1).

Jesus' ministry always looks to the interests of others in an outward movement. His concern for every person who desires to understand and follow his examples has formed priorities that became the basis of true discipleship, i.e. one love, one heart and one scope—his kingdom.

Peter's reply to Jesus when asked about who he is: 'The Christ of God' is so significant that in spite of all the miracles he has done and his teaching made to people, up to this point, he has never publicly announced himself yet as the promised Messiah of Israel. His main reason is simple: he does not want to be a self-proclaimed Messiah. He wants to show his worth as the Messiah through his actions—his works and his whole person. That's how humble he is in many episodes of his ministry. But we have to keep in mind that through Peter's confession Jesus takes the opportunity to prepare his disciples about his coming rejection and death; that he is going to die on the cross for the sake of his love for humanity—for their salvation.

There's an author[177] who once said, "To find your mission in life is to discover the intersection between your heart's deep gladness and the world's deep hunger." I think it makes sense to embrace the challenge where our hearts respond with joy and gladness. Keeping our Catholic presence, for instance, in some places and institutions, is truly an important mission where our faith and our heart are able to articulate charity that is integral to the life of the church.

"Who do you say that I am?" still continues to echo in many contexts and life situations these days. With the presence of consumerism and individualism in today's culture it is evidently the mainstream that brings us to a different realm where the tendency to make personal choice

---

[177]   Frederick Buechner

is given more weight than the common good as the end-all of morality.[178] Who do we think Jesus is in our lives? The latest storm of clerical abuse of minors has been a continuing struggle and we recall what Pope Benedict XVI said when he conducted Stations of the Cross in 2005 before he became pope, "Christ suffers in his own Church. How much filth there is in the Church and even among those, who, in the priesthood, ought to belong entirely to him."[179]

Today's immigrants, for instance, like those who come from non-Judeo Christian faiths—Muslims, Hindus, Buddhists, Taoists, and Sikhs—who is Jesus for them? For the Muslims, Jesus is not divine nor the son of God. But he was sent down as a prophet of Allah (God) and a messenger like Muhammed in Muslim tradition. For them, he was not crucified and they insist that the story of his tragic death is false.[180] They emphasize more on the wonders that surround his birth as 'Jesus Son of Mary.' For many Hindus, however, Jesus is one among many Masters or Prophets or Incarnations. He is understood as a moral principle or an ethical symbol by Mahatma Gandhi.[181] In Buddhism, Jesus is many things as a Jew, prophet, miracle worker, Messiah. Historical evidence says that in Jesus' time Buddhism was already 500 years old and had spread from India. And Jesus' teachings are similar to Buddhism. Non-biblical historical accounts say that Jesus traveled outside Judea during his hidden years between ages 13 and 29. He studied and preached. It is why people were

---

[178] cf. Allan Figueroa, S.J. *You Can't Ignore the Mandate to Evangelize.* The Tablet. Vol. 103, No. 2. April 17, 2010. p 24.

[179] cf. Bishop Nicholas DiMarzio. *Justice and Forgiveness.* The Tablet. Vol. 103, No. 2. April 17, 2010. p 4.

[180] cf. John Casey. Daily Telegraph. London. December 19, 2001.

[181] Felix Machado. *How do Hindus view Jesus Christ?* The Examiner. October 10, 1998.

really amazed to hear him speak and deal with the Jewish doctors of the law in the synagogue.

We are now inundated with many divisions and, like any market place we all have choices to make that somehow along the way fracture Christianity. Hence, our faith in Jesus gets more fragmented than ever. The tension continues both individual and communal. People these days seem to believe that they can be religious even without going to church. The sense of community worship fades slowly and worshippers sit alone in front of computers or flat screen TVs following the rhythms of their faith tenets chosen from a menu of options.

Now, who we think Jesus is in our lives will remain a continuing inspiration, the center of our existence, the reason for all and our source of eternal life. The challenge ahead draws us to remain steadfast in our faith commitment—by being involved and focused on what is essential in our Christian lives. As St Thérèse says, "see our life of time for what it is: A passage to eternity."[182] God bless you.

---

[182] Quoted from *The Gift of Peace*. Joseph Cardinal Bernardin. Loyola Press: Chicago 1997. p 99.

THIRTEENTH SUNDAY IN ORDINARY TIME

Readings: 1 Kgs 19:16b, 19-21; Ps 16: 1-2,
5, 7-11; Gal 5:1, 13-18; Lk 9:51-62

Jesus' Travel Account While Heading For Jerusalem

Like in any history of civilization there are heroes and heroines who are admired for their fame and victory, success and influence. Recall, for instance, the Irish in American Baseball toward the end of the 19th century was the cause of a great deal of competitive spirit of this country. They dominated baseball and won consecutive National League pennants in 1894, 1895, and 1896 with the Hall of Famers Big Dan Brouthers, Jennings, and John McGraw in the infield and Joe Kelley and Wee Willie Keeler in the outfield.[183] Mike "King" Kelly was regarded as the most popular baseball player at that time.[184] It was the height of spectacle and inspiration among the Irish fans and other immigrants in America.

But looking at other aspects of life, there is a pattern that we usually associate with ourselves. This is the human cycle of victory and failure, happiness and sorrow, or excitement and depression. Anyone who is committed to any discipline and even to God, is not excused or immune to being human. And this is a fact of life.

We see this in the life of Elijah who struggled to bring his people to God against worshipping Baal. His victory over

---

[183] Richard F. Peterson. *Slide, Kelly, Slide: The Irish in American Baseball.* 2000. New Perspectives on the Irish Diaspora. Edited by Charles Fanning. Southern Illinois University Press. p 176.

[184] ibid.

the 850 prophets of Baal and Asherah on Mt Carmel[185] draws him to flee to the south of Judah, in Mt Horeb[186] where God reveals himself (1 Kgs 19). It is in this point in time when he decides one day to run away from his post due to depression and he is almost on the brink of giving up his prophetic vocation. The threat of Jezebel to his life, the Phoenician wife of King Ahab, makes him scared and discouraged to continue his ministry. He thinks he would be alone to carry out God's plan for Israel. But God has a plan for him to carry out his mission. He is commanded to anoint Hazael as king of Aram, and Jehu as king of Israel.[187] Then he is also told to anoint and mentor Elisha as his own successor.

It is interesting to note how many great men in the bible were called to carry on the work of God and to speak on his behalf. There are many examples of this: Elijah who denounced worship of Baal and defeated his 450 prophets in a contest on Mt Carmel,[188] Elisha "while he was plowing with twelve pairs of oxen before him, and he with the twelfth," Moses who was pasturing the flock of Jethro his father-in-law, David was tending sheep for his father, Peter was a fisherman, Paul had a trade making tents, and Jesus himself was a carpenter by trade who was trained by Joseph.

But God is not the kind of God who compels us to submit ourselves to his will. He does not force or impose on us to follow his command. He allows us to discern certain things

---

[185]   1 Kgs 18.

[186]   cf. www.answers.com A decisive episode in Elijah's life was the moment when God's word was revealed to him in the cave at Mt Horeb, traditionally identified with Mount Sinai. Here God commanded him with regard to three acts that he was to perform in the future: to anoint Hazael as king of Aram, to anoint Jehu as king of Israel, and to anoint Elisha son of Shafat to succeed him as a prophet.

[187]   ibid.

[188]   ibid.

in our lives and helps us bring to light our response to his message. There are times that he would give us some signs or work in unexpected ways. As we always say, 'with God nothing is impossible.' But he is a God who does not give up on us. He is not like us who can easily turn our back and give up on something that we could no longer afford to cope.

Jesus in today's gospel is very clear in his message to his disciples about the difficulties of itinerant ministry, the so-called flying mission being a pilgrim on the road. He knows that being called to this mission, one does not expect to have a fixed abode—a permanent home where one could live throughout his life. He knows that he is exposed to possible rejection and humiliation by other people who would not receive him.

Since their return from Babylon, Jews and Samaritans had animosity and a feuding relationship. And in those days Jesus, along with his disciples, was heading for Jerusalem and had to pass by Samaria to stay overnight. Samaritans did not want to have anything to do with Jerusalem nor with anyone heading there. The Samaritans shared some aspects of faith with the Jews. Their sacred book was the Pentateuch and they worshipped Yahweh. However, they rejected the significance of Jerusalem. They regarded instead, Mt Gerazim as the locus where Yahweh wanted to build his holy temple—that was eventually destroyed by the Judeans in 128 BC.

This is one of the challenges that discipleship implies in that long journey of commitment to Jesus' new covenant. Like Elisha's preparation for ministry with Elijah being receptive and able to follow directions, Jesus' disciples, too, were reminded of life and service for the sake of God's kingdom. It is like a cross country race where there is a need for endurance and commitment to the mission.

Perhaps our individual stories of vocation have a common denominator of perseverance and dedication to a life of consecration. It is not surprising to say good-bye to our families. Even the prophet Elijah has allowed Elisha to bid farewell to his parents before following him. The argument here is not literal in meaning but rather, bringing with us the baggage of the past which we are asked to leave behind in order to start a new life.

In the eyes of God we are not measured or defined by our past, but by our future. The challenge sets us to be completely focused on the reign of God and our response to his invitation goes forward as we immerse ourselves and get involved in the messiness of life. God bless you.

FOURTEENTH SUNDAY IN ORDINARY TIME

Readings: Is 66:101-4c; Ps 66:1-7, 16, 20; Gal 6:14-18; Lk 10:1-9

Richness in Meaning:
Mission Addressed to the Seventy-Two

"Carry no money bag, no sack, no sandals; and
greet no one along the way. Into whatever house you
enter, first say, 'Peace to this household . . .'"

The most challenging mission for anyone who wishes to follow the footsteps of Christ is to embrace the life of radical discipleship. It is costly and requires discipline of sacrifice, prayer and openness to welcome challenges. To give credible witness that testifies to a life of simplicity and richness in the treasures of God's kingdom defines parameters of commitment that serve as a foundation to vocation or religious calling.

In today's gospel where Jesus appointed seventy-two others to continue his mission to every town and place, the gift of missionary life is evidently the heart of being called to serve. It is giving one's life to Christ through service to others without any strings attached or material compensation. It is a way of living a life that bears the quality and identity of Jesus that is reflected upon missionary works.

I remember when I got my second assignment as a missioner to work with the migrants in Casa del Migrante situated between the border of El Paso, Tx and Ciudad Juarez in Chihuaha, Mexico. For me, it was a difficult mission with poor facilities and scarcity of water. We lived in a desert-like environment. Almost every day I would go with the volunteers to collect left-over food from factories known as 'maquiladoras.' This was the food we served to feed those Hispanics who came to our dormitory. Some of them were deported from the U.S. Others were still in quest for jobs in the States.

How God worked in my everyday circumstances or encounters with other cultures moved me to that deeper level of my religious missionary life. I became stronger and open to welcome any form of challenges that came along my way. I learned to appreciate each culture and became more sensitive to the needs of others. And I came to recognize from the depth of my heart that says, 'where the poor suffer, there I am called to stand fast and be of help to them.' It was a journey of perseverance and commitment to my religious vows.

Being people oriented and responsive to the needs of others, it is important to keep in mind the language of mission that Jesus refers to in the gospel. It is intertwined with cultures, religious traditions, and implications of discipleship.

For a poor country like Haiti, for instance, that has long been known for its political turmoil, for its coups d'état, decades of dictatorship and corruption, what concept of mission cements us to respond to their needs? There are a set of challenges that stymied the current situation of Haitians after the strong earthquake that ravaged the capital city, Port-au-Prince. So many afflicted people lost their loved ones and their own houses. They were completely shattered not only physically as regards buildings and, infrastructure, but they were devastated psychologically and emotionally as well. Our missionary outreach could be expressed in a common vision of loving through an attitude of sharing our resources, skills and talents, including our faith-based communities and the generosity and support of each of us. The power and enthusiasm to bring out the best in us as people of God is our commitment to grow in love through immersion in life experiences of those who suffer. But, of course, first priorities must be food, water, medicine and shelter. Then came the second priority to repair public buildings such as hospitals, schools, roads, electricity, government buildings, and telephone services.

We have also seen in the Daravi area of Mumbai (the setting of "Slumdog Millionaire"), poverty often generates creative responses and initiatives.[189] And I think it is the driving force that strengthens our sense of mission and love for the poor. Jesus has that preferential option, too, for the poor; those who are disenfranchised, afflicted, or marginalized in one way or the other.

This is our calling to be of help to those who are in need. This is our role to play as Christians committed to our vocation. As parents, children, teachers, doctors, or religious, we all share a common perspective of showing our love for one another, caring for one another, and giving witness to what we profess in faith. Though at times there are difficulties connecting the so-called dots and understanding what constitutes missionary outreach, our vision always leads us to the values of God's kingdom and these challenge us to commit ourselves to our calling. God bless you.

---

[189] Thomas L. Firedman. *What's our Sputnik?* The New York Times. Vol. CLIX., No. 54, 922. Jan. 17, 2010. p Wk 8.

FIFTEENTH SUNDAY IN ORDINARY TIME

Readings: Dt 30:10-14; Ps 69:14, 17, 30-31, 33-34,
36, 37; Col 1:15-20; Lk 10:25-37

Who is my Neighbor?

"You shall love the Lord, your God, with all your heart,
with all your being, with all your strength, and with
all your mind, and your neighbor as yourself."

In recent years, there has been a proliferation of popular networking sites. One of them is Facebook[190] which, according to records, has 350 million members worldwide. Members collectively, spend 10 billion minutes there every day, checking in with friends and acquaintances, clicking through photos and keeping themselves up to date.[191] It is a significant source of getting to know who we are in contact with and how we value friendship and family relationship through this world site. It has become part of daily routines and even an addiction to some people.

As we endeavor to reach out to those who are dear to our hearts, those who have been part of our past life, we remember them with gratitude and stay in contact with pictures and lovely notes. Every attempt to touch base or

---

[190] Adam Geller. *Spotlight on Facebook*. The Providence Sunday Journal. Oct. 3, 2010. p B5. With its 500 million users, the world's largest social networking site—began as a tool for communication between people who knew one another and were bound by shared and exclusive interests. Mark Zuckerberg has built Facebook into an international phenomenon by stretching the lines of social convention and embracing a new and far more permeable definition of community.

[191] Katie Hafner. *To Deal with Obsession, Some Defriend Facebook*. The New York Times. Dec. 21, 2009. p A16.

reconnect to some persons is a gesture of caring and kindly attitude while recognizing the gift of relationship.

Today's gospel speaks volumes about the Good Samaritan's caring attitude; his kindness toward the wounded man he met on the road. His heart goes out to him though his action may have put him at serious risk. It is very possible that one who has been robbed has his attackers prowling around the vicinity to assault and rob others. It is still dangerous. But he doesn't think that way. His immediate action is to be of help to this wounded man. This incarnates the real meaning of 'who is my neighbor?'

It tells us that our criterion to show compassion to others should not be conditioned by race, belief, or color. It knows no distinction or running sore of being discriminated against. The spirit of the Law is more important than fulfilling the letter of the Law. It is why he who needs our help, no matter who he is, is our neighbor.

For centuries the overriding stereotypes of Samaritan people have been described with animosity and a rambling note of being discriminated against. In like manner, people of color or men and women who come from other cultures are also labeled as foreigners in the mainstream.

Biblical scholar Robert Funk notes that "a Jew who was excessively proud of his blood line and a chauvinist about his tradition would not permit a Samaritan to touch him, much less minister to him."[192] The depth of animosity between Jews and Samaritans[193] is hard for us to understand but not for the Jewish audience. They were mortal enemies.

---

[192] Robert Funk. (1982). *Parables and Presence.* Philadelphia: Fortress Press. pp 29-34.

[193] *Samaritans* were a Gentile people mostly living in Samaria, Jews thought of them as inferior and hated them. It probably shocked

The priest[194] and Levite,[195] who were supposed to be epiphanies of faith and charity to others especially in this case by aiding the beaten traveler, ignored God's instruction. Instead, it was the Samaritan who assisted the man that was beaten, robbed, and left for dead on the side of the road. He showed more than an exclusive adherence to the Jewish principle. He bandaged his wounds and poured on oil and wine, which was a Middle Eastern form of simple first aid. He fed him, clothed him, and even gave the innkeeper money to finish taking care of the man.[196]

In light of the whole story, we can probably ask ourselves 'who is really my neighbor?' or 'whose neighbor am I?' It may be difficult at times to call to mind the words of John Wesley, the founder of Methodism who used to say, "The world is my parish." With this statement we can also say that "the world is my neighborhood." Let us keep in mind that our religion or faith is empty if it is not well incarnated in life's experiences. We refer to those who are in dire need of assistance in some issues; those who are hurting or grieving

---

the lawyer to hear Jesus speak well of the Samaritan as the only one who acted compassionately toward the beaten traveler.

[194] cf. http://cgg.org. Parable of the Good Samaritan. Martin G. Collins. *The Good Samaritan: Model of* Effective Compassion. *Priest* served God and His law, which encourages mercy. He professed his love for God and human beings, and he played several times a days. This spiritual leader, one of 12,000 priests living in Jericho at that time, had left service to God back at the Temple, having neither time nor compassion for his neighbor. The priest knew that God's law endorses loving God and neighbor, yet he failed to put his faith into action.

[195] cf. ibid. *Levite* was of the same tribe as the priest but of one of the inferior branches. As a servant of the Temple, a custodian of religious worship, and an interpreter of the law, he should also have been eager to assist the battered man.

[196] cf. http://www.bookrags.com-Parable of the The Good Samaritan

the loss of their loved ones; those who have lost their jobs or whose relationship has drifted apart.

Most of us here have had experiences when we could have been a *Good Samaritan* to others in diverse situations. There are numerous opportunities to be of help to others even in a small thing like helping on the computer, shopping for groceries for someone who is unable to walk, accompanying an elderly person to the doctor, or simply giving directions to a stranger who is lost. These are examples of being a Good Samaritan to others. It may be both carrot and stick,[197] but our sensitivity to the needs of others makes the difference.

I would like to close by quoting the words of Pope Benedict XVI. In one of his homilies he described the Church and society in terms of renewal: "Learn to think as Christ thought, learn to think with him! And this thinking is not only the thinking of the mind, but also a thinking of the heart."[198] God bless you.

---

[197] cf. The World Book Dictionary. (1976) Doubleday & Company, Inc. *carrot and stick*, an incentive or reward joined with a threat or risk: profit and loss.
[198] cf. L'Osservatore Romano. November 22, 2006. p 7.

SIXTEENTH SUNDAY IN ORDINARY TIME

Readings: Gen 18:1-10a; Ps 15:2-3, 3-5; Col 1:24-28; Lk 10:38-42

Listening to Jesus—Its Importance

*"Martha, Martha, you are anxious and worried about
many things. There is need of only one thing. Mary has
chosen the better part and it will not be taken from her."*

My love for Homer, the ancient Greek epic poet, reminds
me of countless struggles like those of so many celebrities in
trouble with the law, dying too young, and changing partners
like they alter their clothes. But his focus, on a single unified
theme explains the genesis of hospitality, particularly in the
Odyssey. The theme is homecoming as Odysseus of Troy
tries to get home to see his beloved wife Penelope and to see
his son Telemachus. However, the central theme emphasizes
more on hospitality.

While the Greeks were formed to be hospitable to please
the gods in order to gain favor with them, hospitality was
a major factor in many incidents throughout The Odyssey.
Even Scripture calls us to show hospitality to all kinds of
people: strangers, the poor and homeless, or fellow brothers
and sisters in faith. We are required to offer food, home, or
assistance to them. It is a sacred duty, a moral obligation and
a missionary virtue.

Thinking of hospitality as a major theme in today's
readings, particularly in the first reading, we recall some
memorable incidents when the Lord promised to build a
nation through Abraham. It was the fourth time the Lord
said, "I will surely return to you about this time next year,
and Sarah your wife will have a son." But before that, it

occurred when the Lord specifically promised him a son that would come from his own body.[199] Following that, the Lord changed Sarai's name to Sarah and promised that he would "bless her and give her a son by her."[200] It took 24 years of waiting.

This is described as the foundation of hospitality when Abraham and Sarah welcomed three strangers who turned out to be divine visitors. They were angels sent by God.

Other stories of hospitality abound in the bible. We may recall the story of Lot who offered his daughters to an angry mob rather than allow guests (Sodomites) to conform to the social tenets of hospitality by protecting his guests and their honor (Gen 19:8). Toward the end these guests turned out to be messengers of God. Abraham's servant was received by Rebekah at the well and he recognized her as the perfect wife for Isaac (Gen 24). Then there were the prophets Elijah and Elisha who repaid their hosts by curing their sons and as a token of gratitude that prefigures the Eucharist, Elijah blessed his hostess' grain so that it never runs out (2 Kgs 4).

The Greek word for hospitality means "love to strangers" (*philoxenia, philos, loving, and xenos, a stranger*). The Mosaic law has this mantra "you shall not oppress a stranger . . . for you were strangers in the land of Egypt" (Ex 23:9). Strangers, like the poor of Yahweh (anawim), widows, and orphans, should be treated with special generosity. As it says, "God executes justice for the fatherless and the widow, and loves the sojourner, giving him food and clothing" (Deut 10:18).

---

[199] cf. Gen. 15
[200] cf. Gen. 17. If we recall, when Sarai was 65 years old, she was still beautiful. In fact, to save his own skin, Abram lied to Pharoah and said that she was his sister. Back then it may have still been possible for Sarai to conceive and bear a child, but now it is obviously too late.

According to modern literature, hospitable means a welcoming attitude and environment[201] which are backed by excellent service to create unforgettable experiences.[202]

Looking at the gospel we see the two sisters Martha and Mary being happy to welcome Jesus into their home and to provide him with hospitality. This must have happened toward the end of Jesus' ministry before his passion and crucifixion and straight after the parable of the Good Samaritan. Their brother Lazarus, however, is not mentioned in the story.

Martha is hospitable and a generous homemaker. She exhibits the goodness and hospitality that great hostesses have. Her intentions are so good, albeit, her attitude at that moment is not quite right. The rare occasion to stay and listen to him is of the essence. The spiritual challenge it poses is one must listen to him as Mary does because by listening one learns something that enables her to obey. This reminds us of Samuel's response to God: "Speak Lord, your servant is listening.

On the one hand, Mary is quiet, attentive, and wants nothing more than to be near him, to listen to him. Her contemplative attitude at that very moment with Jesus cements some aspects of faithfulness and legendary meaning in her spiritual life. The implication is clear: to find a space for integration as one may step back and listen to the word of God. This is a fundamental issue to be addressed in this busy world: to sit at Jesus' feet. The need to welcome him to our

---

[201] B. Brotherton. 1999. *"Towards a definitive view of the nature of hospitality and hospitality management."* International Journal of Contemporary Hospitality Management. Vol. 11, No. 4. pp 165-73

[202] N. Hemmington. 2007. *"From service to experience: Understanding and defining the hospitality business."* The Service Industries Journal, Vol. 27, No. 6. pp 747-55.

hearts in prayerful moments is one way to listen to the cries of men and women in suffering. The grace of his presence with us is empowered with love for others. Like Mary we also need contemplation as we own our shortcomings, regrets, admit our mistakes, learn from our experiences and live a genuine life.

When the great German theologian Jürgen Moltmann spoke at the Eucharistic Congress in Melbourne, Australia in 1973, he made a comment: "The active students don't pray and the prayerful students don't act." I think his remarks make sense if prayer and action are complementary in our Christian lives. Its spiritual challenge is to be contemplative in action, i.e. with a heart of service and soul of God's wisdom. God bless you.

SEVENTEENTH SUNDAY IN ORDINARY TIME

Readings: Gen 18:20-32; Ps 138:1-3, 6-8; Col 2:12-14; Lk 11:1-13

Jesus Teaches Us How to Pray

"For everyone who asks, receives; and the one who seeks, finds; and to the one who knocks, the door will be opened."

In the wake of any catastrophic earthquake or flood that may have left thousands dead and countless injured and homeless, our sense of solidarity echoes the living mantra of God's mercy and compassion. We invoke the sacred power in prayer and self-sacrifice. It is a Christian witness in response to the needs of those who are victims of disasters. Our own affinity to the poor like those who live in rickety shacks on steep hillsides or those who have always been afflicted with misfortunes in life is one of great spirituality that helps us own our own regrets, admit our faults and learn from our experiences. They help us fill a perceived need in ways that align us to focus on what is essential in our lives.

It reminds me of St Ignatius' spirituality which, according to many theologians, is incarnational. While it sits well in the heart of God's transcendence, it is deeply rooted in human experience. It is finding God in all things which is a learning continuum; a commitment to countless signs of God's presence in our everyday lives. In other words, there's a core of sanctuary within as one gets involved in life.

In today's gospel Jesus presents to us the way on how to pray along with our attitude that brings about charity towards our neighbor. This flows from and enters into the other, bringing ourselves united with God. The process involves perseverance and discipline to grow in the wisdom of prayer. The spirit and habit of prayer are necessary in living our faith in God. It is persevering in the midst of distractions that eventually lead us to acquire a spiritual culture of intimacy with God. Being confident in Jesus' teaching about prayer, we make every effort to cultivate the little religious practices and exercises that enable us to acquire the habit of prayer.

When we find things difficult to deal with or we do not know what to do or where to find help, we seek help from God who always helps those who turn to him with trust and confidence in our needs. We are confident that God will give us the strength to bear what we could not bear without his sustaining grace.[203]

We are exposed to a variety of human atmosphere, current opinions, pressure of the media and new technology. To educate and discipline ourselves in the practice of prayer is quite difficult as we are affected by distractions that cripple us to the spirit and habit of prayer. We need to acquire the habit of practically always praying and of sanctifying all our deeds and efforts with humble prayer.[204]

I still believe that somewhere in this world—in our lives, there is a spiritual place meant for an act of prayer. Though we may have a number of conflicting issues that plague our society, we still have to develop and cultivate the spirit and habit of continuous prayer. As the prophet Jeremiah says: "You shall pray to me and I will hear you, when you shall seek me with all your heart." And St Paul says "Pray without ceasing" (1 Thess 5:17).

Our interior life reflects our prayer life. God's sustaining grace enables us to triumph over odds and temptations that

---

[203]   Walter Stehle, O.S.B. *Learning to Pray*. The American Ecclesiastical Review. Vol. CXXIX, No. 4. October, 1953. p 227.

[204]   ibid.

beset us on every side of our lives. We are bound in God's love and grace that sustain us to keep going, to keep in the race.

With global challenges we now face our faith has become fragmented, our religion privatized and psychologized. People seem to believe that one can be religious without going to church and praying. Both young and old generations are now attuned to a high-tech way of worshipping God by sitting in front of computers or flat screen TVs and commune to the tenets they have chosen from a menu of options.[205]

A story is told of someone who was asked a question by the local minister. He said, "What do you consider most important for our church?" Without hesitation he replied, "A man who knows God not merely from hearsay. Some of us may know God merely from what they heard at home or in school. We may be equipped with a spate of information about theology and sufficient knowledge of God. But if we don't pray, we would not have this personal intimacy with God. Prayer helps us grow with depth in relationship with God. St Chrysostom wrote: "If I notice that a person does not love prayer, I know that there is little good in him. He who does not pray, has no true life in him. A man is no better than his prayer."[206] God bless you.

---

[205] David Gibson. *Religion is losing ground to spirituality*. San Jose Mercury News. January 15, 2000. p 3E.

[206] cf. The American Ecclesiastical Review, Vol. CXXIX, No. 4. October 1953. p 227.

EIGHTEENTH SUNDAY IN ORDINARY TIME

Readings: Ecc 1:2; 21-23; Ps 90:3-6, 12-13;
Col 3:1-5, 9-11; Lk 12:13-21

Faith and Trust in God

"But God said to him, 'You fool, this night your life will be demanded of you; and the things you have prepared, to whom will they belong?' Thus will it be for all who store up treasure for themselves but are not rich in what matters to God."

Through the centuries modernity has shaped the world and everything else. Science has become very powerful and increasingly influential especially in today's contemporary world. The better way of life seems to be associated with earthly treasures that money, possessions, or status can make. Continuous economic growth seems to be the main goal of most countries today as they come to grips with the growth ethic of the business world.

While it is true that we all invest our time and energy to earn a living, to plan as best as we can for our families, there are certain things in life that can only be seen with our hearts—our treasures in heaven. These things are reflected in our happiness and satisfaction and even in our great sense of deeper meaning as committed Christians.

Today's gospel is profound in meaning. It shows us the values that Christ cares about being in complete accordance with our journey to be with God. This aspect gives much prominence to discipleship calling each of us to focus our main concern on heavenly treasures. These are things which are not subject to decay and cannot be stolen; they are like our road map to eternal life.

We put our faith and trust in Christ. Faith is a gift from God and trust is something we develop through time and space. Living with our own spirituality and in our journey to know the language of mystery is like the pilgrimage of an exile to the unknown or someone who finds himself in a foreign land with no knowledge of the language. Through people around us we acquire learning that enables us to use the resources we have.

Perhaps you have watched the movie 'The Talented Mr. Ripley.'[207] It's a 1999 American film with Matt Damon, Jude Law and Philip Seymour Hoffman and the setting was mainly in Italy with landmarks in the cities of Rome and Venice. Tom Ripley is a young man struggling to make ends meet in 1950s New York City. One night while working at a party as a piano entertainer, he is approached by wealthy businessman Herbert Greenleaf (James Rebhorn), who believes he is a graduate of Princeton University and a friend of his son Dickie (Jude Law) since he's wearing a Princeton jacket which he borrowed from someone. He is asked to travel to Italy and convince his son to return to the States to help run the family business. He agrees, notwithstanding that he never went to Princeton and has never met his son Dickie.

The story revolves around deception, murder, and ambition to acquire material things such as money, prestige, status, and possession. During an incident that happens while Ripley and Dickie hire a small boat and travel together for a short holiday to Sanremo, Dickie tells Ripley that he has

---

[207] It is an adaptation of the Patricia Highsmith 1955 novel of the same name, which was previously filmed as Plein Soleil (Full Sun, 1960).

grown tired of his company and his dependence on him. As a result, a violent fight follows in which Ripley kills Dickie. Ripley tries his best to conceal his crime by sinking the boat with Dickie's body still on board.

In the wake of a tragic death that was followed by another scenario of killing Dickie's friends—Freddie and Smith-Kingsley, there's one statement that Ripley says in his conversation with one of Dickie's friends: "It's better to be a fake somebody than a real nobody." Underlying everything is the language of lies and deception, the make-believe revelation and the power of material quest deep within. But in that context his guilt always haunts him. He is never at peace nor relaxed in any way.

I am saying this because at times our craving for material wealth, recognition and power goes beyond proportion. Greed and selfish concerns continue to afflict us. They keep us bound to this world and we cannot let things go because we are so attached to them. We have to keep in mind that wealth or money cannot suffice if we have to continue in this world. All of us are going to die and Jesus' words challenge us 'for those who store up treasure for themselves but are not rich in what matters to God.'

Perhaps these days you notice that the new world religion seems to be either shopping or sports. And the new cathedrals and shrines are the sprawling, huge shopping malls where people across cultures spend more and more of their time and money.

The Beatitudes are the classic example; the map of life with a series of directives helping us on our journey to focus on what is essential in the eyes of God. Mindful of our calling as men and women of the gospel, we are challenged to live our lives according to the ideals of our faith; to the teachings of Jesus that we follow his way—'both his character and his blessedness'.[208] And one fundamental attitude he shows us in his ministry is his 'love for the poor.' He sees what is in each human heart and he invites us to strive to be Christ with and for others. This is one of the so-called brushstrokes of life—*las pinceladas de vida*. God bless you.

---

[208] Rob Warner. 1998. *The Sermon on the Mount*. Kingsway Publications. p 42.

NINETEENTH SUNDAY IN ORDINARY TIME

Readings: Wis 18:6-9; Ps 33:1, 12, 18-19, 20-22;
Heb 11:1-2, 8-12; Lk 12:32-48

To be Faithful and Committed to God

*"... For where your treasure is, there also will
your heart be ... Blessed are those servants whom
the master finds vigilant on his arrival."*

From the humble beginnings of the foundation of the
United States of America, Catholicism has continued to
grow in legendary proportions. This remains true despite
persecutions and other challenging problems when all facets
of American experience are being dealt with scrutiny and
division. However, the high priority support of the people to
move toward integration of cultures in their faith or religious
interrelationships has evidently been proven as witnessed by
the increase of immigrants in this country.

Faith communities have come to grips to find the grace
and the wisdom of nurturing the cultural, economic and
spiritual roles in the context of dialogue with other segments
of the Christian world. And there is one thing that I envisage
looking at the increasing pattern of coexistence and faith in
God. This is our joint effort in strengthening our mission to
churches of the Third World—to the poor.

As in today's gospel, the command is to be dressed
for work, for action, for something concrete that requires
commitment and faithfulness. It allows us to see beyond
with a significant focus in life. This is God's revelation that
explores the implications of discipleship, our understanding

of God's priority in our journey as committed men and women of the gospel.

The gospel passage has profound awareness of what is essential in this world. It has another horizon, too, which is the second coming. Hence, we are called to be prepared. It is similar to what John the Baptist echoes in his teachings which we usually read at the time of Advent and this enables us to deepen our perception about spiritual treasures and insights about our faith.

Our starting point on the road to understanding the mystery of God's revelation about his kingdom through Jesus Christ is, first and foremost, our attitude of conversion. This starts from the heart that draws us to show our allegiance to God; our faithfulness to the epiphanies of the one God as Scripture shows many of his images.

We may recall in history during the first three centuries when Christians showed their faith commitment to God, they wound up in martyrdom. In those times, Christendom was a political reality as we saw in the Middle Ages when religion and state were combined as one entity. The Crusaders came to the fore and their original plan was to get rid of Islam from the Holy Land. As a result, many Jewish people were killed, both in Europe and in the Holy Land. Christianity started to lose its flavor with the Renaissance. Then the French Revolution took place and one important legacy we can recall is when the separation between State and Church was introduced. Equality of all men and women before the law came out as the major result, along with religion as a private choice of an individual.

In moments of great crisis, especially during this electronic age when innovative technologies become the norm and restructure the global village, we need to tap the mind of God—our dependence on his divinity as someone above us and our appreciation of his gift of faith which we all share. After all, God loves us so much that he gave us His only Son to save us and be part of his kingdom in heaven. Hence, as we re-align our focus in life with our eyes set into the future, let us engage ourselves in seeking out God's agenda or his will for us. It is our Christian hope and what we hope for tells us who we are.[209] This is captured beautifully in Matthew's Gospel: "Seek first God's kingdom and righteousness and all these things will be added to you" (Matt 6:33).

I would like to close this with a short story about St Francis of Assisi. Legend has it that the devout Francis was approached by a certain man while doing some work in the garden. He was asked about the coming of Christ if in case he comes like a thief in the night, what would be his first thing to do. Although quite reluctant to answer him, Francis dropped his gardening material on the ground and looked up at the man and replied, 'Young man, first and foremost, I would finish my work in the garden.'

St Francis has his own wisdom to tell us in a very simple way as he would finish up his gardening because he had no regrets about how he lived out his commitment to Christ. For us, too, we find the grace and wisdom where we are called to commit ourselves though in the eyes of men ours may be little and insignificant. But in God's standard, it is where our treasure is, our heart that makes us blessed to partake of his divine nature in the life hereafter. God bless you.

---

[209] Rowanne Pasco and John Redford, Editors. 1994. *Faith Alive—A new presentation of Catholic belief and practice.* Twenty-Third Publications. Mystic, Connecticut. p 73.

TWENTIETH SUNDAY IN ORDINARY TIME

Solemnity of the Assumption of the Blessed Virgin Mary

Readings: Rev 11:19a; 12:1-6a, 10ab; Ps 45:10bc,
11, 12ab, 16; 1 Cor 15:20-27; Lk 1:39-56

There was an incident in a catechetical class one Sunday morning when a teacher asked her pupils about those who want to go to heaven to see Mamma Mary and Jesus. She tells them to raise their hands. This is actually the time when she just finished their lesson on the feast of the Assumption. All of them raised their hands except little Maria Pilar who sat in the corner of the second row. "Don't you want to go to heaven Maria Pilar to meet our Blessed Mother and her Son Jesus, our Lord and Savior?" asked the teacher. "I can't," said Maria Pilar as she's fidgeting. "My mother told me to go straight home after catechism class."

It is a child-like response that has its own humor but I think it is worth reflecting as we embrace the great solemnity of the Assumption of our Blessed Mother and let her shining example flow into our everyday lives. Time and again, her unique role in the mystery of salvation reminds us of our journey here on earth that has its sequel in the life hereafter—our heavenly destiny with God. This is our faith. Her Assumption widens our hope that as mortal beings there is resurrection for us and the final chapter that awaits us is that we will also assume into heaven during the Last Judgment.

Mary's Assumption into heaven is a sign of salvation promised to all of us. Her role in God's plan to redeem us enables us to understand that there is hope; that life does not end in death but it is a new beginning to mark our heavenly birth in God's kingdom. We firmly believe that our true home is not in this world but in the true presence of God in his kingdom. Following this, it also reminds us that we, too, as members of the Body of Christ must be pure and holy in body and soul since our bodies will be glorified on the day of our resurrection. In this way, we come to believe that our true home is not in this world but in the true presence of God in his kingdom.

Although there is no direct reference to Mary's death and assumption in the bible, particularly in the NT, but there are two incidents of assumption that we find in the OT: and that of Enoch (Gen 5:24) and Elijah (2 Kgs 2:1). These citations or references support the possibility of Mary's bodily assumption into heaven. Other important citations are also indirectly suggested by Matt 27:52-53 and Paul's letter to the Corinthians (1 Cor 15:23-24). In his official declaration of the dogma, Pope Pius XII also cites these biblical verses from Ps 131:8; Cant 3:6; Rev 12; Is 61:13 and Cant 8:5.

Our Tradition on Mary's Assumption has been greatly supported and promoted by the Church Fathers and theologians. Some theological reasons they raised to support our belief on her Assumption are the following: Mary was born without original sin and it is not God's plan that her body would degenerate in the tomb. Since she is full of grace, God's celestial home is the appropriate place for a sinless mother of Christ. Like Elijah who was taken into heaven in a fiery chariot, it is possible that Mary would also have been taken into heaven.

Mary's role in God's plan of salvation echoes her faith which makes a great deal in fulfilling the promise of redemption. Through her 'fiat' the whole history of salvation was made possible because, through her, the Son of God became human and won for our redemption.

We are mindful of her openness to God's challenge. She is indeed a model of discipleship. Her faith and obedience are two inspiring qualities that she has and these make us realize that we, too, are called to trust and obey in our respective calling.

During these days that we continue to brace for problems especially concerning economy, religious commitment, and human relationships, we need to go beyond the boundaries of our comfort zone to care for others whom we meet on our journey through life. This is a sign of openness to others and at the same time obedience to the call of charity and compassion. Like the Visitation of Mary to her cousin Elizabeth, the element of truth here is service to someone who is in need. Elizabeth, the mother of the last OT prophet, is pregnant and needs assistance especially in her age as an old woman. This is like the meeting of the two covenants— Jesus in the womb of Mary is the fulfillment of the promise foretold and John the Baptist in the womb of Elizabeth represents the last OT prophet who is going to prepare the way of Jesus by telling his people to repent.

One of my favorite spiritual writers, Henri Nouwen, had a tremendous love of people and was gifted with profound insight into the longings of a human heart. His vision and openness to the Spirit enabled him to put into writing what it means to be God's instrument in the plethora of opportunities that has become available to him over the years. Like many immigrants across the world, he felt the celebration and beauty of being human suffused with hope and sensitivity to the needs of others.

I would like to close this with a short anecdote which I heard from other priests about Mary's maternal love for her children. There was a time when God the Son made a round in heaven—like a canonical visit of the superior in his province to make sure that everything was in order. In heaven it was fine—the surroundings are clean, buildings, including the roofs, are well taken care of. Jesus came upon one of the side streets and chanced upon people who are not supposed to be in heaven but rather they are supposed to be in purgatory. So he went to see St Peter and asked him about those people. "Peter, by being in charge I thought you knew of people who come to my kingdom," Jesus told him. "Well, my Lord, don't blame me," he replied. "How did they get here?" asked Jesus. "I turned them down, but, your mother told them to take the back door and so they're here," he confessed. And Jesus just turned his back and scratched his hair.

I am saying this to illustrate Mary's role and influence in our lives. She intercedes for us and helps us lead a holy life. She is our Mother, our inspiration.

TWENTY-FIRST SUNDAY IN ORDINARY TIME

Readings: Is 66:18-21; Ps 117; Heb 12:5-7, 11-13; Lk 13:22-30

Our Faith Commitment to Loving Others

*"For behold some are last who will be first,
and some are first who will be last."*

A significant step forward in meeting the challenges posed by the new immigrants in this country has been crucial to some initiatives organized by the government vis-à-vis church involvement in her mission to integrate them through specific service. Our diverse experience within the immigrant groups has taught us about a vision of what the Church ought to be—a church of the poor. Of course, with greater exploration, we think about our institution, programs, and service that we can provide for them. But a substantial part in finding a model more beneficial to our times and to the vision of our institution as a church is to bring the restructuring process back to the mainstream. And that highlights the nature of loving and giving.

We are a community who cares for one another and in loving relationship we grow as persons. It is like putting new wine into old bottles with a sense of vision that we are still one family and growth-oriented people (cf. narrate the story of St Thérèse of Liseux).

This is what we are bound to do as we keep a clear hold on principles of our faith. And this is our mission to be addressed as the gospel today reminds us to focus on the essentials and to set our priorities straight according to our faith commitment. As a community, we are God's Little

Flock. As an institution, we provide services that define our commitment as caring and loving people of God.

Jesus' invitation to endeavor more in building relationships as foundation for our life of witness evidently shows our commitment to the gospel. And the narrow gate imagery is Jesus himself. He says, "I am the way and the truth and the life. No one comes to the Father but by me." His teachings that bear witness to the call of endless service and loving others without measure put us into that perspective. His challenge allows us to see beyond and limit our options to what is essential and to live our lives according to the gospel values. As humans, we have this tendency to elevate ourselves above others and we make use of God's gifts to accomplish our goal.

Jesus is our way of living and loving; a way of losing ourselves for the sake of loving others. We strive to be Christ-like to others, mindful of others' needs, human in dealing with others; receptive to change; and authentic men and women of the gospel.

As we go forward toward the future with confidence and courage, I am reminded of some thoughts that came to my mind while reading Henri Nouwen's article in America (March 13, 1976). It was about the story of a very old man who used to meditate every morning under a huge tree on the bank of the Ganges River in India. One morning, as he has just finished his mediation, he chanced upon a scorpion floating helplessly in the strong current of the river. The scorpion was caught in the long roots that branched out far into the river. The scorpion struggled to save his life but got more and more entangled in the complex network of the tree roots.

So as soon as the old man saw this, he immediately stretched his hand out to rescue the drowning scorpion.

Each time he touched the scorpion the animal jerked and stung him wildly. Instinctively, the man withdrew his hand, but then, after having regained his balance, he did it again to save the agonized scorpion. But every time he came within reach, the scorpion stung him so badly with its poisonous tail that his hands became swollen and bloody and his face distorted by pain.

While he was struggling with the scorpion, a passer-by saw him and yelled at him: "Hey, stupid old man. What's wrong with you? Don't you know that you kill yourself to save that ungrateful animal?"

But the old man just turned his head, and looking calmly in the stranger's eyes, he said, "Young man, because it is the nature of the scorpion to sting. Why should I give up my own human nature to save?"

I think he makes sense in bringing to the fore our inherent concern to care for others; our caring presence even in today's climate of secularism; our nature of saving and loving deepens our faith as we incarnate them in our journey of relationships. Because each of us has a mission to fulfill and that is our mission to loving others. We are committed to focusing on what is essential before the eyes of God—our love for our brothers and sisters. God bless you.

TWENTY-SECOND SUNDAY IN ORDINARY TIME

Readings: Sir 3:17 20, 28-29; Ps 68: 4-7, 10-11;
Heb 12:18-19, 22-24a; Lk 14:1, 7-14

Messianic Images of the Banquet in God's Kingdom

*"For everyone who exalts himself will be humbled, but
the one who humbles himself will be exalted."*

A relevant issue that makes contemplate the life of St Ignatius of Loyola, founder of the Society of Jesus—the Jesuit Order, was his attitude of humility. It was at the height of his conversion when he sought God's will to follow him more closely as he made his pilgrimage from Montserrat to Manresa in Spain.

One incident in his life was when at age 30 he had to sit in class with small boys learning their Latin lessons.[210] That was one of the major requirements at that time to become a priest. His journey from being a former soldier who fought in the Battle at Pamplona in 1521 to start anew his academic commitments was a great challenge and his humility in many aspects enabled him to move on and embrace God's will in his religious calling.

Today's readings, particularly the gospel, explore the inner value of humility with its enduring strength in our journey of relationships with the poor. What is in our hearts is something that echoes the spirituality of the poor and affinity to those in need. It is like Ignatius, who found God everywhere either in the life of the poor, in his prayer, work,

---

[210]   James Martin, SJ. 2006. *My Life with the Saints*. Loyola Press, Chicago. pp 81-88

or his confreres in the community. It is often described as a way of coming to understand the church's preferential option for the poor. It is a kind of spirituality that provides a perspective in focusing on the essentials of being men and women of the gospel.

Two parables in the gospel illustrate the messianic images of the banquet in God's kingdom. These pose a challenge which is implicit in loving God through our brothers and sisters. In essence, to love God is to engage the wisdom of our Christian paths to loving others. Christ himself freely chooses to become poor (2 Cor 8:9). And the poor are reflections of God's presence in our midst. This is what Christ teaches us over and over again: to equate Christian spirituality with our caring presence or attitude towards those in need; the poor of Yahweh known as *anawim* in Hebrew.

Many familiar figures from Christian history have shown their great love for the poor. Their humility and genuine appreciation for simple things in life have brought them to the altar. Others continue to be emblazoned in the annals of history. Their lives and writings have shown their holiness and love for the poor. Karl Rahner wrote: They are the initiators and the creative models of the holiness which happens to be right for, and is the task of, their patronal age. They create a new style; they prove that a certain form of life and activity is a thoroughly genuine possibility; they show experimentally that one can be a Christian even in this way; they make such a person believable as a Christian type."[211]

Perhaps these days we may find it difficult to put into practice what Jesus says in the parable as far as open table fellowship with the poor and marginalized is concerned.

---

[211] Robert Ellsberg. 1998. *All Saints*. The Crossroad Publishing Company. New York. p 2.

There are, of course, certain limits to avoid disproportionate consequences especially when the host runs out of food or if safety is brought to the fore. There are good and bad people; this is a fact. Indeed, experience has taught us this.

However, Jesus tells us something that goes beyond that category—the celebration of a faith community in the context of the Eucharist where everyone takes part in the sharing of relationship, worship, thanksgiving, or even the values of belonging to a family. We are encouraged to rediscover countless gifts of our brothers and sisters in faith. Implicit in our discipleship is the welcoming culture we show them. We are all part of God's family.

As Jewish prophet Abraham Heschel once wrote: "Holiness is not the monopoly of any particular religion or tradition. Wherever a deed is done in accord with the will of God, wherever a human thought is directed toward Him, there is the holy."[212] I seem to believe him because of the fact that God's love encompasses all regardless of color, creed, or culture. We belong to his family as his own people by virtue of faith.

In reading the lives of saints, we can see that in their own struggles and difficulties, they lived the life of poverty in a variety of lifestyles; they incarnated the value of humility in their quest for greatness in the eyes of God. Their faith commitment enabled them to see beyond the light of Christ focused on their prophetic witnessing. This is the aspect of their lives that perhaps may inspire us as we write our own stories with the hiddenness of the desert or the humility of our unseen witnessing.

We come to know that what inspires us is the immortal teaching of Jesus that always draws us to struggle with human

---

[212]   ibid. p 4.

weaknesses, deformities, and pride. It is what makes us true disciples that enable us to allow God to work in and through our lives. Our quest for becoming authentically human in our identity is to continue with humility as each day we discover our mission to care for the poor; our compassionate witnessing in different settings and life relationships. God bless you.

TWENTY-THIRD SUNDAY IN ORDINARY TIME

Readings: Wis 9:13-18b; Ps 90:3-6, 12-17;
Phil 9:10, 12-17; Lk 14:25-33

Commitment to the Implications of Discipleship

"If anyone comes to me without hating his father and mother,
wife and children, brothers and sisters, and even his own
life, he cannot be my disciple. Whoever does not carry his
own cross and come after me cannot be my disciple."

There was a time in history when heroism and doctrinal orthodoxy were mainly the defining measure toward sainthood. The aura of transcendence and sacred power were taken with the utmost seriousness, along with higher principles that speak volumes about human capacity for love, for sacrifice, and generosity.

One night as I was aimlessly flipping through the channels, I stumbled across a documentary featuring the life of St Ignatius of Loyola. My own admiration for him is not one of great personal closeness compared with other famous saints. But his spirituality—his Ignatian spirituality is something that reminds me of being grounded in the real-life experiences as I endeavor to 'find God in all things'—in the everyday events of my life. His principle and foundation (Exercises or examination of consciousness) lead me to search for signs of God's presence in my everyday life. And it is a commitment with discipline especially in prayer and contemplation in action.

At the time when I struggled with my own "dark night" as a missioner, I learned to cement my intimacy with God as part of my spiritual journey. And I think it is also true to anyone who strives to seek an answer or commits to life and love relationship.

We are constantly challenged to allow God to work in and through our own humanity. In reading the gospel today, Jesus makes use of two short allusions or parables that describe the implications of discipleship. One illustrates the plan in building a tower and the process involved in doing it. The other one refers to a wise ruler who calculates the cost it may require to go to war where it has to be studied carefully. These are good planning strategies and assessment of the whole situation in a military context. But towards the end, Jesus concludes with strong affinity to giving up their possessions as they carry within themselves the pull toward the life of discipleship.

True discipleship is maintained by faithful service (1 Cor 15:58). This reminds me of one of the most famous sayings of Mother Teresa of Calcutta: "Silence begets prayer, prayer begets faith, faith begets love and love begets service on behalf of the poor."[213] Indeed, the key to follow Christ's footsteps requires sacrifices. It is costly and the path leads to perfection. It is remarkably compelling to embrace the flesh and blood of the cross with an intense spiritual storm in the process similar to what St John of the Cross used in his mystical writings—the dark night of the soul.

Jesus himself speaks with clarity and truth about the aftermath of following him. He underscores the integrated life in defense of Christian principles and to put him as top priority in fulfilling their vocation or call of discipleship.

---

[213]   Quoted from Bishop Thomas J. Tobin. *Lessons from the Christian Life of Mother Teresa*. Rhode Island Catholic. p 3.

After years of butting heads with the Romans, the Jews are stretched with challenges as regards the identity and mission of the so-called Messiah. Their concept of messiahship is conditioned by their literal meaning of a political liberator; someone who would free them from the Roman dictatorship. In their long awaited expectation they are able to get back their own land and restore their own country. However, they still consider themselves not completely free as they are dominated by the Romans.

While they have to work unwaveringly in the political process, Jesus tells them that his messianic presence in their midst does not aim to bring their liberation to a complete halt from Roman cruelty. But rather he challenges them to follow him through the language of the cross. This is the moral tone of his surrender that makes salvation work on each of us—on every level of service and commitment.

As disciples of Christ, our love for him has to be our top priority in this world. And this becomes concrete as we put it into action through our brothers and sisters. The implication to serve and preach the good news is interwoven in the context of loving.

Today we notice that a lot of people have gone through lengths in their journey of moral relativism that has replaced the moral certitudes of the past. We have a prominent issue on the battle for marriage that continues to be attacked on all fronts. We have witnessed the battle over an Islamic center at Ground Zero in NY City that provoked furor and outrage among American people.

When I was thinking about these things and reflecting on Jesus' call of discipleship, I was reminded of the vision of the mystics who see through the eyes of faith in their intense spirituality that God is still supreme over all creation, ever-greater than us or our ideologies. God's transcendence and sacred power surrounds our lives.[214] With his presence in us the call for all seasons enables us to respond to what we really desire in life and what God asks of us as we come to grips with countless distractions and temptations along the way. It is not necessary that we succeed in everything but how we have put love into our actions, i.e. our human capacity for love, for sacrifice, and generosity. God bless you.

---

[214] Robert Ellsberg. 1998. *All Saints*. A Crossroad Publishing Company. New York. p 5.

TWENTY-FOURTH SUNDAY IN ORDINARY TIME

The Parable of the Prodigal Son

Readings: Ex 3:7-11-11, 13-14; Ps 51:3-4, 12-13,
17-19; 1 Tim 1:12-17; Lk 15:1-32

*"My son, you are here with me always; everything I have is yours.
But now we must celebrate and rejoice, because your brother was
dead and has come to life again; he was lost and has been found."*

More than a hundred years ago when Cardinal John Henry
Newman was on a ship bound for his native England after
a visit to Rome, he found himself and other passengers
stranded at sea. At that time he was not yet a Catholic but
he was already interested in the Catholic Church. Which
is why, he went to Rome to gain a first hand knowledge of
Catholicism.

Because he was in such darkness, dissatisfied with his
own religion, that incident when they were unable to move,
and drifting for over a week in the midst of the sea, Newman
prayed hard for light and he wrote his immortal poem, "Lead
Kindly Light"

> Amid the encircling gloom
> Lead Thou me on!
> The night is dark, and I am far from home.
> Lead Thou me on!
> Keep Thou my feet; I do not ask to see
> The distant scene—one step enough for me."

There is more to think about in Newman's poem, but he
was indeed groping for the Light—the light of God.

Like the gospel today, the parable of the Prodigal Son, shows us the light of God in the context of forgiveness, love and compassion. It is a beautiful story of relationship, the greatest story in the world; best known and best loved of all Jesus' parables because it is a "Gospel with the Gospel.[215] It tells us the genesis of God's compassion and his willingness to welcome each of us regardless of our past, or backgrounds.

Through the centuries it has been the favorite gospel text for many occasions and religious celebrations. It has generated legions of interpretations; countless images, themes, and illustrations across the world. Some have suggested that a more appropriate title for this story could be "The Waiting Father," "Joy and Repentance," or "The Parable of the Merciful Father."

The word "prodigal" comes from the Latin "*prodigere*" meaning to "drive forth or away" or "to waste." It can be construed as either liberal generosity or extravagance in spending or showing one's love and care.

The Christian meaning of this parable also has a Buddhist parallel in one of the major writings of Mahayana Buddhism.[216] Both parables seem to give the same message regarding the character of God as a merciful Father, however, a closer look will reveal something about the fundamental differences in their teaching. In the gospel

---

[215] William Barclay. 1975. The Daily Study Bible Series, revised, ed. The Gospel of Luke. Philadelphia. Westminster. pp 203-206.

[216] cf. Wikipedia, the free encyclopedia. The source of the name Mahayana is polemical, having its origin in a debate about what were the real teachings of the Buddha. Although the Mahayana movement claims that it was founded by the Buddha himself, the consensus of the evidence indicates that it originated in South India in the first century. It was propagated through China by *Kushan Lokaksema*, the first translator of a Mahayana sutra into Chinese

the father represents God, while in the Lotus Sutra,[217] the father is Buddha (or more specifically, the Buddha nature— *Dharmakaya*), the individual struggling to become an enlightened *bodhisattva*[218] being.

It is very interesting to follow the sequence of the story which depicts the example of a wayward young man who wastes his inheritance with lavish spending while living in a foreign land (Lk 15:13). When a severe famine plagues his new homeland (v. 14), he hires himself out to a man who lets him feed his pigs (v. 15). He starves and feels humiliated with this kind of work. Then he decides to go home to his father who receives him with open arms (vv. 17-24).

This is particularly significant with that ardent desire to be reconciled with his father to the full. The sanctity of each moment, with every effort to himself and pledge to spend himself in loving service of his father are evidently God's power to help him make changes and be reunited with his Father.

We see here the wonderful glimpse of God the Father's compassionate, even lavish love for the son in his role in the parable. We see here too how differently God views things than we do. "For thoughts are not your thoughts, neither are your ways my ways," declares the Lord. Because God's ways are not ours (Is 55:8-9). It is when we repent that God makes us whole again and restores us to the full honors due a child of God, regardless of our sins (Acts 3:19: 1 Jn 2:1-2). His forgiveness and mercy abound and no matter what we have done, he will always accept a truly repentant sinner. When

---

[217] It is the famous *Saddharmapundarika Sutra* also called the Lotus Sutra composed at the end of the second century A.D. which revealed the new teaching of Mahayana Buddhism regarding the *bodhisattva* beings.

[218] Buddhist worthy of nirvana who postpones it to help others.

the prodigal son was working and starving no one dared to give him anything. His father gave him a ring[219], the best robe, and sandals and held a big banquet.

When we flick through the news of every day, we notice that many of our issues are clouded with anger, fear of rejection, and greed. Exactly what caught my attention was the unique web of mental pictures of those who repented and confessed publicly about their transgressions; apologized for their shortcomings and negligence as an institution. Like every person, we consider ourselves forgiven because of our faith in God. We consider ourselves sinners, but because we believe in God's mercy and compassion, we need God's power.

Countries like Canada, Australia, Spain, and Great Britain have provided us some materials in regard to asking for forgiveness. For the past centuries they have lorded over their inferiors—the Aborigines, the natives (indigenous people), the blacks. The history of Ireland is also a good example. For the past two centuries, it has been an area of export for people especially after the potato famine of the 1840s. High emigration rates continued throughout the 19th century after they struggled for almost 800 years against the British. In 1922 they gained their political independence but their stories of struggle may still be present because of their sense of remembering. One thing is certain, however: they are whole again with their deeply experienced gift of national identity.

We all need to return to God in repentance and faith. He never compels us; it is our initiative as a personal decision to step up to the plate of healing our relationships. His

---

[219] It symbolizes the knowledge and understanding of eternity. Eternity is movement without beginning and without end.

forgiveness is not gained through spiritual performance but only by repentance. Our time of healing may take its course and there are rays of light like that inner quest of Cardinal Newman while he was groping for the Light. They are symbols of hope; Jesus' promise that a new chapter in our lives is going to be whole again, restored and strengthened as we turn over a new leaf and bury the hatchet.

I'd like to close this with these words: Christianity has no room for complacency and an easy life. Christianity invites us to be extraordinary." And I think to be extraordinary simply means to be faithful to the values of the kingdom of God. One of them is our continuing attitude of forgiveness and compassion to our neighbors. God bless you.

TWENTY-FIFTH SUNDAY IN ORDINARY TIME

Amos 8:4-7; Ps 113:1-2, 4-6, 7-8; 1 Tim 2:1-8; Lk 16:1-13

The Parable of the Dishonest Steward[220]

"A rich man had a steward who was reported to him for squandering his property. He summoned him and said, 'What is this I hear about you? Prepare a full account of your stewardship, because you can no longer be my steward."

There's an Italian philosopher, Antonio Gramsci who said: 'it is difficult to maintain the optimism of the will in the face of the pessimism of the intellect.' Pessimism of the will is what we are living today in a global village where the sin of pride, dishonesty, and selfishness run deep within our system. It is pessimism that conditions us not only of the danger of a growing culture of secularism, but of division that may provoke the collapse of our Christian foundation in various disciplines.

There are so many sad examples of notable people who have shown their disgrace by lying for fear of rejection, for fear of impeachment, or for fear of losing their power and richness in this world. History has taught us the principle of integrity and sharing in countless situations where proper perspective gets its priority to reflect upon.

Today's gospel 'The Parable of the Unjust/Dishonest Steward' deals with the issue of wealth. It has a number

---

[220] Others call it the Parable of the Clever Villain. The crafty steward is considered wise to tell the two people not to pay all they owed his master. Using a couple of old sayings, good Christians do not believe in "anything for a buck" because they know that "you can't take it with you."

of points that allow us to discover more deeply about Jesus' continuing exhortation for his disciples and for us to be resourceful; to figure out a way to do what needs to be done especially in times of difficulty. And he tells them to deal with it courageously and wisely with regard to the use of possessions, money or other business transactions. It is a lesson in Christian discipleship which is pretty much emphasized in Luke's gospel.

This is actually a story that is difficult to understand. It has been called 'the most difficult of all the synoptic parables' probably because it has conflicting morality messages since Jesus appears to be commending dishonest behavior of the steward. Many NT scholars have struggled to understand its allegorical interpretation for centuries. But Jesus, being a member of the lowly peasant class, picks up the idea of a steward to deal with what the Pharisees and scribes are missing in regard to honesty and dishonesty in the context of money dealings or the use of material possessions. He brings to the fore the need to have a proper perspective and sight of spiritual goal as a priority while living in this world.

As a student one of my favorite moments was when we read 'The Merchant of Venice' in a class on Shakespeare. It is a kind of morality play on the subject of honesty. The story itself is all about the worst stereotype of the Jew as portrayed by Shylock. He is a Jewish usurer who demands a pound of flesh from the debtor Antonio, who, due to ill fortune at sea, cannot pay the money back. Though Shakespeare may not have intended Shylock, the Jew, to be the central character of the play, there is truth in it. Jews, for instance, were the only people who could employ usury in those days—during the Middle Ages. They were hated for being rich and shrewd in their business. They were known in their profession of lending money, which the Christians by religion were unable to do. At the center of Venice, for instance, there was a great tension between Jews and Christians. And this led them to control big chunks of the World Economy.

Even if we look at their own history, their Jewish-ness, we find that theirs is a story of connection. As in Europe their history is centered on money—business. We recall in today's parable that Jesus is telling the Jews to use their money during the age of the Gentiles to make friends. In Britain many of them have their names all over the banking system and they are prominent in various disciplines, particularly in business and finance. Their sense of being Jews, their identity and commitment to their religion are still pretty strong. In Germany, for instance, they are regarded as the richest and most exclusive community. As a consequence native Germans are deprived of their wealth. Whether correct or not, that perception contributed significantly to Anti-Semitism and eventually the Holocaust.

We see in the parable that the steward betrayed the trust he was given. He is supposed to work for his master's best interests, but instead he mismanaged and squandered his master's possessions. Like the story of the Prodigal Son who squandered his own inheritance, the steward, too, squandered and wasted his master's property. But toward the end, both of them get credit: one for true repentance and the dishonest steward for his worldly wisdom. The material reasons of the world and the wisdom of this generation are combined for the good of spiritual teachings. One has to make a choice and the challenge is to be responsible as 'children of light' to resolve the problem.

The steward's dishonesty is definitely not commended. What is commended in his behavior is the way he deals with the problem; his quick judgment with the money of the debtors to win their favor. That makes a difference. When faced with a dilemma or in deep crisis, the steward acts shrewdly to take care of himself. Apparently, he knows the tricks on how to get out of his mess. It is why the steward is compared to the "children of this world/light who are wise and resourceful to get on in life. Jesus tells the crowd that the time would come when they also would be responsible for their actions like how they use their finances and help others who are in need.

It is the same thing in Christian discipleship when one needs to be creative and resourceful to make ends meet. He may need to explore other possible resources or means to enable him to figure out the best way to do what needs to be done. This is the perspective of discipleship—being able to cope with difficulties, to weather many storms of life and to show God to be alive in his ministry. And we have a lot of examples who stand out in history. They show to the world that in spite of struggles they have had, they still commit themselves to service and faith in God. God bless you.

TWENTY SIXTH SUNDAY IN ORDINARY TIME

Readings: Amos 6:1a, 4-7; Ps 146:7-10;
1 Tim 6:11-16; Lk 16:19-31[221]

The Parable of the Rich Man and Lazarus

"When the poor man died, he was carried away by angels to the bosom of Abraham. The rich man also died and was buried, and from the netherworld, where he was in torment, he raised his eyes and saw Abraham far off and Lazarus at his side."

An incident that reminds me of the former British Prime Minister Clement R. Attlee[222] in the late 1940s was when he was asked by Winston Churchill about what his predecessor had done to win the war. Attlee shrugged his shoulder and said: "Talk about it." Perhaps we also need to talk about something not in the context of war but certainly something that has to do with our faith vis-à-vis the teachings of Christ.

We have every reason to believe that our faith episodes are densely layered with allusions to sources as varied as sacred scriptures. In reading the signs of the times, it seems, the call of conversion continues to echo in our hearts; to

---

[221]   This is the only gospel that carries the parable of Lazarus and the Rich Man. Luke was the companion of Paul, the apostle to the Gentiles. It showed a specific message that Gentiles could now inherit the promises to Abraham provided they were faithful as Eleazar had been. Yet Paul did not want the Gentiles to be conceited in their new relationship with God.

[222]   Clement Richard Attlee. The Prime Minister of UK from 1945-1951, and the Leader of the Labor Party from 1935-1955. He was the first Labor Prime Minister to serve a full Parliamentary term, and the first to command a Labor majority in Parliament.

abound around the world. It is one of the great mysteries of being human endowed with faith in God.

Today's gospel, the Parable of the Rich Man and Lazarus,[223] speaks to our hearts with the light of faith as Jesus continues to preach the kingdom of God. He reveals salvation for all and resurrection to eternal life. It is the continuation from the parable of the dishonest steward that we read last Sunday. It comes after a series of four other parables: parables of the lost sheep, lost coin, prodigal son, and dishonest steward.

As parables are a form of storytelling that relate an essential spiritual teaching, Christ himself is always in the habit of speaking to his people in parables. It was a common mode of instruction in the Semitic world of the first century.[224] The story of this parable has been used countless times by many within traditional Christianity to prove that sinners, the unrighteous will go to hell where they will suffer eternal damnation with fire. But it is not the story of heaven and hell. It is not a story of afterlife, though it may give us a glimpse into the nature of life after death. Rather, it is a story to further illustrate what proper stewardship is since Jesus had just given his teaching about the unjust steward who mismanaged his master's property (Lk 16:1-13). It is about being able to cope with difficulties; being creative and

---

[223]   This is the only time in Christ's parables that a person's name is used. The name "Lazarus" is a transliteration of the Hebrew *"Eleazar"* (which means "God has helped"). The name was a common Hebrew word used for eleven different persons in the Old Testament.

[224]   cf. Matt 13:34-35: "All these things spoke Jesus unto multitudes in parables and without a parable he spoke not unto them. That it might be fulfilled which was spoken by the prophet, saying, 'I will open my mouth in parables; I will utter things which have been kept secret from the foundation of the world."

resourceful to get on in life and how to help others who are in need. And we read that last Sunday, didn't we?

Following this, we notice that a common theme to several of Jesus' parables is to highlight the treatment of the least of society—the poor, those who don't flow in the mainstream. The rich man, however, is 'indifferent to the needs of the poor.'[225]

The context of the story tells us that Jesus is being mocked by the Pharisees because of what he told them before in the preceding parable of the Unjust Steward: that one cannot serve two masters—God and riches.[226] The Pharisees, who were known in those days as "lovers of money" (Lk 16:14), had failed to provide the religious leadership which was entrusted to them. In fact, Jesus wants to show them through parables that they, too, are in need of salvation. Hence, when they realized that he is referring this parable to them, immediately, they scoffed at him. Their self-righteousness has blinded them to their own wicked ways.

The Jewish mentality, especially among the Pharisees, believed that being poor and sick is a curse from God. And being rich, on the one hand, is a blessing from God. It is a sign that one is loved by God. As we can see, the Rich Man is described to be a Pharisee because he is dressed in purple, a symbol of kingship, a sign that the Davidic or Messianic Kingdom was his. He wears fine linen, the symbol of priesthood, showing that God's ordained priests and the Temple were his.

---

[225] Arland J. Hultgren. 2002. *The Parables of Jesus: A Commentary.* Eerdmans. pp 110-118.

[226] "No servant can serve two masters; for either he will hate the one and love the other, or else he will be loyal to the one and despise the other. You cannot serve God and Mammon."

The gospel is replete with symbols; instructive and significant which is why it should not be taken literally. If we analyze the story, the name Lazarus (which means "God has helped") is a transliteration of the common Hebrew word used for eleven different persons in the OT. He is one who must have had some kind of affinity or relationship with Abraham because the story places him in Abraham's bosom after death. He is Eleazar of Damascus, the chief steward of Abraham.[227] Lazarus represents Abraham's faithful steward Eleazar.[228] But probably Eleazar is a Gentile who must also be associated with stewardship because Christ teaches this parable for the crowd to explain what stewardship really means.

Eleazar's faithfulness to Abraham brings his own disinheritance from all the promises of blessing which God has given to Abraham. It is given to Isaac and his future family. That inheritance includes wealth, prestige, kingship, power, priesthood, and the land of Canaan as an eternal possession. Now Eleazar is cast out. Hence, the parable calls Lazarus a "beggar", a "pauper" who possesses nothing of earthy worth.

The Rich Man symbolizes the actual son of Abraham— Judah who had all the material blessings promised to Abraham's seed like the kingdom, priesthood, and the tribe of Israel. We remember that Judah had "five brothers" (They

---

[227]   cf. Gen 15:2-3. "And Abram said, 'Lord God, what wilt thou give me, seeing I go childless, and the steward of my house is this Eleazar [Lazarus] of Damascus, and lo, one born in my house is mine heir."

[228]   Gen 15:3 ff. Chief steward of Abraham, not an ethnic part of the Abrahamic family. Though he had been the legal heir to receive all of Abraham's possessions, Abraham gave him an assignment which was to result in his own disinheritance. But Scriptures show he carried out the orders of Abraham in a precise and faithful way.

are the sons of Leah: 1) Reuben—Jacob's firstborn, and 2) Simeon, and 3) Levi, and Judah, and 4) Issachar, and 5) Zebulun.[229] The Rich Man also had the same (cf. v 28).

Judah and the Rich Man each had "five brothers," along with Moses and the prophets in their midst. Albeit, the Rich Man and Judah have been given the actual inheritance of Abraham's blessings, Christ is telling us that the Rich Man has been unfaithful to his responsibilities. When the true inheritance is to be given, Judah is in 'Hades' and 'in torment' while Lazarus (Eleazar, the faithful steward) is now in Abraham's bosom. He is finally received into eternal life.

With all these allegorical allusions to the Old Testament, particularly in the Book of Genesis, we get to know the true stewardship that Christ is trying to convey in his parable. Lazarus who symbolizes Eleazar finds after death his true inheritance to be in Abraham's bosom. However, the Rich Man who symbolizes Judah has inherited all the material blessings while on earth, but when he dies he is not allowed to pass the spiritual Jordan into the final inheritance of heaven because of his unfaithfulness.

The challenge seems to point out how we must live our lives according to the values of God's kingdom. Our concern for the needs of the poor, for instance, is fundamental in our sense of stewardship; a reflection of God's love for humankind. Proverb tells us that God identifies with the poor. "If you do it to the poor, you do it to me." Matthew 25 says also the same thing.

We are challenged to care for those who have less than we do and to help those who are helpless and marginalized. That's the call of stewardship—being able to care for others

---

[229] cf. Gen 35:23

and being faithful to the covenant of life and love. Let's say in our own families, poverty is not only in terms of materials things but, can be reflected in terms of relationship—scarred, wounded, neglected, or abandoned, are indeed realities of Lazarus in our midst. Rather than despise them, we show them our caring presence, like we are their sibling souls. After all, it is not for us to judge them; God will judge all of us. God bless you.

TWENTY-SEVENTH SUNDAY IN ORDINARY TIME

Readings: Hab 1:2-3; 2:2-4; Ps 95:1-2, 6-7,
8-9; 2 Tim 1:6-8, 13-14; Lk 17:5-10

The Parable of the Unprofitable Servants
(Attitude of a Servant)

When you have done all you have been commanded, say, 'We are unprofitable servants; we have done what we were obliged to do."

One of our conferences held years ago, focused the theme on servanthood and leadership. It was dealt with clarity and emphasis on certain areas that need to be addressed. The profile of the problem involved a litany of concerns in regard to the priests' morale today, their sense of ecclesiology and spirituality. However, a highly sensitive barometer to what is going on in church and society is evidently a gospel cry. There is sorrow and pain inflicted upon their identity, leadership, and credibility. The lack of a unified vision has grown steadily with opposition to the decisions and directions of Vatican II.

Speaking about churches in first world countries, they are now gradually graying and emptying. Without new immigrants, for instance, churches across the nation can no longer continue their operations. Children in this generation no longer walk the path of faith with us. They want to be in their own; to be free and independent.

As we come to grips with the reality of today, we realize how necessary it is to be constantly challenged by the word of God. It is within the context of discipleship where we establish a relationship to Christ and a living out of the paschal mystery. Otherwise, we will always ask God why he allows so much pain and trouble and we start to doubt God's existence.

It is the same principle rooted in the historical context from the first reading where the prophet Habakkuk cries out: "How long O Lord? I cry for help but you do not listen! I cry out to you." We recall the sufferings of the ancient Israelites when they were punished for their sin of idolatry. They were enslaved by the Babylonians for 79 years of cruelty and injustice. They ruined the city of Judah and destroyed their Temple, stealing all their treasures and artifacts. It is the reason why the prophet Habakkuk complained to God when he allowed the Babylonians to grow and prosper in Judah and then make them slaves.

The state of being and doing comes across as an element that relates well to faith perspective because it is in today's gospel that the apostles ask Jesus to increase and strengthen their faith.[230] Their quest for that gift of faith will enable them to cope with the implications of discipleship; challenges of being called to a mission without any fixed abode. They are itinerant preachers or missionaries that peddle the word of God.

The apostles are honest enough to acknowledge their own limitations. Like what psalm 46 says: "In you, O Lord, I have hoped, and I will never be disappointed." They need faith that, although small like a mustard seed, is the substance of things hoped for, the evidence of things not seen (Heb 11:1). It is faith in deep appreciation of how mysterious God is; it is

---

[230] It is faith that has more to do with what kind of faith it is than with how much faith there is. A small amount of faith—as much as a mustard seed (a very small seed) can accomplish great things, if that small amount of faith is placed in a great and mighty God. It was not quantity they needed but quality.

something that embraces different facets of God's mysteries and grows best when immersed or deepened in trials and tribulations—in this valley of tears.

Jesus knows his apostles because he has direct experience with them. With that, he constantly reminds them of the challenges they may encounter as they draw near Jerusalem. He is aware that in their journey their faith will be challenged and thus, tested in fire. As a consequence, they will step back and feel disillusioned. It is reminiscent of that incident when Simon Peter and his companions told Jesus: "Everyone is searching for you." Because they need him badly and they cannot afford anymore to bear the brunt of rejection and animosity from people they minister to.

As the first community of faith and ministries of the Gospel in the New Testament Church, the apostles themselves have no clear understanding about the Messiahship of Jesus. They cannot accept the fact that their Master will suffer and die on the cross. They think of Jesus as a political Messiah—one who will overthrow the Roman government and re-establish a new nation that reflects total freedom and independence from foreign dictators. It is how they perceive the agenda of Jesus. But his kingdom agenda is not in this world but in the life hereafter. It is faith in his words and promises; his deeds and actions that one has to trust him with determination like the roots of the mulberry tree which are extremely strong. His vision-mission agenda are focused on God's kingdom.

Jesus' figurative language, especially in this parable, has symbolic meaning in terms of service and discipleship. The agricultural background that bears the images of farm life (v. 7) like plowing fields, the mulberry tree, mustard seed and tending sheep represent spiritual labor, to which Christ called his own followers (Jn 21:16; Acts 20:28; 1 Pt

5:2-3). Christ tells us to do work to the hilt; to leave no stone unturned in fulfilling our respective tasks and assignments without expecting in return. As members of Christ's mystical body—his Church, we have no right of ownership of anything because God owns us, we belong to him, and everything we have is his, even our time. And whatever we do in his service, we have to be humble; not to brag about it (cf. story of St Jerome).

As committed Christians we can be compared with the worker in today's parable who expects to be paid for his day's work. We cannot do as we claim that Jesus owes us something. We should always think that we are God's stewards, his servants[231] with proper attitude of faith as we serve our master.

Looking in today's context where almost everything has to be bought, paid off in certain amounts, as regards products or labor done, I think the spirituality of stewardship, servanthood, or discipleship in general, share a commonality of focus which are anchored in our personal identity with Jesus and his mission.

If we think, for instance, about our Catholic media networks such as EWTN, Veritas, Catholic newspapers, journals, and magazines, all of them offer their services and provide us with dependable information and opinion. And they are described as joyful servants of God's pilgrim church. Let us share our contribution especially to our families by doing our obligation and responsibility with hardly any ostentatious display of bragging or to exaggerate it with so

---

[231] Servants at the time of Jesus were the property of masters and were more akin to slaves than employees or workers. They were doing all the drudgeries such as planting crops, looking after the sheep or preparing and serving meals. However, they were taken care of by their masters.

much publicity. Let us humbly acknowledge ourselves that we are Christ's stewards in this world who care for our brothers and sisters. We are all called to serve. Just as he came "not to be served, but to serve" (Matt 20:28), so do we.

Though our faith this time may be compared to the size of a mustard seed, with our commitment to serve and dedicate ourselves to the person, teaching and mission of Christ, we can certainly develop it and be productive where we are called to be. God bless you.

TWENTY EIGHTH SUNDAY IN ORDINARY TIME

Readings: 2 Kgs 5:14-17; Ps 98:1, 2-3,
3-4; 2 Tm 2:8-13; Lk 17:11-19

The Cleansing of Ten Lepers

"Ten were cleansed, were not? Where are the other nine? Has none but this foreigner returned to give thanks to God?" Then he said to him, "Stand up and go; your faith has saved you."

There was an incident in the life of Eli Stanley Jones, a 20th century Methodist Christian missionary and theologian who gave thousands of his inter-religious lectures to the educated classes in India, who once asked Mahatma Gandhi why he refused to become a Christian when he always quoted the words of Christ in the gospel. Gandhi replied, "I really don't reject your Christ. As a matter of fact, I love your Christ. The problem is that many of you Christians are so unlike your Christ.

I think he makes sense as far as our Christian witnessing is concerned. We continue to struggle with a number of deeply troubling issues related to tragedies and moral decadence. It seems they are like 'leprosy of sin' that range from greed and power, sex and money, pride and rebellion against God that burst each day into public view.

As we endeavor to develop our institutions, along with the package of reforms for cleaning up the system, we need to be anchored in faith seeking more spiritual healing. This is the challenge as we all take on the journey toward spiritual healing.

In this challenging context, do we see any spiritual signs or implications to what we long for like our 'second spring' or 'great rebirth' in this world? As we step into the crossroads, we come to know the great need as well as priorities.

The healing of Naaman in the first reading is not just a story of being cured or healed from one of the most dreaded diseases of ancient times. It is also a story of salvation—spiritual salvation as an inward experience of faith reborn through the power of God. We see here the classic illustration of what God would later do in the ministry of Jesus in the NT. It brings to light how God reaches out to people who live in darkness and uses their struggles and afflictions to draw them to him as they respond to his invitation.

In biblical times Naaman[232] was the chief commander of the Syrian army (Aram). He was a pagan from Damascus (2 Kings 5). It says that he was "honorable" and a mighty warrior but he was a leper. That's the main problem of Naaman. We have a picture of Naaman as a sinner before he comes to God. When he obeyed Elisha's instruction to wash seven times in the Jordan River he was healed.

---

[232] It comes from the Hebrew verb name, "be delightful, pleasant, beautiful." It has the idea of "gracious" or "well informed." His name suggests he had undoubtedly been a handsome man, at least before the leprosy. But his name became a reproach and a striking contrast to his appearance and probably also to his disposition because of the disease which had attacked his body. He was the General of the Syrian or the Aramean Army, second in command to the King.

We really don't know what biblical leprosy[233] was. While it may be described today as "Hansen's Disease,"[234] other skin diseases may also be included such as psoriasis, elephantiasis,[235] HIV, or cancer. In Scripture, leprosy is a portrait of sin and its effects as described to us in Leviticus 13-14. The leper was considered unclean, an outcast, and had to be separated from society. Because of the nature of the disease, the leper was often considered as dead. The person had to be isolated and segregated from the rest so that his disease would not spread (cf. Lev 13:46; Num 5:2-3). If the sores went away, the leper had to go to the priest to see if he could go back to normal life with his family. If the priest said that he was no longer contagious, then he could go back to his home, restore his religious and social status as a person and live with his family.

---

[233] cf. New Leprosy Bacterium: Scientists Use Genetic Fingerprint To Nail Killing Organism. Science Daily. November 28, 2009. Leprosy or Hansen's disease, named after physician Gerhard Armauer Hansen, is a chronic disease caused by the bacteria Mycobacterium leprae and Mycobacterium lepromatosis. It is an infectious disease that has been known since biblical times. It is characterized by disfiguring skin sores, nerve damage, and progressive debilitation. It is not very contagious (difficult to transmit) and has a long incubation period (time before symptoms appear), which makes it difficult to determine where or when the disease was contracted. Children are more susceptible than adults to contracting the disease. Contrary to folklore, leprosy does not cause body parts to fall off, although they can become numb and/or diseased as a result of the disease.

[234] cf. www.wikipedia, free encyclopedia online. Sasaki S., Takeshita F., Okuda K., Ishii N (2001). Microbiol Immunol 45 (11): 729-36.

[235] cf. The Columbia Encylopedia. 2008. Sixth Edition. It is the abnormal enlargement of any part of the body due to obstruction of the mymphatic channels in the area, usually affecting the arms, legs, or external genitals.

We can imagine the disfiguration and pain of leprosy[236] that a person has, at least in certain forms. It kills the nerves in the affected area, disfigures or disintegrates the victim's body joint by joint, and keeps him restless, filthy, and miserable, as if he were wearing the scarlet letter, bearing its social stigma.

According to Scriptures, some people get the disease because they disobey God. Miriam, the sister of Moses and Aaron, for instance, got leprosy for seven days as a punishment for speaking against Moses' leadership (Numbers 12:9-15). She and Aaron were supposed to be instruments of God to speak on his behalf, but instead, they spoke against Moses and disobeyed God. Miriam was healed though when Moses implored God for her healing. In a similar vein, King Uzziah,[237] king of Judah, got leprosy because he rebelled against God. At his early reign as king, he was very good but later he began to disobey God. He started to incense God in the temple which was only restricted to priests at that time and he was not a priest. He had leprosy the rest of his life and lived in isolation.

---

[236] The term "leprosy" (including leper, lepers, leprosy, leprous) occurs 68 times in the Bible—55 times in the OT (Hebrew = *tsara'ath)* and 13 times in the NT (Greek =lepros, lepra). In the OT, the instances of leprosy most likely meant a variety of infectious skin diseases, and even mold and mildew on clothing and walls. After the end of the 17th century, Norway and Iceland were the only countries in Western Europe where leprosy was a significant problem. During the 1830s, the number of lepers in Norway rose rapidly, causing an increase in medical research into the condition, and the disease became a political issue. Norway appointed a medical superintendent for leprosy in 1854 and established a national register for lepers in 1856, the first national patient register in the world.

[237] Hb "my strength is Yahweh, king of Judah 783-742 B.C., son and successor of Amaziah. He is also called Azariah (2 Kg 14:21; 15:1, 6-8).

Today's gospel echoes the same argument with a common theme of gratitude in the context of healing. When Jesus was on his way to Jerusalem, he was approached by the ten lepers who asked him for healing. What makes us reflect here is that out of ten who are healed, only one comes back to express his gratitude to Jesus. He is the Samaritan, a stranger to the commonwealth of Israel who returns to give glory to Jesus (vv 17-18). He is the Samaritan, a stranger to the commonwealth of Israel who returns to give glory to Jesus (vv 17-18). Both Jews and Gentiles are offered cleansing, but it is the Samaritan[238] who exhibits better response—to say 'thanks' and acknowledge the healing power of God.

Along this line, Jesus makes reference to Naaman, a Syrian (foreigner) with leprosy whom Elisha cured. In this context, Elisha tells Naaman to go and wash in the Jordan seven times (2 Kgs 5:10). He obeys him and is cured.

But the principle it gives us is more than physical healing as God often uses the sicknesses and problems of humanity as a means to bring us to salvation; to draw us to his redeeming love and compassion; to make us whole again. Like us too, in some ways, we are grateful for that and for every blessing we receive from God. Alongside, our sense of appreciation to people who make a difference in our lives makes us whole again. Our journey of thanksgiving[239] has an implicit grammar of gratitude that is automatic in our genetic coding, in our humanity as we're inclined to say 'thank you', to count our blessing, to express our

---

[238] A Samaritan, a man from the region of Samaria. He was a despised, heathen foreigner. Samaritans looked to Mt Gerizim as the place to worship God, not Jerusalem. They were hated by the Jews.

[239] The Greek word for thanksgiving is *eucharist*. At the heart of it is *charis*, which means "grace" God's provision as a manifestation of his grace to us.

appreciation to everything and everyone we encounter in our lives. Indeed, we are blessed.

I would like to close with a story that I also heard from other priests. It's about a mother who was walking along the seashore with her baby son. While walking, a huge wave descended upon them and carried the child out to sea. The mother cried, so distraught that she began begging to God to save her child. Shortly afterwards, another huge wave deposited the child, unharmed, right at her feet. The mother took the child and embraced him. She said to God, "Thank you, Lord. Thank you so much for saving my child." A moment later, she looked at her child and she noticed one thing and asked God again: "Where is the hat he was wearing?"

I think there are times that we forget the most important thing in our life and focus instead on trivial things like in this story. Let's focus more on what is essential. God bless you.

TWENTY-NINTH SUNDAY IN ORDINARY TIME

Readings: Ex 17:8-13; Ps 121:1-2, 3-4, 5-6,
7-8; 2 Tm 3:14-4:2; Lk 18:1-8

The Parable of the Persistent Widow[240]

*"While it is true that I neither fear God nor respect any human
being, because this widow keeps bothering me I shall deliver
a just decision for her lest she finally come and strike me."*

I recently stumbled upon a riveting message of Cardinal
Francis George that says: Hispanic Catholics have now
become more mainstream members of the U.S. Catholic
Church. The ongoing American immigration drama has
indeed been good for the country. It has also been an asset
in various other aspects. However, it needs to be better
managed with due process protections of individual rights
and an immigration system that highlights the American
sense of fairness.

There are, of course, conflicting demands and missions to
accomplish but, as a Church, we are committed to providing
assistance to those who are poor and marginalized. The
vital nuts-and-bolts information about undocumented
immigrants, narcotrafficking and rampant lawlessness
may have engendered fear and hostility by some immigrant
groups, particularly in the Hispanic community. This is a

---

[240] Many scholars view this parable as Luke's editorial comments. It is
similar to the parable of the Friend in Need only this time the request
is not being made of a friend, but of someone who is indifferent. And
the request is not for a material item, but for justice.

noxious chemistry that needs to be addressed. Tensions are at play. Justice has to take place.

Today's gospel, the parable of the Persistent Widow, tells us a story with a familiar relation in the contemporary world that seeks justice through persistence in prayer more than a midnight epiphany. The goal is clear and the process involved has taken its shape through persistence. Furthermore, it has become a testament to sustain hope in the language of faith.

As English is the common tongue that we all need to learn to participate in civic and economic life in this country, persistence in prayer is the language that is mighty and powerful. It gives wings to the hopeless spirit, heals the wounded heart, and sets the afflicted free from injustice. With faith we profess that God alone is our hope: "therefore, we must be saved by hope."

God grants justice to those who continue to cry out and the key to its meaning leads us to the principle of developing those habits of the heart and mind intrinsic to the incessant journey of prayer. At its core lies the attitude of the widow who never ceases to fight for what is just in a given context. She exhibits persistence in her commitment to social justice, social responsibility, or perhaps social change as she implores the judge who does not fear God nor care for his people.

Like an editorial page in Luke's gospel, this episode of the gospel reflects the spirit of persistence—its power with two evolving issues of faith in God's goodness and God's chronology of actions. The widow's faith knows no surrender. She continues to bother the corrupt judge to enable her to achieve what is in store for her that would make a difference in her life and the lives of others. And that's to bring about change. However, being poor and defenseless, weak and vulnerable, her only option is to convince the judge through her persistence. In this regard echoes the historical context of the gospel, e.g. the church being persecuted and Christians bereft of individual rights and travesty of justice.

As a woman and member of the Jewish community in those days, she had little hope to ever be heard because she had no husband or relative to represent her in court. But she made a difference as she persistently nags and badgers the judge until eventually he gives in and grants her justice.

In Scripture, widows, orphans, children, and foreigners were among the most vulnerable in society. They were an easy target of exploitation. In a Jewish society that was conditioned by patriarchy and machismo, women were highly dependent upon men for their well being. They were identified only with their husbands. In the Dead Sea Scrolls there is a written recount of a widow named Babatha[241] who was persistent in protecting the legal rights of her household. Several of Babatha's arguments bring out her legal battle

---

[241]   cf. Wikipedia, the free encyclopedia. *Babatha* was a Jewish woman who lived in the port of *Maoza* in modern day Jordan at beginning of the 2nd century CE. In 1960, archeologist *Yigael Yadin* discovered a leather pouch containing her personal documents in what came to be known as the Cave of Letters, near the Dead Sea. The documents found include such legal contracts concerning marriage, property transfers, and guardianship. These documents, ranging from CE 96 to 134, depict a vivid picture of life for an upper-middle class Jewish woman during that time; furthermore, they provide an example of the Roman bureaucracy and legal system under which she lived. (cf. Goodman, Martin David 1996. "*Babatha*", Simon Hornblower and Antony Spawforth: The Oxford Classical Dictionary, Third Edition). By 124 CE, she had been married and widowed with a young son, Jesus. She was remarried by 125 CE to Judah, owner of three date palm orchards in *Ein Gedi*, who had another wife and teenage daughter. (cf. Freund, Richard A. 2004. "A Tale of Two Caves: *Babatha* and Her-story", Secrets of the Cave Letters: Rediscovering a Dead Sea Mystery. Humanity Books. ISBN 978-1591022053.

against two appointed guardians of her son for control of her deceased husband's land. As with Babatha, the parable implies the widow in Jesus' parable was claiming her right to obtain support from her late husband's estate.

I once heard from an old parishioner who told me once that "the squeaky wheel gets oiled" If the undocumented immigrants, or teachers' union make so much noise, with protests and rallies, then, others who don't care for their cause will probably pause and listen to them just because they make a lot of noise. But most of the time they simply look for a way to stop their noise. But we should not think that God would have that same attitude. He listens and he has his own chronology of action. He has his own way—his own time and he hears our persistent cries especially for justice, even though it may take a while or long in coming (Ecclesiasticus 35:14-22).

God is willing to hear and answer the supplication of his elect (Lk 17:8), he responds when they offered according to his will. Jesus tells us long prayers and useless repetitions will not make God hear us any better (Mt 6:7). He already knows our needs.

God's justice is very different from human justice. His justice is always tempered with mercy. He favors the weak and those who are unable to help themselves. He is always there for us. And we need to complement our prayer with our feet ready to walk and take an extra mile to reach out to those who are in need.

We recall our history when Columbus, for instance, arrived in this country. His triumph was the voyage itself. He did not discover the new world in America because millions of people have lived here for thousands of years. The Indians, the indigenous people, e.g. Cherokee and Choctaw, were here already. What happened to them? They were treated like slaves. Punishment was appalling. Their bodies were hung in markets to be sold and fed to European dogs and many times their hands were cut off because they didn't bring enough gold to Europe.

Our historical and cultural issues reflect the cry of the poor and indeed, the protagonists of this country struggled to define the American identity that continues to move forward. God really is in the details of our history, especially when some of them take the form of human encounters like in our worshipping community, family meals with a real welcoming culture and not being discriminated against.

With tons and tons of lawyers in this country, justice has gone by the wayside and has been replaced by greed and business-like maneuvering—'let's make a deal.' Some of them are more concerned with draining one's wallet. It's like the process of making a mountain out of a little molehill. Some of them already make good income but that doesn't seem to be enough.

Moses, in the first reading, prays fervently for his people[242] who keep murmuring and complaining about their hunger and thirst in the desert. It is that kind of prayer that embodies persistence in faith and trust in God which also reflects the widow's persistence in the gospel. Let us be men and women committed to our search for justice, willing to sacrifice for those who suffer in many forms. I would like to quote what Winston Churchill once said, "Never, never, never, never give up." God bless you.

---

[242] This is the testing of covenant love. They challenged God rather than praise Him. They said, "Is the Lord among us, or not?" Moses built an altar, and called the name of it Jehovah Nissi, for he said, "Because the Lord has sworn that the Lord will have war with Amalek from generation to generation" (Ex 17:14-16).

THIRTIETH SUNDAY IN ORDINARY TIME

Readings: Sir 35:12-14, 16-18; Ps 34:2-3, 17-18,
19-23; 2 Tim 4:6-8, 16-18; Lk 18:9-14

The Parable of the Pharisee and the Tax Collector

*"I tell you, the latter went home justified, not the
former; for whoever exalts himself will be humbled,
and the one who humbles himself will be exalted."*

Not long ago I ran across a story about a little girl who, while playing in the garden noticed a beautiful flower—a gardenia. She wanted to take it. She exclaimed, "This flower is so pretty to be planted in such a dirty place." So she pulled it up by its roots and washed it in the water faucet. Not long after, the flower started to die. When the gardener came by and saw what the little girl did, he said: "you destroyed my beautiful plant!" "I'm sorry Sir, but I didn't like it to be planted in a filthy environment," she said. Then he replied, "But you don't know, my child, that I chose that spot and mixed the soil because it was only there that the plant could grow to be a beautiful flower."

As some of us may work unwaveringly in defense of certain principles, I think God has placed us where we can be a delight to one's heart; where we can be effective or be of great help to others. We just have to trust him. And he allows us to experience difficulties, trials and tribulations to enable us to see beyond the surface the wealth of meaning about what life really means in relationship with God.

Today's gospel presents another historic value of Luke's editorial commentary that speaks about the nature of prayer and relationship with God. As a sharp word of clarity and connection between two different attitudes toward prayer, the familiar challenge deals with one's humility.

Keenly aware of the challenges that human pride entails, Jesus addresses the ability to see oneself as he really is and to allow God's grace and mercy to shape his inner self. He reminds his disciples of who they are in the eyes of God and their dependency on him. He argues that God favors those who recognize their own sinfulness and welcome him with humility in his heart. If one is full of himself or suffused with self righteousness and knows no space for God to help him, it is possible that God's grace will not stand out to perfection as he endeavors to make himself a living reflection to others.

The Pharisee in the parable, who represents those who take pride in their religious practices and laid secure claim to the oral interpretation of the Law of Moses as the basis for Jewish piety, is here given a highlight for his attitude to boast about his own righteousness and exalted himself at the expense of others. He appears to have relished his journey through memory lane with pride, and has aimed to impress God with his accomplishments. While the tax collector, who represents those who are in connivance with the Roman authorities to deceive Jewish taxpayers by charging them more, presents himself as a sinner before God.

This reminds me of King David when he asked God for forgiveness. Yahweh forgave him. Later his son Amnon raped his half-sister Tamar and another son Absalom committed adultery with David's concubines on the same palace roof from which David had seen Bathsheba, the wife of Uriah the Hittite, while taking a bath. David was forgiven, but, he was unable to reverse God's punishment for his sin of adultery and murder when he sent Uriah, Bathsheba's husband, to die in the battle (cf. 2 Samuel 11 & 12; 2 Sm 11:27; 2 Sm 12:9).

God is really in the details, especially when those details take the form of human encounters that have to do with our moral lives. In the face of all kinds of trouble and the unknown, our shame and moral transgressions continue to afflict us, yet we have the humility to ask for pardon; and the abiding 'blueprint' for higher purposes is our transforming spirituality. It is an attitude that is reflected in our day-to-day encounter with our lives and the lives of those who surround us.

Over the years our image of ourselves as Americans, Italians, Filipinos, or Hispanics, has sometimes blinded us to the way others may perceive us. Widespread secularization in many aspects has certainly enchanted our culture. Here in our country, for instance, our foreign policy, our corporate export of raw capitalism, our good standard of education, our status as the leading supplier of munitions across the world, have made us superior over the rest of the world. We forget that there is still God above us; the Prime Mover and author of everything we have.

Just as we're inclined to tell others that we're doing marvelous things and that we have accomplished a lot of things, with God, however, we have to be humble enough to allow him to speak to us; to shape us from within while thinking that we are better than others. We constantly seek our need for his blessing. God does not need to be impressed because he already knows who we are. In life we hold fast to God who keeps us aligned to his teachings and to his call of humility that serves like our window into spirituality.

There was a time when Mother Teresa of Calcutta met a young woman who asked her if she could do some mission work in India where she had a center for the sick, and other impoverished people. And she told her, "You must find your own Calcutta." It dawned on me that we all have our own calling; we may not be fit or called to a certain state of life either in single blessedness or religious life, but oftentimes these "Calcuttas" that Mother Teresa referred to, are those who live in our own backyards. We just have to immerse ourselves in the grassroots of our people—their own struggles, their poverty in many forms.

As we celebrate Mission Sunday, let us humbly ask God's mercy and blessing for those who find it difficult to reach out to others; those who are struggling to commit themselves to relationship, unable to see beyond the horizon, and hard to forgive. God bless you.

THIRTY-FIRST SUNDAY IN ORDINARY TIME

Readings: Wisdom 11:22-12:2; Ps 145:1-2,
8-14; 2 Thes 1:11-2:2; Lk 19:1-10

Zacchaeus the Tax Collector

*"Today salvation has come to this house because this
man too is a descendant of Abraham. For the Son of
Man has come to seek and to save what was lost."*

There has been an abiding conviction among today's leaders
that we have to move beyond preconceived boundaries, do
what has to be done, to risk and trust and sometimes upset
the status quo. Just as we are now heading for election politics
in action, candidates for various positions have vowed to
commit themselves to their political agendas if elected. They
have a dream that shapes up challenges and new possibilities
that stretch out from the center to the margins.

This political journey offers a major focus on how we
can face the future and set out on our present situation
as opportunity. Likewise, it is a metaphor for our lives as
Christians committed to our faith. There is language of
mission and solidarity with the poor as we strive to make
God known and loved through our lived-experience in this
world.

The story of Zacchaeus in today's gospel is about bridging
the gap between what we heard or knew about Christ and
our own experience of God in the historical figure of Jesus
of Nazareth. It is a first hand account of an encounter with
Jesus. It tells us how God's grace works in our lives and the
call that his grace places in our hearts. As Jesus explains,

"We are people of God's family and the Messiah seeks out and saves the lost as well as those who are found."

Zacchaeus,[243] a chief tax collector in Jericho,[244] apparently knows very little about Jesus. He is a Jewish citizen who sold out his countrymen to be a puppet for the Roman Empire. His actions provide us with an extraordinary example on how to receive Jesus.and his journey of conversion enables us to understand the manifold ways God reveals his love for us. Like the three Wise Men, Zacchaeus searches for vital answers in his faith. And he finds his way home to God. He finds Jesus, his Savior.

---

[243] The name **Zaccheus** "from the Hebrew ZKY means "the righteous or pure one". First century Jews would have called a tax collector, one who collaborated with the unclean enemy, something besides "the righteous or pure one." Scripture tells us that he was a very wealthy man. He was a penitent man who resolved on the spot to act differently in the face of Jesus' acceptance of him. He symbolized the kind of person that Jesus came to seek and to save. He was the chief tax collector of the region and therefore very rich. A chief publican such as Zacchaeus would contract with the Romans directly and then farm out each section of the district to subcontractors. He would pay the procurator a fixed sum which they could recover by charging whatever they wanted for taxes to the people. This led to terrible abuse and dishonesty and they were hated by everyone, Jews and Gentiles alike. They were not allowed to enter the temple or the synagogue.

[244] It is a fertile area, with Balsam wood and date palms. People referred to the city as the Eden of Palestine. It is located in the southern end of the Jordan valley on the north shore of the Dead Sea. It is the **oldest city in the world**. Ever since people have learned how to trade one commodity for another, Jericho has been the center for trade routes that have gone through that part of the world. The caravan routes of that day went through Jericho. The markets of that day would be filled with wine and wheat from the north, gems and grain from Egypt, spices and silk from India. Anything you wanted in the world at that time could be found in the city of Jericho. It seemed that all of the roads led to Jericho.

This whole incident is the heart of Jesus' ministry as regards his work of salvation and his quest for the lost like Zacchaeus. Salvation[245] comes to Zacchaeus, not by his initiative, but by God's. It is the entire authentic realm that bristles with faith and stands out to perfection.

A priest once said, "What we dream alone remains just a dream, but what we dream with others can become a reality."[246] I think it makes sense as God made us a community for connections. We become part of the community of faith as we make our wise choices in faith.

In retrospect, the whole story takes place one Friday afternoon, four hours before sundown and the beginning of the Jewish Sabbath. In the life of Jesus, Palm Sunday is only two days away. Jesus is on his way to Jerusalem passing through Jericho. And Jericho is rightly called the City of Palms in the OT. It is described as the oasis in the desert.

Jesus knows already what's going to happen to him in the following week of his life. As he walks through Jericho, he is struck by something that he sees in the life of Zacchaeus: his crimes to his heart, his current behaviors about money.

Jesus' popularity has reached its legendary proportion. He's like the heart throb, the stellar celebrity in the Jewish

---

[245]   **Salvation** (*soteria*) is a rare word in Luke. All the other occurrences are in the *Benedictus* (1:69, 71 & 77), which are in references to John the Baptist's ministry. The related word also translated "salvation" (*soterion*) occurs in the *Nunc Dimitis* (2:30) and in a quote from Isaiah (3:6). Salvation is having sins forgiven. This is certainly part of the salvation Zacchaeus experienced. It comes from Keeping and believing the Word—and then bearing fruit. Sozo also carries the meaning, "to make whole". Some translators try to combine both the physical and moral implications by translating it with phrases like "to give new life to" or "to cause to have a new heart."

[246]   Ronald Rolheiser, OMI. *Religious Life in America Faces a Change of Epoch*. Paper prepared for the Inter-American Meeting in Toronto. May 1999, p. 13.

film industry. There is a huge crowd and Zacchaeus merely wants to catch a glimpse of Jesus. It is because he has heard rumors at the tax collector's union a few months earlier that his friend Levi, a tax collector in Capernaum, has quit his lucrative larceny to enable him to follow Jesus of Nazareth.

Levi had thrown a party which Jesus attended and that somehow prompts or intrigues him to see who this Jesus is. Because he is short he climbs a sycamore[247] tree to get a good view of the celebrity—Jesus himself. Jesus has never met him before but calls him by name: "Zacchaeus, hurry down, for I mean to stay at your house today." Jesus shares a meal with him and spends his last Sabbath night with the least, the despised and the lost.

Zacchaeus, being completely transformed reminds us that Jesus comes to seek and to save the lost. It tells us that conversion is the main issue; Jesus' preferential option for the poor, sinners, and outcasts of society. Like Zacchaeus, we also need conversion, a change of heart. After the Lord beckoned to Zacchaeus, "He made haste, and came down, and received him joyfully" (Lk 19:6).

Christian tradition tells us that toward the end, Zacchaeus sold everything he had and distributed it to the poor. Then he moved up to the town of Caesarea with other Christians. Before he died, he was made the first bishop of Caesarea. According to Clement of Alexandria, in his book Stromata, Zaccheus was surnamed Matthias by the apostles, and took the place of Judas Iscariot after Jesus' ascension.[248]

---

[247] A sycamore tree would have large branches near the ground like an oak tree and would be fairly easy to climb. These trees reach a height of some 50 ft (about 15 m). A sycamore fig tree is the very tree that was ironically a symbol of the nation of Israel and of blessing.

[248] cf. wikipedia, free encyclopedia online.

The pressure of our past, the challenge of wealth, prestige or relationship can be roadblocks to more sublime action of following Jesus. But like the prayer of the publican of last Sunday's gospel we present ourselves to God with humility and continue to ask for his mercy and blessing. Let's open our hearts to God and listen to the sounds of life that allow us to discover more that we also need conversion like Zacchaeus.

In closing, I would like to share with you what the late Pope John Paul II stressed in meeting with the Latin American bishops years ago: 'that the new evangelization requires a new language, new methods and new attitudes. The church in the past had stressed sociological solutions to poverty whereas now the emphasis should be on conversion. Once converted and brought to a personal encounter with the living Jesus Christ, the laity will then fix all these problems.' God bless you.

THIRTY-SECOND SUNDAY IN ORDINARY TIME

(1)

Readings: 2 Mc 7:1-2, 9-14; Ps 17:1, 5-6, 8,
15; 2 The 2:16-3:5; Lk 20:27-38

The Problem of the Resurrection[249]

*Jesus said to them, "The children of this age marry and
remarry; but those who are deemed worthy to attain to the
coming age and to the resurrection[250] of the dead neither marry
nor are given in marriage. They can no longer die, for they
are like angels;[251] because they are the ones who will rise."*

I'm pretty sure all of us have had some rough times in our
lives whether it be in family life, marriage, school, work, or

---

[249] The question of the resurrection of the body was important in Greek
philosophy (cf. 1 Cor. 15). Luke used this incident in his narrative to
bring Jesus' confrontations with his critics in the temple courtyard
to a climax. Most Greeks denied the resurrection of the body too (cf.
1 Cor. 15;12). Greek psychology viewed the body as the temporary
prison of the soul that was immortal.

[250] R. A. Edwards. *A Theology of Q.* 1976. Fortress Publications.
Philadelphia. pp 41, 50f., 113 f. Many popular treatments of
resurrection often presume that it reflects a "Jewish" view of the
unity of the human person over against a Greek dualism of soul
and body. cf. Pheme Perkins. *Resurrection—New Testament Witness
and Contemporary Reflection.* 1984. Doubleday & Company, Inc.
Garden City, New York. pp 38-39. Resurrection emerged in response
to particular crises in the fate of the nation. The most consistent
context for resurrection remains that of a judgment to establish
divine justice. However, there is no well-defined doctrine or
symbolism of resurrection. Nor is there a consistent anthropology
in the writings of this period.

[251] Pheme Perkins. *Resurrection—New Testament Witness and
Contemporary Reflection.* 1984. Doubleday & Company, Inc.

friendship. We have weathered the storms and so far some of us are still hanging in there; strong and undaunted by difficulties in life.

I recall an incident in my life when I went with a friend to visit a family in Manhattan, NY. It was after my 7 p.m. mass in the parish. We took the subway which was a walking distance from our place. My friend had epilepsy and I forgot to check with him if he had taken his medication before we took off. While riding the train, I noticed that he was restless. Something strange was beginning to surface. And that was the time when I started to worry about him because I was afraid that he might have a convulsion. I was right. He fell on the floor and started convulsing. There was commotion, some passengers started to scream and everybody was focused on him. The train stopped and someone called 911. At the dust of a hat, the paramedics came and took him to the hospital where I stayed with him until he got back to normal. When he opened his eyes, he was very apologetic to me. He said, "Father, I'm so sorry; I forgot to take my medication. Thank God I'm still alive though I may be forever the same like this—*semper eandem*." But God is the ground of my hope.

With that incident it dawned on me what the Roman poets once wrote: "While there is life there is hope." And

---

Garden City, New York. pp 74-75. Luke's version has expanded the phrase "are like angels in heaven" by incorporating it into an explanatory sentence, "for they cannot die anymore because they are equal to angels and are sons of God, being sons of the resurrection" (v. 36). This explanation has put together several metaphors, the unusual "sons of the resurrection," which had been attached to the apocalyptic paraenesis about marriage in Luke; becoming like angels, which appears to have been the story's original understanding of resurrection; and the combination of "sons" of God and immortality, grounded in the wisdom tradition.

this is best described in the Book of Ecclesiastes, "He who is joined with all the living has hope" (9:4).

It is in today's gospel that the promise of hope holds the first avenue to an inner knowledge of God's revelation in the resurrection and what that means in our lives as partakers of the divine nature. The question about resurrection evokes profound meaning as we come to grips with this question: What will life be like after we are resurrected? This is one hidden treasure of our salvation—to believe in the mystery of resurrection. Our faith tells us that there is victory over death and the promise of eternal life.

Jesus' triumph over his public ministry was also complemented with instances of confrontation, moral battle for interpretations of the law of Moses, his knowledge of Scripture, and his Messianic identity. How the chief priest, scribes, elders, Pharisees and Sadducees[252] test him, his encounter with them was replete with challenging attacks against his teachings and his deeds. They challenged his authority and trap him by his answers. They were crafty and self righteous. It is in this light that Jesus in today's gospel is being challenged by the Sadducees in connection with the meaning of resurrection which they don't believe in. Jesus, however, contrasts the dichotomy of "the current age" with "the age to come" seen by Jews as the Messianic

---

[252] The name "**Sadducee**" seems to derive from the name "**Zadok**," who was high priest at the time of David and Solomon. Actually we don't know a great deal about them since none of their own writings survive, only those of their opponents. They were Jews of a particular party or persuasion. They were the priestly aristocracy among the Jews by whom the political life of the people was largely controlled from the time of Alexander the Great onwards. Their belief system includes: **belief in the Torah, belief in free will over the idea that everything is predetermined, denial of the resurrection and of the immortality of the soul.**

period. They are both different. The "present age or earthly life" evidently implies material relationships with honor, wealth, status, and prestige. While "that age to come" evokes the spiritual meaning of what holds for us in the future— in the life hereafter. It is marked with mercy, compassion, peace, and eternal bliss. This is God's time and promise for our resurrection: that there's hope for us all of rising again. And we will mark our entry into God's kingdom which he promised to us through faith and Scripture. It says further that: "All of the OT saints died, without having received the promised blessings of God, but by means of the resurrection of the dead, they will" (cf. Heb 11).

The Sadducees, however, were a conservative religious group who only based their beliefs on the first five books of Pentateuch, the Torah. They rejected the immortality of the soul, angels, and spirits (cf Acts 23:8) and other traditions. Their belief in God's kingdom was similar to what the present world looks like. They were very much influenced by the Greek culture and had good connections with the Romans.

Their trick question 'whose wife will she be at the resurrection' is based on the passage of Dt 25:5 which says: "If brothers are living together and one of them dies without a son, his widow must not marry outside the family. Her husband's brother shall take her and marry her." This is the practice of levirate marriage in the ancient Israel.[253] We find

---

[253] It comes from the Latin *levir,* "husband's brother"—brother-in-law. According to Culpepper (Luke, NIB), such laws are found in Ugarit, Middle Assyrians and Hittite codes as well as in Deut. 25:5-10 (cf. Gen. 38:8, Lv 18:16; Ruth 3:9, 12-13). For the ancient Israelites, before a belief in the resurrection of the dead, "eternal life" was understood, as producing heirs (sons) who would continue the family's ownership of their land. If the husband died before producing sons (Dt 25:5), it was the responsibility of his brother

in the bible a curious relationship between Judah, his son Onan, and Tamar, his widowed daughter-in-law (Gen 38:8-26) and the story of the Moabite widow Ruth, her mother-in-law Naomi and her kinsman Boaz that she married.[254]

Resurrection is one of the major mysteries of our faith. We belong to an immense family with a great cloud of witnesses, so to speak. It is part of God's plan for us. And our destiny is to have our final rendezvous with God in his kingdom where there is eternal happiness and joy; where one does not have to marry again just to ensure that the family name will continue and will never die. When that time comes in God's kairos, one becomes like an angel and is no longer liable to death. This is our faith.

Over the course of time we have been struggling in every step along the way, with fears of every sort. These are fear of rejection, fear of old age, fear of death, or fear of insecurity. In times of crisis, when we are pressured by the daily grind, our fears are much stronger. Life does not always present us the way we want it to be with all the logical facts and or rational explanations. God doesn't think the way we do. He has his own way, a mysterious way. We may say that he never writes in straight lines. Rather, he writes in crooked lines and some of these lines are our own witness and lives. We can simply trust in him, trust that God is at work in the silence and serenity of our lives.

In closing, I would like to share with you an incident when the Rev. Billy Graham turned 80. He was asked by a young student about the most significant thing that

---

to "perform his duty" to her to produce offspring and continue the name of his brother.

[254] "The Marriage of Boaz and Ruth," Journal of Biblical Literature 59. (1940): pp 445-54.

surprised him in his life.[255] His answer was: "brevity of life." That's wisdom that is realized only with age.[256] We need the eyes of faith to enable us to see beyond and come to know that God is at work in our lives. Life is too short to neglect it without spiritual nourishment, without a balance of God and action where charity reaches and shares. As I mentioned before, "He who is joined with all the living has hope." It's not only in this world but also hope in the life hereafter. God bless you.

---

[255] Effie Caldarola. Reflection on Turning 60. The Tablet. Vol. 103, No. 25. Sept. 25, 2010. p25.

[256] ibid.

(2)

Readings: 2 Mc 7:1-2, 9-14; Ps 17:1, 5-6, 8,
15; 2 The 2:16-3:5; Lk 20:27-38

The problem of the Resurrection[257]

*Jesus said to them, "The children of this age marry and
remarry; but those who are deemed worthy to attain to the
coming age and to the resurrection of the dead neither marry
nor are given in marriage. They can no longer die, for they
are like angels; because they are the ones who will rise."*

The current crop of American films dealing with immigration
is as diverse as the immigrant experience itself. It shows
the continuing phenomenon of the American dream that is
the magnet to most cultures in this world. With tolerance
of differences, fairness, equal measures of hard economic
analysis, and compassion, it is evidently clear that the
process deserves to be addressed. It is indeed good for us—as
a country of immigrants. But it is also an asset like in any
business transaction that needs to be better managed.

I'm saying this because we are a nation created by
immigration and we are people of hope. As our liturgical
year is now getting closer to its conclusion, our journey with
Jesus in the next four weeks will highlight that hope in the
midst of fear and conflicting demands in our missions or
calling.

---

[257] The question of the resurrection of the body was important in Greek
philosophy (cf. 1 Cor. 15). Luke used this incident in his narrative to
bring Jesus' confrontations with his critics in the temple courtyard
to a climax. Most Greeks denied the resurrection of the body too (cf.
1 Cor. 15;12). Greek psychology viewed the body as the temporary
prison of the soul that was immortal.

An English poet William Blake observed about seeing the world in a grain of sand and eternity in an hour. I think it makes sense when we look more deeply into the heart of what's going on in our lives, in our society, in the world, at large. Because the more we do that, the more we enter into the mystery of every human being.

It is the same thing in the teachings of Jesus like in today's gospel which require commitment to faith and trust in God's providence. If equal opportunity fires the engines of achievement, our witnessing enables us to bring about transformation that culminates in union with God. We enter into dialogue with those whose faith traditions differ from our own. Our way of life, simple and focused is a form of commitment, a way of discipleship that Jesus himself stresses with his community of disciples.

The theme of hope holds the fundamental covenant of God with man. It is the first step to an inner knowing of God's revelation in the resurrection and what that means in our lives as partakers of divine nature. The principle is this: God became human so that we would become divine. But the imprint he left in our lives by Christ's resurrection power is the Cross. Suffering with him is a daily reality; that our Christian life is not only a question of believing (cf. Phil 1:29) but also a matter of suffering.

The question about resurrection evokes a profound meaning as we deal with this question: What will life be like after we are resurrected? We really don't know. It is God's mystery in his plan of salvation for humankind. But our faith tells us that there is victory over death and the promise of eternity. And our destiny is to be with God in his kingdom where there is eternal happiness and joy. Which is why, one does not have to marry again just to ensure that the family name will continue and never die. When that day comes in God's chronology of time—his kairos, those worthy of the resurrection do not have to marry again to ensure continuity of the family name or heritage. As the gospel says, one becomes like an angel and is no longer liable to death. This is our faith.

But the Sadducees, who were the Jewish conservative religious who only based their beliefs on the first five books of Pentateuch, the Torah, don't believe in the immortality of the soul, angels, and spirits (cf. Acts 23:8). Their belief in free will over the idea says that everything is predetermined and for them God's kingdom is similar to what the present world looks like. They are very much influenced by the Greek culture and have good connections with the Roman officials.

Jesus is telling us that the dead will rise even the saints in heaven in the Final Judgment; that our relationship with God does not end in death. We really do not know what it is exactly going to be. Only God knows. And the challenge for us is not to worry so much over certain things like the last four ends—eschatological ends that our minds cannot comprehend.

Over the course of time we have been struggling in every step along the way, with our fears of every sort. These are fear of rejection, fear of old age, fear of death, or fear of insecurity. In times of crisis, when we are pressured by the daily grind, our fears are much stronger, aren't they?

I'd like to share with you an incident when the Rev. Billy Graham turned 80. He was asked by a young student about the most significant thing that surprised him in his life.[258] His answer was: "brevity of life." That's wisdom that is realized

---

[258]   Effie Caldarola. Reflection on Turning 60. The Tablet. Vol. 103, No. 25. Sept. 25, 2010. p25.

only with age.[259] We need the eyes of faith to enable us to see beyond and come to appreciate life's blessings that God has bestowed on us. As Roman poets once wrote, "He who is joined with all the living has hope." It's not only in this world but also hope in the life hereafter. God bless you.

---

[259] ibid.

THIRTY-THIRD SUNDAY IN ORDINARY TIME

Readings: Mal 3:19-20a; Ps 98:5-6, 7-8,
9; 2 Thes 3:7-12; Lk 21:5-19

Jesus' Discourse on the Future of Jerusalem and the Temple

"Before all this happens, however, they will seize and persecute you, they will hand you over to the synagogues and to prisons, and they will have you led before kings and governors because of my name. It will lead to your giving testimony."

I would like to share a story about Oliver Wendell Holmes, Jr., the famous American jurist who served on the Supreme Court of the U.S. from 1902 to 1932. He was a brilliant man and one of the most influential American common-law judges.[260] One day he took the train and was immediately recognized by the conductor who greeted him. "Good morning, Sir." "Good morning," Mr Holmes replied. He told him that he didn't have to worry about his fare; the railroad company would be pleased to cover his it. But Holmes said, "That's not the problem, young man. The problem is that without that ticket I have no idea where I'm supposed to be going."

I think it's the same thing in our lives when we ask ourselves, "What's my goal in life? What's my vision as a Christian? Where am I supposed to be going? My life is crammed with page upon page of tests and trials.

From the beginning of this year, I counted the turning pages of the calendar and I noticed that there was always

---

[260]   cf. www.wikipedia, free encyclopedia online.

something that makes us aware of issues we are facing on a particular day. In matters of faith, we are now experiencing the decline of religion which evidently reflects secularization of society, moral decadence, poverty, and the resurgence of Islam and other religious sects. They define what the world looks like now amid new technologies and a modern way of life. Dominant culture and thinking are in continuous search for a meaningful and comfortable lifestyle.

Over the course of time we have walked with Jesus through liturgical readings of infancy narratives, his public ministry, his death and resurrection. At this point in time as he prepares his disciples for a challenging ministry that would require them to put their hearts and souls into it while striking a balance of prayer and action, Jesus announces one of the most remarkable prophecies of Holy Writ in regard to the end of time—the destruction of the Temple.[261]

For many centuries Sacred Scriptures have warned of the coming end of time. The Book of Revelation, for instance, confirms that at the end of time, Israel will once again lose control of Jerusalem. The book of Daniel in the 9th chapter, however, tells us a prophecy about the coming end times known in the NT as Great Tribulation and in the OT it is called the time of Jacob's trouble.

Jesus' followers ask him when it is going to happen. But first he warns them against those who will claim themselves

---

[261] The temple in Jerusalem was originally built by Solomon. The temple has been destroyed twice. The first destruction was made by Nebuchadnezzar of Babylon and the rebuilding after 70 years. It offered a vision of what the temple was to be: the locus of the presence of God. In Judaism, the temple was the religious, cultural, and national center; indeed, the temple was a microcosm of the universe. The power of the temple as a symbol is especially seen in its ability to continue long after the temple building itself was destroyed in 70 A.D.

as Christ's messengers or prophets announcing that the end of the world is near. They raise three questions: 1) when will the Jerusalem Temple be destroyed? 2) what will be the sign of the coming destruction? 3) when will this generation end and the new age to begin?

Described as the city of the great prophets and the capital of the Kingdom of Israel and Judah under King David and his son King Solomon, Jerusalem has been the apple of discord—the longtime target of conflict in the Middle East. Muslims across the world wish that someday Jerusalem will no longer be under Israel's control.

The first temple was originally built by King Solomon. But it was destroyed twice; first during the reign of King Nebuchadnezzar of Babylon. Then the Romans came under the armies of Roman Emperor Vespasian. They crushed the rebellion of the Jews, destroyed the city and burned the temple in 70 A.D. However, Rome fell. The Byzantine Empire followed and controlled Jerusalem until Muslim armies conquered the city in 638-199. The First Crusade came and passed it to European invaders who held it until 12th century (1187) when it was taken by the Muslim General Saladin whose successor al-Khamil turned over the city to Emperor Frederick II of the Roman Empire in 1228.[262] The Egyptian rule came when armies of the Ottoman Empire seized Jerusalem.

After four centuries at the height of World War I in 1917, the British forces defeated the Ottoman Turks and occupied Jerusalem. From 1947 to 1967, West Jerusalem remained under Israeli control while Jordan administered

---

[262] cf. Meir Ben-Dov. 1982. *In the Shadow of the Temple: The Discovery of Ancient Jerusalem*. Trans. Ina Friedman. San Francisco: Harper & Row, Publishers.

the territory of East Jerusalem.[263] Today, Jews worship at the Western Wall, or Wailing Wall, which they believe is the only surviving element of the Second Temple destroyed by the Romans.[264]

In Judaism, the temple represents the heart of God, Israel, and the heart in each person where the Divine dwells. It is the center of worship and for them the majority of the commandments of the Law of Moses, the Torah deal with Temple worship, sacrifices, and spiritual transformation.

Jesus gives many signs that will mark the end of the world. These include earthquakes, famines, plagues, wars, and the mighty signs that will come from the sky. But we really don't know when it is going to happen. However, he tells his disciples to remain steadfast in their faith and keep their lives focused on the values of discipleship. His legacy is commitment to his teachings and trust in God.

Many forms of death in our life have taught us so many things. This was a central theme of Cardinal Bertone's homily to mourners of earthquake victims that devastated the mountainous Abruzzo region of central Italy in 2009. There were 290 people dead and 28,000 homeless. He said, "Death teaches us that "everything can stop in a moment. When everything ends, all that remains is love."[265]

In difficult times we always invoke God's mercy and compassion. We also ask his blessing on us that we may not be led astray nor misread the signs of the times. Our experiences and interests bring us to deeper learning and

---

[263]   cf. www.tomorrowsworld.org. Richard F. Ames. *The Future of Jerusalem*. Vol. 9, Issue 3

[264]   ibid.

[265]   cf. Rachel Donadio. *Flowers, Tears and Rows of Coffins at a Funeral in Italy for Earthquake Victims*. The New York Times. CLVIII, No. 54, 642. April 11, 2009. p A4.

discovery of life without shortchanging the essentials and vitality of our Christian faith. We move ahead in darkness, sustained in our faithfulness by what we once glimpsed when, if only for an instant, everything was clear.[266]

As we deal with our priorities in life, let us open our hearts to everyone who is in need of help. Let us keep our vision focused on what the gospel teaches us and renew our commitments as we abide in relationship with Jesus that is constant, profound and growing.

While we recall the reconstruction of the second temple and the veil of the temple that was torn from top to the bottom when Jesus died, let us also reconstruct our inner temple with faithfulness to our conscience, the divine voice within us. It is our individual hearts that can have that vision, too, as God's windows to our brothers and sisters in faith. God bless you.

---

[266] John Fullenbach. *Proclaiming His Kingdom* (Manila: Divine Word Publications, 1992), 190.

SOLEMNITY OF CHRIST THE KING[267]

Readings: 2 Sam 5:1-3; Ps 122:1-5; Col 1:12-20; Lk 23:35-43

The Crucifixion

"Jesus, remember me when you come into your
kingdom." He replied to him, "Amen, I say to you,
today you will be with me in paradise."

During the course of Europe's long history of kingship,
authority has never been an easy affair. European monarchies
have slowly become Christianized and kingship was defined
with divine right and absolute power. English and French
kings in the twelfth century since the time of Charlemagne

---

[267]   cf. Calendarium Romanum (Libreria Editrice Vaticana, 1969), p
63. It dates from the Middle Ages, Pope Pius XI added it in 1925
in response to growing nationalism and secularism. In his 1969
motu proprio Mysterii Paschalis, Pope Paul VI gave the celebration
a new title: "D.N. Iesu Chrsti universorum Regis" (Our Lord Jesus
Christ King of the Universe). The name is found in various forms in
scripture: King Eternal (1 Tim 1:17), King of Israel (Jn 1:49), King of
the Jews (Matt 27:11), King of kings (1 Tim 6:15; Rev 19:16), King of
the Ages (Rev 15:3) and Ruler of the Kings of the Earth (Rev 1:5). It is
a day to celebrate and remember Christ's kingship over all creation,
as well as remind us that all mankind must submit to Christ's rule.
Jesus turned the whole concept of lordship and primacy on this:
'whoever wishes to become great among you will be your servant;
whoever wishes to be first among you will be the slave of all. For the
Son of Man did not come to be served, but to serve, and to give his
life as a ransom for many (Mk 10:42-45). Jesus' kingship is closely
connected with his role as Judge. He looks at the heart and does
not judge by human standards. His justice is designed to lead to
repentance and salvation through the Sacraments of the Church.
He is all loving, all-merciful and in a loving relationship with his
people. His kingship is proclaimed multiple times while he is on the
cross. It is still a primary defining point of Christ's kingship.

(742-814), for instance, claimed themselves with a quality of divinity. They ruled by divine right and retained their dynasties. However, during the 16th and first half of the 17th century, religious reformation started to shape the distinction that brought tension between papacy and the cult of kingship especially when King Henry VIII, priest-king of the English Church, broke with Rome. It greatly enhanced the power of the king.

Obviously a great deal of leadership among kings has a strict hereditary succession with absolute monarchy or political power. History is replete with legends and folktales, along with many significant battles and wars. We think of Zeus, Pelops, King Arthur and the Knights of the Round Table, Robin Hood, Romulus and Remus, Sir Gawain and the Green Knight as they strive hard to attain the Holy Grail. Then we have the Battle of Lepanto, the Battle of Marathon, the Battle of Waterloo, and the Battle of Pharsalus. They have provided us with images and characteristics of kings or kingdoms, founders or institutions that bring to the fore the distinguishing nature and meaning of their role in society. In all utterance and in all knowledge,[268] they also have their limitations and imperfections, but, with a definite objective to realize. Most of them took a journey and they successfully weathered their worst struggles, their spiritual storms, and their anxious moments.

Today, as we celebrate the solemnity of Christ the King, we recall the curious chain of circumstances that bring to light the prominent feature of Christ's kingship over all creation. It reminds us that Christ's kingship is not like that kingship of the ones from many legends and myths of literary sources. Yes, they have demonstrated their

---

[268]   1 Cor 1:5

courage, chivalry, and intelligence but, the central focus on Jesus' kingship is servanthood in light of love and sacrifice. Except in sin Christ humbles himself (kenosis) to become human like us and show us the cup of suffering by dying for our sins that eventually brings his triumphant glory—his resurrection.

Many important elements go into this principle that Christ's identity is marked with a sign of service and self-giving. His spiritual kingship is demonstrated not in control and domination like that of the Roman Empire, David's kingship, English monarchy, or the Carolingian Empire.

We now live in an era when disintegrating Christian values continue to afflict our moral lives. With the growing influence of secularism and modern technology, our way of life has changed dramatically. It seems there is more intense stimulation to attain some level of greater satisfaction, let's say in sports, politics, business, and many other areas. Our concept of leadership or kingship has even been challenged with a variety of concerns and priorities that lobby for justice, peace, and equality. The running sore of discrimination or racial profiling continues to generate violence and animosity.

Our experiences in life offer new opportunities to encounter another challenge. They weave through all aspects of our life and enable us to understand the heart and soul of our commitment; our attitudes in relation to power and authority.

Looking at our own context today, we have made great strides in understanding terrorism and putting in place protections against it. Under Transportation Security Administration rules, for instance, there are now new machines that show the body's contours on a computer stationed in a private room from security checkpoints.[269] It's a big deal to confront the emerging terrorist threats in our country. If we look at our own backyard, we see protests among students in regard to university costs. Rhode Island Department of Education has alerted the attention of local communities that they have to ramp up their efforts and meet higher expectations by 2012. Our neighboring countries, too, show that there are thousands of people dying in Mexico's drug wars, and Haiti is suffering from a deadly cholera epidemic.[270]

These are realities that speak to us about the fundamental issue that becomes our foundational issue to reflect on the larger context where we ask ourselves: what's wrong with the world? One aspect of our faith in Christ the King is to be able to take an extra mile to reach out to those who are in need or to roll up our sleeves and dirty our hands.

As people of hope we commit ourselves to the gospel values and oppose any dehumanizing forces that go against the true meaning of Christ's kingship which is service, love, and sacrifice for our brothers and sisters. We need to realign ourselves to the foundation of God's kingdom here on earth and to take part in many situations that generate redeeming actions and service to our brothers and sisters.

As we welcome a new liturgical year, we commit ourselves to altering what patterns in our lives need conversion. We are challenged to turn over a new leaf because life does not end in death. There is hope that awaits us and that's the gift of eternal life. God bless you.

---

[269] cf. The Providence Journal. November 15, 2010.
[270] Andres Oppenheimer. *Region ignores Venezuela coup threat*. The Providence Journal. Nov. 16, 2010. p. B6.

THANKSGIVING DAY

Readings: 1 Kgs 8:55-61 (943-1); Ps 145:2-3,
4-11; 1 Cor 1:3-9; Lk 1:39-55

Gratitude to God Through Centuries

*"I give thanks to my God always on your account for the grace
of God bestowed on you in Christ Jesus, that in him you were
enriched in every way, with all discourse and all knowledge, as the
testimony to Christ was confirmed among you . . ."*
(1 Cor 1:3-9)

Over the centuries our celebration of Thanksgiving has
taken its shape in two different traditions—with the native
Indians in Plymouth County, Massachusetts and Pilgrim
settlers[271] from England. Harvest festival and gratitude to
God for victory or survival during those difficult times in
the 17th century were reasons to celebrate until it grew into
the full-fledged American holiday of Thanksgiving.

---

[271] Teaching about Thanksgiving. Sept. 1986. State of Washington.
With an introduction by: Chuck Larsen Tacoma School District.
Originally written and developed by Cathy Ross, Mary Robertson,
Chuck Larsen, and Roger Fernandes Indian Education, Highline
School District. They were a sub sect, or splinter group, of the
Puritan movement. They came to America to achieve what their
Puritan comrades continued to strive for in England; and when
the Puritans were forced from England they came to New England
and soon absorbed the original "Pilgrims." The Puritans were not
just simple religious conservatives persecuted by the King and the
Church of England for their unorthodox beliefs. They were political
revolutionaries who not only intended to overthrow the government
of England, but who actually did so in 1649. Mainstream Englishmen
considered the Pilgrims to be deliberate religious dropouts who
intended to found a new nation completely independent from non-
Puritan England.

As many writers and editors have claimed, especially Sarah Josepha Hale, who succeeded to convince Abraham Lincoln, after so many attempts, to proclaim Thanksgiving a national holiday, there is a balance of historic truth and inspiration that defines a common national history of this country. They are far above and beyond that which we hold special in our hearts.

There is much to say about the story of Thanksgiving Day. It is not just the story of the founding of the Plymouth Plantation or the Pilgrim image we have of them. But rather, we come together to count our blessings and to focus on the strength we get from our families, communities, or others around us.

As a nation we have much to be grateful for. The cornucopia of blessings bestowed upon us reminds us not to lose sight of the grassroots nature of our beginnings. Our sense of history, our wounded past is a great deal of what mobilizes the body and soul of our nation, our freedom that continues to shine for future generations.

With family members, friends and relatives sharing the gift of relationship, a generous meal and other delectable trimmings, we now partake in this significant event of thanksgiving celebration as men and women committed to our faith. We give thanks to God for many blessings in our lives.

Happy Thanksgiving Day!

SOLEMNITY OF THE IMMACULATE CONCEPTION OF THE BLESSED VIRGIN MARY

(1)

Readings: Gen 3:9-15, 20; Ps 98:1-, 2-3ab,
3bc-4; Eph 1:3-6, 11-12; Lk 1:26-38

*"I will put enmity between you and the woman,
and between your offspring and hers; he will strike
at your head, while you strike at his heel."*

One thing I still remember in Hasidic tradition is the great stress put on the idea of hiding. It says that after Adam and Eve had eaten the forbidden fruit, God did not ask them if they are being good or evil? Instead, God asked them, "Where are you?" For Hasidic teaching, any transformation for men and women begins after they stop hiding.

Perhaps we can also ask ourselves, "Where are we now?" We are part of human history; part of an interesting narrative which may be allegorical as biblical scholarship and science cast serious doubts about the story of Adam and Eve; they deny the Fall of Man and the concept of original sin which was commonly understood in Augustinian terms. However, it is not all that allegorical since there is literal and authentic truth of the Fall in Genesis[272] where our first parents—a man and a woman were tempted to eat the forbidden fruit. As a consequence, the whole humanity has to struggle with life and experience death.

As God's narrative and not ours, our faith in Him shaped our conviction that God is more important than we

---

[272] cf. CCC. para. 360; emphasis in the original

are. His revelation in history changed the whole human race that gave birth to the presence of the divine—the promise of redemption. And Mary was given a special privilege to carry out her role or mission in the mystery of human salvation. God's intervention at the first instant of her existence was to preserve Mary from the original fault committed by our first parents—from original sin.

As an affirmation of what had been, in some schools of thought, popular devotions for centuries, the faith proclamation (doctrine) of the Immaculate Conception was officially articulated in the mid-19th century (1854). Four years after Pope Pius IX declared Mary's sanctification as a doctrine or dogma of faith, our Blessed Mother appeared herself as the Immaculate Conception to Bernadette Soubirous at Lourdes.

According to historical records, the Immaculate Conception was supported and pushed by the American bishops at that time. In another quote from Rocco Palmo— "On August 15th, 1791, in the small chapel of an English castle, Father John Carroll was ordained America's first Catholic bishop, assigned to the newly founded Diocese of Baltimore. In his own Inaugural address, Bishop Carroll dedicated this country to the Patronage of the Mother of God, entrusting to her another earthly journey that continues to this very day. Even before this, as far back as 1643, the King of Spain dedicated his newfound lands in the Americas to the special care of the Mother of Christ and Mother of the Church.

In the mid-19th century later, the Holy See summoned American bishops to Rome for the solemn pronouncement of the Immaculate Conception as a definitive teaching of the Church. In 1866, it was declared that Dec. 8th was to be observed as a holy day of obligation in every diocese of the U.S. and Mary's new journey was officially underway. Our early bishops were truly committed to Marian devotion and above all, the Immaculate Conception. They were convinced beyond any doubt that God loved this nation as he loved Mary, as he loves each of us.

Four days from now and we're going to celebrate the feast of Our Lady of Guadalupe. Mary's intervention in our lives has redeeming elements of inclusion and liberation that conveys a powerful message to the local bishop to understand well that to be catholic is to be universal. There may be some theological dissonance or disagreement between the doctrine we affirm this Dec. 8 and the ecclesial practice but, we have to keep in mind that some of our faith experiences fall into the category of mysteries. Like Mary, her Immaculate Conception wasn't a license for her to be free from life's difficulties. She remained steadfast and faithful to her mission as the Mother of God and the first disciple of her Son.

Let's ask her intercession that we, too, may remain faithful to our commitment with a grateful heart for all the graces and blessings we have received.

(2)

THE SOLEMNITY OF THE IMMACULATE CONCEPTION OF THE BLESSED VIRGIN MARY

Readings: Gen 3:9-15, 20; Ps 98:1, 2-3,
3-4; Eph 1:3-6, 11-12; Lk 1:26-38

The story of a woman who is chosen and blessed from
the beginning . . . «*potuit, decuit ergo fecit*» (God could
do it, it was fitting that He did it, and so He did it).

*"I will put enmity between you and the woman,
and between your offspring and hers; he will strike
at your head, while you strike at his heel."*

Today's feast of the Immaculate Conception can be traced
back from churches in the East in the seventh century when
they started celebrating the Feast of the Conception of St
Anne, the mother of Mary. Many centuries have passed and
both churches in the East and West have kept that belief that
Mary was conceived without original sin.

Catholic theology maintains that since Jesus became
incarnate of the Virgin Mary, it was fitting that she be
completely free of sin for expressing her fiat.[273] Hence, the
Immaculate Conception represents Christ's saving grace in
the life of Mary in anticipation of humanity's redemption
and in God's plan that connects to Mary's acceptance of his
will during the Annunciation. It's God's grace in mysterious
ways that made possible Mary's exemplary life of faith.

The proto-evangelium "I will put enmity between you
and the woman, between your offspring and hers; he will

---

[273] Ludwig Ott. *Fundamentals of Catholic Dogma*. Bk3, Pt 3, Chapter
2, § 3.1.e.

strike at your head, while you strike at his heel," explains to us that this was a prophecy that foretold of a "woman" who would always be in animosity with the serpent. It means that a woman would never be under the power or influence of sin, nor be a slave to the serpent.

As a Christian nation, our true devotion to Mary is measured through imitation of her virtues, particularly her faith (cf. Lumen Gentium no. 67). She may not have preached like Peter and Paul or planted churches in many places. But her claim to fame, honor and role in the mystery of salvation is her 'fiat' her 'yes' to God. She believed that nothing is impossible with God.

Let's keep our faith intact as we reflect on Elizabeth's final words to Mary "blessed are you among women.' This, however, holds the key to our understanding why she is to be proclaimed with honor and sanctity—because of her faith. Our faith tells us in terms of theological axiom, '*lex orandi, lex credendi* that the law of prayer is the law of faith. As we pray, so do we believe.

ADVENT SEASON

T he word advent means "coming" or "arrival" and the season of Advent is focused on the "coming" of Christ as Messiah (Christ or King). Our worship, scripture readings, and prayers not only prepare us spiritually for Christmas (his first coming), but also for his eventual second coming. This is why the Scripture readings during Advent include both Old Testament prophecies predicting the Messiah and New Testament passages concerning Jesus' second coming as Judge of all people.

Advent has a two-fold character: as a season to prepare for Christmas when Christ's first coming to us is remembered; as a season when that remembrance directs our mind and heart to await Christ's second coming at the end of time. Advent thus is a period of devout and joyful expectation (General Norms for the Liturgical Year and Calendar [henceforth, General Norms], 39).

It is a time to recall the cry of the early Christians: *Maranatha!* "Come, Lord Jesus!" The Advent wreath, a popular symbol in many churches, may be placed in the gathering area, or near the ambo. Each Sunday the candle (s) of the wreath might be borne in procession, following the thurible and cross, or just ahead of the Book of Gospels. Other creative uses are encouraged.[274]

The first reference to the celebration of Advent occurs in the 6th century. Prior to this time, there were celebrations and fasts resembling our current Advent season. St Hilary of Poitiers (d. AD 367) and the Spanish Council of Saragossa (AD 380) spoke of a three week fast before Epiphany. Pope St Leo the Great preached on "the fast of the tenth month (i.e. December)." The Gelasian Sacramentary (AD 750) provided liturgical material for the five Sundays before Christmas as well as Wednesdays and Fridays. The Western Church eventually settled on 4 Sundays of Advent, which has the season beginning at the very end of November or the very beginning of December, starting immediately after Ordinary Time. Until the 12th century, in many geographical areas, Advent had a more festive tone, and white vestments were still occasionally used. However, Advent became more closely related to Lent as Christ's second coming became more and more a prominent Advent theme, as seen especially in the seventh century Bobbio Missal. Advent proper is unknown in the East, although the Eastern Churches have a long fast before Christmas. This fast lasts longer than the Western Advent season and begins in mid-November. Advent, or the Eastern equivalent fast, is celebrated in all Catholic and Orthodox Churches.

During the Reformation, many Protestants assaulted or de-emphasized many Christian holy days and seasons, disconnecting Protestantism from the rhythms of the Church Year. However, some Reformation churches, like the Anglicans, retained Advent. Possibly because of the

---

[274] cf. The Order of Prayer in the Liturgy of the Hours and Celebration of the Eucharist 2007. compiled by Rev Peter D Rocca, C.S.C. Paulist Press Ordo. Mahwah, New Jersey, p 1.

liturgical movement or maybe as a reaction to the excesses of secular Christmas values, celebrating Advent has become more popular in non-Catholic and non-Orthodox churches. Lutherans, Anglicans, Methodists, Presbyterians, and even many evangelical groups have incorporated Advent into their worship service to varying degrees.[275]

---

[275]   cf. Catholic Encyclopedia in ChurchYear.net (online)

FIRST SUNDAY OF ADVENT

Readings: Is 2:1-5; Ps 122:1-9; Rom 13:11-14; Matt 24:37-44

The Unknown Day and Hour—The Coming of the Lord at the End of Time

"Therefore, stay awake! For you do not know on which day your Lord will come. Be sure of this: if the master of the house had known the hour of night when the thief was coming, he would have stayed awake and not let his house be broken into."

The advent of Christianity on the American continent echoes some controversies concerning the religious significance and purpose that witnessed conquest and powerful influence by the Western warriors and colonists. Indeed, the pages of our history are stained with the blood of believers that became the seed and foundation of Christian faith. And what is instilled in our minds is to recall when Christ stood on earth and became human. He said: "The thief does not come except to steal, and to kill, and to destroy. I have come that they may have life and have it more abundantly" (Jn 10:10).

The full grasp of Christ's message teaches us that salvation belongs to us and it is a gift, though its fullness will be realized only when the Lord returns. Which is why, it heightens the ideal of living the Christian life and inspires us, too, to pray more fervently with the saints of old awaiting the fulfillment of Christ's promise. This is particularly true with the Apostle Paul as he closes his First Letter to the Corinthians (16:22) quoting this Aramaic expression, "Maranatha![276] Come Lord Jesus!"

---

[276] Walter Riggans. *The Parousia: Getting our Terms Right.* Themelios Journal Vol. 21.1 October 1995. pp 14-16. This Aramaic expression

Today, as we begin anew our liturgical journey for Advent season[277] we commit ourselves more spiritually to the covenant with God who reminds us of his coming. Jesus in the gospel speaks at length about the end of the world and the Great Day of God, 'the Day of Judgment.' He also testifies about his return on the last day as the God-appointed Judge of the living and the dead (cf. Matt 24:14; 26:64; Acts 1:11) with no time perspective nor scriptural ground for setting dates for the Lord's return[278] as no one knows about the day or hour of his return in the clouds (cf. Matt 24:36). Even saints in heaven wait for the time when he returns to fulfill the promise of the resurrection of the dead. This is their hope and our hope too as mortals.

For centuries the issue of the nearness of the Parousia[279] or Jesus' return to earth has been one of the most important

---

is only found once in the NT, at the end of Paul's first letter to the Corinthians: If anyone does not love the Lord—a curse be on him. Come, O Lord! (1 Cor. 16:22). The expression itself is capable of two interpretations, each of them based on the two Aramaic words, *maran/marana* (=our Lord) and the verb *'ata'* (=to come). We are either dealing here with a simple perfect form of the verb (*maran ata*), giving us the proclamation that 'Our Lord has come!' or with an imperative form (marana ta), expressing the longing, 'Come, our Lord!'. Terms apart from parousia: *The Day of the Lord, Maranatha, Epiphaneia, Apokalypsis.*

[277] Advent literally means "coming". This opens the new liturgical year. The Church begins an intense period of waiting. She awaits the coming of the Lord Jesus. As the French proverb goes, "Everything comes to those who wait." And Advent is the season of waiting, of expectation.

[278] John F. Walvoord. 1990. *Armageddon, Oil and the Middle East Crisis.* Grand Rapids: Zondervan. pp 21-22.

[279] cf. Walter Riggans. <u>Themelios Journal</u>. p 16. Firstly, the parousia brings about the final conquest of the devil and his forces (1 Cor. 15:23-24). Secondly, it brings about the final judgment of the world (1 Cor. 4:5). Thirdly, it completes the redemption of the redeemed (1 Jn. 3:2); 1 Thes. 4:16-17; Heb. 9:28). Fourthly, it brings the whole

teachings in the NT. It has also been a thorn in the flesh among NT scholars in their defense of Jesus against prognosticators or millennialists[280] in regard to Jesus' return. The anticipation of his return has been a vital part of our faith. It makes us reflect on the purpose of Jesus' return, along with the fact that he will come suddenly and will be in public appearance; his presence will vindicate the faith and the hope of Christians everywhere.[281]

As we trace back some apocalyptic signs in the bible, one predominant issue is the fall of Jerusalem as "the day when the Son of Man is revealed" and secondly, Jesus' return at the end of the world. Those believers who are alive will be resurrected without physical death, while believers who have previously passed on will be resurrected first. Jesus' "coming on the clouds" is a metaphorical phrase which we can also find in the OT judgment on ancient wicked nations and cities.

There are several ways of God's many returns in judgment often referred to as "the day of the Lord."[282] Among them

---

of history to its climax and fulfillment (Rom. 8:19; 2 Pet. 3:13; Rev. 21:1). Fifth and finally, it establishes, once and for all, the public vindication and glorification of Jesus (Mk 15:62; Rev. 1:7). It will also fulfill God's purposes for the Jewish people; that when Paul states in Romans 11:26 that 'all Israel will be saved', he is preparing the Jewish people for a massive turning to faith in Jesus when he returns.

[280] Known as chiliasts, a name derived from the Greek word for "thousand" believe that a period of universal peace and prosperity lasting a thousand years will precede the end.

[281] ibid.

[282] 1). The deliverance from Egypt (Ex. 3:14); 2). The destruction of Judah by Assyria (Amos 3, 5, 8); 3). The destruction and captivity of Israel by Babylon (Zeph. 1; Jer. 2:25); 4). The destruction of Egypt by Babylon (Eze 30-32); 5). The destruction of Babylon by Medo-Persia (Is. 13); 6). The judgment upon Edom by Arab tribes (Is. 34; Mal 1:2-5; Obad).

are apocalyptic revelations about collapsing universe, sun and moon darkened, fire, stars falling, sky rolling up, earth moving and shaking. It reminds us of Noah's flood, in the days of Lot when people were eating and drinking, buying, selling, planting. But the day Lot left Sodom, fire and sulfur rained down from heaven and destroyed them all. It will be just like this on the day when the Son of Man is revealed (cf. Lk 17:26-30). These things illustrate an emphasis on suddenness and repentance.

The destruction of Jerusalem served both as an eye opener to that type of devastation of the world. The unknown period of time between the Day of Wrath and the Second Coming when all that's visible in the sky is the sign of the Son of Man not the Lord Himself (Matt 24:30). Date predictions abound but time is his creation; God lives in eternity (Is 57:15). With him "day is like a thousand years, and a thousand years are like a day" (1 Peter 3:8).

We have heard about some prophecy teachers and prognosticators of doomsday and related catastrophes that have captured the headlines across the world. One of them was a group of millennialists who believe that a period of universal peace and prosperity that last a thousand years will precede the end. Then, we have Nostradamus, Charles T. Russell, founder of the sect now known as Jehovah's Witnesses, made claim that Jesus had come back invisibly in 1874 and predicted that in 1914 Satan would be destroyed and a new utopian era would start. The most recent incident was the Family Radio's Harold Camping who claimed that Christ would return sometime in September 1994. There are many of them who claim that the end of the world is near or has come. But no one really knows when the Son of Man returns.

Nowadays reports of wars, disasters and catastrophes are like screaming headlines that accost us daily from the pages of our newspapers, television sets, and internet websites. Our generation has advanced by leaps and bounds, particularly in science and technology. Let us draw ourselves back to repentance, to God's transforming love and mobilize our mission as we keep in mind that God's perspective differs from ours. God bless you.

SECOND SUNDAY OF ADVENT

Readings: Is 11:1-10; Ps 72:1-2, 7-8, 12-
13, 17; Rom 15:4-9; Matt 3:1-12

The Preaching of John the Baptist

*"A voice of one crying out in the desert, 'Prepare
the way of the Lord, make straight his paths."*

There is an interesting story about Thomas Edison when he was a child at Milan, Ohio in the 19th century and his mother fell ill. It was winter time and the doctor couldn't help her since it was already getting dark. At that time candles and lamps were the only source of light in many homes. They just added gas or whale oil to have more light. What Edison did was carry the big mirror 'girandole', a popular mirror in those days, and candles into his mother's room so the candlelight was reflected in the mirror that added more amount of light.[283] Hence, the doctor was able to continue treating Edison's mother and in due time she recovered.

Candles lit in front of a mirror magnify the light. It makes a difference and can be a great help to everyone. This year's Jewish Festival of Lights, aka the eight days of Hanukkah, started the beginning of December to recall the biblical miracle that took place more than two thousand years ago in the temple of Jerusalem that was sacked by the Syrians[284] in 165 B.C. It will end sundown on Thursday,

---

[283] Terry Kovel. *Before there was electricity, girandoles helped light the
night.* The Providence Journal. Oct. 9, 2010. p E3.
[284] cf. Arielle D'Auguste, Amanda DeLalla and Ricardo Hernández.
Let's Celebrate! Staten Island Advance. Sunday, December 2, 2007.
pp A 1 & A 4. There was a Syrian king, Antiochurs, who ordered the
Jewish people to reject everything they believed in to worship the

December 9. History says that their one day's supply of oil for the temple menorah lasted for eight days. They believed God made a miracle and as a sign of gratitude, Jews observe it every year.

As Catholics, too, we have our own celebration in preparation for Christ's Nativity. We call it Advent where John the Baptist,[285] sometimes called John in the wilderness, prepares the coming of the Messiah. For us, it has strong implications and certainly provides us with significance and importance that John held to the people of his time. He is out there in the wilderness of Judea baptizing those who come to him. In Jewish messianic tradition, however, the word *messiah* refers to a leader anointed by God; a future King of Israel.

John the Baptist was an itinerant preacher, an important leader, and a major religious figure who led a movement of baptism at the Jordan River. He was frequently shown in Christian art especially by the Italian artist Caravaggio by his bowl, reed cross, camel's kin and lamb. He had his own followers. He lived in the wilderness of Judea during the period of Classical Antiquity, which lasted roughly from the 8th century BC to the 2nd century. His mission could be

---

Greek gods. Although some did as they were told, most of them did not.

[285] John the Baptist's name was divinely given. It was to be "John" (Lk 1:13), which derives from a Hebrew term signifying "*Jehovah is gracious.*" He was known familiarly as "the Baptist" (bearing no relation to the modern sect), which simply means, "an immerser, one who administers the rite of immersion (see Mt 3:1; 11:11; etc). The Jewish historian Josephus even refers to John by the designation (Antiquities 18:5.2). John was born to aged Jewish parents Zacharias and Elizabeth, who were of a priestly family (Lk. 1:5). Elizabeth was related to Mary, the mother of Jesus (Lk 1:36). This devout couple lived in the "hill country" of Judaea (Lk 1:39), perhaps Hebron, a priestly city of the region.

summed up as someone who is a forerunner; one who will prepare the people for the coming Messiah. Both prophets Isaiah and Malachi had announced that he would prepare the way for the coming of Jesus. He made it clear to the people that he was not the promised Messiah, nor the reincarnated Elijah. Rather, he was the fulfillment of Isaiah's prophecy, the voice of preparation for the coming of God in the flesh (Jn. 1:19-23). His role was to highlight the need for the completion of God's promises to Israel in sending the Messiah. His message had a biting edge. He made use of figures of speech in his message. He talked about the "ax" that lies at the root of the trees, "unquenchable fire," and "fan" in the Lord's hand (Matt 3:10-12). Perhaps he referred to the impending destruction of Jerusalem.

John the Baptist baptized Jesus in the Jordan, officially the Hasemite Kingdom of Jordan. Back then it shared control of the Dead Sea with Israel and the Palestinian authority.

If we look at traditions found in the OT regarding the expectation of a messianic king or ruler, the idea of anointed ones came with the time of Moses when he was instructed by God to make oil from cinnamon, cassia, spices, etc. and how to anoint an individual, making him a Messiah. Psalm 45: 7 speaks about the "oil of gladness." Moses started to symbolize an anointed one as a rite of passage. There are quite a number of examples in the Book of Exodus, e.g. Moses anoints his brother Aaron (a Levite) making him the first messiah in the biblical traditions as a priestly messiah (priestly: Ex 40:13), Samuel anointed Saul (1 Sm 10), David, and later Zadok anoints Solomon as kingly messiahs. The ritual of taking oil and pouring it onto the head of another to anoint him was strictly observed in those times. They see the anointed one as coming on the scene with a mission from God that needs to be carried out. As Ps 110:4 says: "you are a priest according to the order of Melchizedek (one who blesses Abraham).

In biblical studies there is an expression that says: 'where the Scriptures are silent it is best that we remain silent.' Basically, I refer to the silent years of Christ since we are now dealing with John the Baptist. How about the remaining years of Christ as a teenager, or a young man in his early or late 20s? Nothing was recorded since he was 12 years old when Joseph and Mary found him in the Temple—the 4th Joyful mystery: the finding of our Lord in the temple. In the books of Apocrypha there are stories of the early life and boyhood of Jesus like that of the healing of little birds with broken wings. But I think Christ has preferred to just leave his hidden life in silence. And so we skip that part in Christ's journey of adolescence and adulthood.

Perhaps you remember an incident when Christ was with his disciples. He was hungry and while walking, they chanced upon a fig tree with no fruit. Jesus cursed the fig tree and the next day as they were heading out the same direction, the disciples were astounded when they saw the fig tree had withered and died overnight. If we look beyond the image of the fig tree, we find its symbolism being referred to the nation of Israel. Christ expects something more from these people living here being the focus of his ministry that will eventually grow and bring fruit. But what happened was—they did wicked things. They were adamant to accept him as their Messiah. They were suffused with pride, envy, greed, and selfishness.

In the time of John the Baptist, spirituality and politics were closely interwoven. Judaism could be roughly divided into a trichotomy that reflects the current spiritual fashion of Christendom: Sadducees,[286] Pharisees and Essenes.

It is this line of thought that ties up with the preaching of John the Baptist who says: repent for the kingdom of God is at hand. The moral challenge is in the details of our lives that take the form of human relationships or encounters that come alive with a real spirit of being human and Christian to our brothers and sisters. What stands out most in our preparation will be the time to deal with our personal issues that need to be addressed and in the silence of our hearts we humbly say: Jesus, help me repent for all my shortcomings and failures. Help me understand that preparation for Christmas is not only material in terms of food, gifts, decorations, and new clothes, but, it is also a way of learning to transform my life into a place of Christian significance.

The other day I was reading the news about that gruesome home invasion in Connecticut by a man who was sentenced to death for killing the wife and 2 daughters of Dr. William Petit Jr. Steven Hayes sexually assaulted and strangled Petit's daughters in their beds, poured gasoline on or around them and set fire to their Cheshire, Connecticut home in 2007.[287] Dr. Petit fought back tears as he talked about his family as he misses them, his home, and everything they had together. He lost his entire family, along with the records of their shared lives together due to the fire.

With great empathy and sympathy to only survivor of the home—Dr. Petit Jr., the Advent message is justice,

---

286 Josephus, War 2. 165. Josephus notes that the Sadducees shared this belief ("They maintain that each man has the free choice of good or evil, and that it rests with each man's will whether he follows the one or the other.

287 John Christoffersen. *Convicted murderer Hayes says death will be a 'relief.'* The Providence Journal. December 3, 2010. p B1.

peace, and compassion. There are, of course, many other cases but, the common denominator or the clarion call of all these is to be prepared at all times: to let our Christian values speak to us in the ordinariness of our daily life. God bless you.

THIRD SUNDAY OF ADVENT

Readings: Is 35:1-6a, 10; Ps 146:6-7, 8-9,
9-10; Jas 5:7-10; Matt 11:2-11

The Message from John the Baptist—Jesus as the Messiah

*"Are you the one who is to come or should we look for
another?" Jesus said to them in reply, "Go and tell John
what you hear and see: the blind regain their sight, the
lame walk, lepers are cleansed, the deaf hear, the dead are
raised, and the poor have the good news proclaimed to
them. And blessed is the one who takes no offense of me."*

Perhaps you remember the time when construction of the
National Shrine of the Immaculate Conception began on the
grounds of The Catholic University of America in Washington,
D.C. It took place ninety years ago as a victory memorial
to our soldier dead of World War I, and as a tribute to the
patroness of the United States. There were millions of dollars
invested. Members of the hierarchy were asked to appeal
to priests and religious to contribute. The National Marian
Confederation, too, pledged to raise funds for the Shrine.
For them it was symbolic of their devotion to our Blessed
Mother. And to be symbolic the Shrine had to be enormous
and had to be comparable to sister-shrines in Europe such as
Notre Dame de Paris, Santa Maria Maggiore of Rome and the
Catholic Westminster Cathedral of London.

There was a long debate and discussion while construction
was still in progress. Criticisms were brought to the fore as
regards the altars, the mosaics, the pillars and the symbolism
of the crypt. Others were already getting impatient about the
length of time they still had to wait before it was going to be
ready for public worship.

This is one example that St. James tells us in the second reading. "Be patient, brothers and sisters, until the coming of the Lord. Make your hearts firm, because the coming of the Lord is at hand. Do not complain, about one another, that you may not be judged." And in our own lives there is so much concern about preparations especially this Christmas. In many dioceses like ours, there is preoccupation with regard to current plans for realignment, twinning two parishes, and closing of schools. The coast to coast protests by immigrants and their supporters provide us a pathway of reform for them and their families.

Each of these things occupies a singular place in American consciousness. As a church we are committed to helping those who are in need. From many different angles and viewpoints, there's anger, hurt, violence, and cynicism. Perhaps it is much easier to deal with the reality of poverty or affliction in this country than it is to respond to questions as to why this reality exists.

And if we look at the context of the gospel today, John and his followers also have difficulty recognizing Jesus as the Messiah. Being committed to seeing through those prophecies and hearsay about the coming of the Messiah, they were conditioned by the popular notion of a Messiah as someone who is going to be a political revolutionary and who will liberate them from the Romans' atrocities. But that's not the real essence or concept of Jesus' messiahship. It is service to humanity. This is what the gospel reminds us—Jesus is the Messiah! He is a humble servant willing to show the way to the Father.[288] He reflects the radical nature of his call to serve others; his flesh (incarnation), his sacrifice on the cross

---

[288] cf. Gil Alinsangan, SSP. Editor. 366 Days with the Lord—Liturgical Biblical Diary 2004. St Paul's Publications, Philippines. ISSN 1655-5457.

(crucifixion), and his subsequent vindication (resurrection) and exaltation at God's right hand (glorification).[289] This is what is going to be a scandal (*scandalon* in the Greek). As he says: "Blessed are those who are not scandalized at me." His sublime purpose abounds with love and faithfulness to his mission—to the will of his Father.

Being in prison John the Baptist seems to think that he is already at the tail end of his chapter—end of his ministry. King Herod Antipas,[290] the tetrarch of Galilee, has put him in prison because he rebukes his adulterous marriage with his brother Philip's wife (Mt 14:1-11). It is why he wants to be reassured that his life and ministry will not end in vain. Hence, he sends two of his disciples to Jesus to inquire whether he is the Christ, the promised Messiah. He says: "Are you the one who is to come or should we look for another? He even doubts but later, he finds that he is really the Messiah.

Jesus tells the disciples of John the Baptist that his healing ministry with the poor and marginalized will prove that he is indeed the promised Messiah. He sets the record straight about the role of John the Baptist. He honors and speaks highly of him by saying that he is among the greatest

---

[289]   Ronald D. Witherup, P.S.S. *The Emerging Priesthood*. St Anthony Messenger. March 2010. pp 36-40.

[290]   John L. McKenzie, S.J. Dictionary of the Bible. The Bruce Publishing Company, New York. 1965. p 356. He is the Son of Herod the Great and Malthace, tetrarch of Galilee under the terms of Herod's will. Herod rebuilt and fortified the city of Sepphoris N of Nazareth and founded the city of Tiberias, named after the emperor Tiberius, on the West shore of the Sea of Galilee. Herod was unwilling to execute him, but the dance of the daughter of Herodias at his birthday dinner so enchanted the intoxicated ruler that he promised her anything she desired. Salome at her mother's prompting asked the head of John the Baptist on a platter and his head was brought to the dining hall (Matt 14:3 ff; Mk 6:17 ff).

prophets of the OT prophets. He is the privileged one to announce the coming of the Messiah, the forerunner[291] and messenger who would prepare the way of his coming.

People at that time cried for justice. They wanted to overthrow the Roman government because of their cruelty and oppression to the Jews. But they had difficulty reconciling the concept of Messiahship that Jesus tells them about servanthood with the evolving deal of political leadership.

For us Christians, too, as we await and prepare ourselves for Christmas, we may find it difficult to see Jesus' presence in our midst especially if we are constantly bombarded by problems. Life holds many facets and we strive to keep our spirits up. Let us allow God to speak to us and transform us through trials. Let us invite him in silence by developing a deeper relationship with him. As we affirm our commitment to helping others, we keep that focus on developing a loving and faith-filled response to our brothers and sisters. God bless you.

---

[291] Jesus refers to Malachi 3:1. That Scripture predicted that a forerunner to Messiah would come. John was that person.

FOURTH SUNDAY OF ADVENT

Readings: Is 7:10-14; Ps 24:1-2, 3-4, 5-6,
7c, 10b Rom 1:1-7; Matt 1:18-24

The Angelic Annunciation Made to Joseph

*"Behold, the virgin shall conceive and bear a son,
and they shall name him Emmanuel."*

Almost any discussion of the subject of what Christian faith brings to us and inserts into the orbit of time evokes a response to remind ourselves that we are presented with a story of salvation. The power behind allows us to continue in time and live for Christ the great wonders of redemption.

While it is important not to lose the religious meaning of our liturgical year in circular movement, our mental review of the various mysteries of faith teaches us that Christianity has sprung from an historical event. To bring the plans of God into the realm of time, today's gospel is one example of how the mystery of Incarnation comes once into time, continues in time, and will bring us from time to eternity. It is with Christ that brings to light the hope of a glorious future.

Evidently the experience of Joseph at the annunciation when the angel of the Lord appeared to him in a dream puts him in a dilemma. He is betrothed to Mary,' but before they lived together, she was found with child through the Holy Spirit . . . He doesn't want to expose her to shame, and decided to divorce her quietly. That was his intention. However, God has his own plan and tells him to take Mary his wife into his home because she will bear a son and he is going to be named Jesus. He will save humanity from their sins.

On the part of Joseph, the extraordinary weight given to his dilemma reveals the challenge of openness and obedience to the will of God. With a mysterious process in biblical narratives that we will never understand, time and again, God has his own way that pertains to eternity—the so-called divine, eternal *mysterium tremendum* of salvation. Scripture tells us that Jesus' birth through a virgin[292] echoes exactly the fulfillment of Isaiah's messianic prophecy as Matthew quotes Isaiah 7:14: "therefore, the Lord himself will give you a sign, look, the young woman (KJV, NIV "virgin") is with child and shall bear a son and shall name him Immanuel." Our faith in the virginal conception of Jesus and his entry into human experience, into the womb of Mary, is the reason—the core truth of Christmas. We believe with profound truth that God became human in Jesus.

As we now get closer to the Christmas celebration,[293] we acknowledge in many ways the religious diversity of peoples in our country. We love to share our faith, our biblical roots with all those that believe in celebrating life. The ecumenical and interfaith celebrations of faith reflect inclusion as a matter of justice. We make every effort to understand from our hearts the true story of what God has actually done for

---

[292] The Hebrew text of Isaiah 7:14 uses a word "*almah,*" which is translated as "virgin" or "young woman. The standard Greek translation of Isaiah 7:14, however, used the word *parthenos*, which had a clearer connotation of "no sexual experience" than *almah* (yet even *parthenos* could mean "young woman" or "unmarried woman" without a primary sense of "virgin").

[293] The Catholic Encyclopedia states, "the word for Christmas in late Old English is Christes. Maesse, the mass of Christ, first found in 1038, and Christes-messe, in 1131." It explains "Christmas was not among the earliest festivals of the Church," pointing out "first evidence of the feast is from Egypt" around A.D. 200 with attempts by theologians to assign not only the year of Christ's birth but also the precise date.

us—to redeem us from our sins. Jesus' incarnation enables him to show us how much he loves us. He understands what it is to be human. And his love for us even brings him to the horror of Calvary that makes possible the saving power of passion, death, and resurrection.

Like Joseph who had a difficult time to discern and weigh things according to God's will while caught up in a dilemma, we, too, are called in certain situations to act on God's behalf; to be risk takers with a heart open to all seasons of life; to human challenges while allowing trust in God's providence. Our love of God should well up in the soul of countless men and women that are always on the edge, the margins of society. Generosity in many forms is our watchword.

Through the centuries our Christmas celebration in this country has witnessed an exponential growth in various spectrums of society. We have changed the ways we behave and articulate our faith in public. Now it seems new trends are converging as others split hairs with animosity and dictate their culture of argument against Christian themes in some schools or religious literature in public.

I remember the death of Tyler Clementi of Rutgers University who died in fall of 2010.[294] His death intensified concerns on the problem of school bullying with those who identify themselves as gay, lesbian, or questioning. Being taunted by his peers and caught up in a dilemma, fear of rejection caused the victim, Tyler, to commit suicide. He lost the sense of meaning of his life and opted not to season against hurt.

In our families we say kids are kids. And the rule of the thumb is: we will always have kids with disagreements. But

---

[294]   September 22, 2010.

sometimes these are good because they allow them to talk things out and appreciate their sense of worth.

The challenge comes along in countless situations of our lives. To be in a state of predicament or in a dilemma requires us to seek God's assistance to guide us in our decision. At times we find ourselves mentally tortured or taxed by the everyday stresses of doing our tasks as parents, teachers, or students. Let us be strong in our faith and make every effort to put love into our actions. As St. Augustine once said, "the perfection of religion is to imitate whom we adore."[295] May our Christmas preparation be meaningful and focused on the essential.

---

[295] cf. De civitate Dei, VOOO. 17. MPL, 41:242.

CHRISTMAS SEASON

C hristmas also known as the Feast of the Nativity, literally means "Christ Mass." The feast celebrates Jesus' birth and the Incarnation of the Son of God on December 25. Christmastide is another name for the Christmas season, and currently extends from the first Vespers of Christmas Eve until the Feast of the Baptism of Our Lord.

Christmas is the feast of the Incarnation, the feast celebrating the birth of Jesus Christ, true God and true man, as a little baby in Bethlehem within the realm of history. While many Christians recognize Christmas as celebrating Jesus' birth, unfortunately many fail to see it as a festival of the Incarnation.

The history of Christmas ultimately goes back to the miraculous virgin birth of Jesus Christ around 4 BC. At least by the time of St Matthew and St Luke's Gospels, Christians began to reflect on the birth of Jesus Christ. A few of the early Fathers speculated about the bith of Jesus but the actual celebration of Christmas cannot be fixed with certainty before the very early 4th century. Some scholars think that the celebration of Epiphany (originating in the East), which included the nativity and modern Christmastide themes, was celebrated much earlier (possibly late 2nd century). The celebration of Christmas uniquely as the nativity of Jesus Christ, however, originated in the West, probably in North Africa. The earliest surviving reference to December 25th for the celebration of Christmas is in the Philocalian calendar which shows the Roman practice in AD 36. The celebration of Christmas spread throughout the whole of the East and the West in the 4th century. By the fifth century, almost all of the Church was observing December 25th as the Feast of the Nativity and Epiphany on January 6th, although some Christians still kept January 6th as a holy day which included the nativity. The West was slower to embrace Epiphany but by the fifth century Rome included it as a feast. Today, in the Western Church, the season of Christmas, called Christmastide, includes the Epiphany (the manifestation of Christ to the wise men) and the baptism of Jesus. Also, in the Catholic Church we remember and celebrate the divine Motherhood of Our Lady, the Blessed Virgin Mary, with the solemnity of Mary, the Mother of God, falling on January 1st.[296]

It says that during the Creed on Christmas itself, at the words "and became man," all genuflect on one knee if they are recited, and on both knees if they are sung.[297]

---

[296]   cf. Church Year.net (online) & The Oxford Dictionary of the Christian Church (Cross and Livingstone, eds.).

[297]   cf. The Order of Prayer in the Liturgy of the Hours and Celebration of the Eucharist 2007. Year C. Compiled by Rev. Peter D. Rocca, C.S.C. Paulist Press Ordo, Mahwah, New Jersey 07430. p 17.

SOLEMNITY OF THE NATIVITY OF THE LORD AT THE VIGIL MASS

Readings: Is 62:1-5; Ps 89:4-5, 16-17, 27, 29;
Acts 13:16-17, 22-25; Matt 1:1-25

The Long Ancestry of Jesus—A Connecting Link to our Human Family

"Abraham became the father of Isaac, Isaac father of Jacob, Jacob the father of Judah and his brothers . . . All this took place to fulfill what the Lord had said through the prophets."

There's an old saying that goes, "you can't see the forest for the trees." I wonder if some of us are so particular with the details that at times we miss the point; we fail to understand the whole situation or we overlook the main essence of the entire story.

Over the centuries there has been tremendous debate and confusion about the ancestry and blood lines of Jesus culled from the lists of two sources: Luke and Matthew. Matthew shows Joseph to have come from David's son Solomon (Matt 1:6) while Luke declares Mary to have come from David's son Nathan (Lk 3:31), the older brother of Solomon. Matthew gives us the line of Joseph, the adopted father of Jesus, and Luke gives us the genealogy of Mary, the mother of Jesus.

Perhaps to write Jesus' genealogy the way modern historians would write their family trees today would be different as Matthew wrote it not in the modern theological sense, but simply as a record of legal inheritance—showing us the succession of Jesus in the royal line with forced symmetry or genealogical abridgment. There are problems of missing names, questions about Levirate marriage and the rabbinic usage of gematria which is the practice of giving each letter in the alphabet a numeric value and symbolic meaning. Then Matthew himself skipped a great number of generations with a purpose of establishing that Jesus was descended from these two men—Abraham and David. There are 14 names during the first group, i.e. Abraham to David, 14 names in the second group, i.e. David to the time of the deportation to Babylon, and 14 names from the deportation to Babylon to Jesus Christ.

Looking at the background of Matthew some suggest that since he was a tax collector and spent his profession tallying up lists and numbers, he just wanted his three lists "to balance." As he writes for a Jewish Christian audience, his goal is to show Jesus as the direct, true descendant of Abraham through David.

From the Jewish custom it was very common to list only the major figures in a genealogy. For us Christians, however, records provided in the NT documents are very important as this enables us to establish in faith that Jesus is the Christ promised in the OT. Jesus was not just an ultimate hero or the greatest gift to Judaism, but he is the goal to which other stories are highlighted and to which Israel has remembered history with great significance.

We trace human ancestry of Jesus either in a descending linear list from Abraham to Jesus Christ as Matthew did or in an ascending linear list culminating in the assertion that Jesus was "the son of Seth, the son of Adam, the son of God (Lk 3:38). His genealogy includes 4 women (Tamar, a prostitute is unclear, Rahab, a Canaanite harlot, Ruth, a Moabite foreigner is sometimes seen as seducing Boaz; and the wife of Uriah, Bathsheba who's married to a Hittite was an adulteress).

As we reflect on the inclusion of foreigners—their Gentile origin, prostitutes, an adulteress, and a murderer, Jesus' genealogy reminds us that they are part of his mission—his ministry. Their sinfulness emphasizes God's locations of grace and it reminds us that his birth fulfills the hopes and stories of Abraham, Jacob, Joseph, Moses, David, and Solomon—down to the last righteous person in Israel.

With many names in the list, along with those familiar and unfamiliar names, great and sinners, we come to know that God, indeed, accomplishes his mystery of salvation through these kinds of people such as the extraordinary and ordinary, the saints and sinners, the weak and the strong.

Let us keep in mind that God's history continues with you and me. He is the Lord of History whose mysterious plan has to go on until the final return of his Son—Jesus Christ, the coming of his kingdom. Let us also celebrate our stories of faith, our gift of relationship as blood relatives, friends, or acquaintances. Christmas is the feast of the family; a family that generates peace, love, and joy.

Merry Christmas!

CHRISTMAS MASS AT MIDNIGHT

Readings: Is 9:1-6; Ps 96:1-3, 11-13; Lk
2:11; Titus 2:11-14; Lk 2:1-14

A Savior has been Born in the City of David

*And suddenly there was a multitude of the heavenly host
with the angel, praising God and saying: "Glory to God in the
highest and on earth peace to those on whom his favor rests."*

Just the right time to come and behold the light of Incarnation, Jesus' birth fulfills the promise of salvation. With the new covenant God gives himself for our sake, his human form is his mystery and his purpose is his great love for us. And he will continue on earth until the end of time. This is the whole meaning that Scripture teaches us. From knowledge flows love, and love, in turn, prompts imitation.[298]

Today, Christmas celebrations abound throughout Christendom. I think there are no other feasts in the church calendar which is more festive and colorful than Christmas. Traditions characterize joyful songs, special liturgies, generous meals and gifts wrapped with variegated colors. Our church and our homes are festooned with festive signs and symbols of Christmas. Beautiful!

In all of the euphoria and preoccupation surrounding the familiar rhythms and obligations of Christmas festivities, the poor have once again become the centerpiece of our concern as we share a spotlight and wrap ourselves with kindness and generosity. The presence of the Infant Jesus

---

[298] John H. Miller, C.S.C. *The Theology of the Liturgical Year.* The American Ecclesiastical Review. Vol. CXXXVIII. No. 4. April, 1958. Published by the Catholic University of America Press. p. 225.

in our midst inspires us to be men and women of humility and simplicity.

What the angel said to the shepherds about the Infant Jesus being wrapped in swaddling clothes and lying in a manger reminds us of a sign that the royal son of David, the Messiah, is born in a humble setting. Many have romanticized the image of poverty in Jesus' humble birth. Others have focused on its sign that shows he is indeed the true Son of David.

We may recall Solomon, the first son of David, when he was born he was also wrapped in swaddling clothes. Before he turned away from God, Solomon did not ask for wealth, glory, or power, but only Wisdom. Although he may be the greatest of all the kings of the earth, he was born like all others. In his humble words, he also breathed the common air, stumbled, cried, and was nursed with care in swaddling clothes. For no king has had a different beginning of existence. There is one entrance to life and a common departure.

As we reflect on what implication it may tell us, it is of interest to note that humility is the watchword. Our mental review prompts imitation to be ordinary and simple, but focused on treasures of the kingdom and examples of virtue.

Many Christmas greetings bear similarity to the Pope's very own, especially his "Urbi et Orbi" message—Latin for "to the city and to the world" to pilgrims and visitors in St. Peter's Square. A recurring theme was the courage to create islands, oases, and then great stretches of land of Catholic culture where there is life of simplicity and the Creator's design is lived out.

We remember during the Dark Ages (the 8th-10th centuries) when Roman civilization was on the brink of falling apart, faith was kept alive in Europe by the monasteries. The monasteries became oases and islands in a culture of war and division. Humble and simple lifestyles were reinforced across cultures. As a challenge for us in today's world, we are also called to do the same in our institutions as we face the growing influence of secularism and moral relativism that belittles life, love, and dignity of the human person.

The Church is an oasis in this world that continues to echo the essentials of faith with humility and simplicity. God's presence in our lives is the eternal oasis and we nourish our lives with sacrifice, faith, and affirmation of God's love for all. May God's choicest blessing continue to abound in your families. Merry Christmas!

CHRISTMAS DAY

Readings: Is 52:7-10; Ps 98:1, 2-3, 3-4, 5-6;
Heb 1:1-6; Jn 1:1-18 or 1:1-5, 9-14

Solemnity of the Lord's Birth

*"In the beginning was the Word, and the Word was with God,
and the Word was God. He was in the beginning with God."*

Several fascinating decorations and sets of scenery for Christmas have truly captured my appreciation as they bring us into the splendor of God's light, into the true celebration of the mystery of Christ's incarnation—the very heart of Christianity. If in our own perspective and looking at things around us says 'eyes are the window to the soul,' light, in the language of faith, reflects a path similar in behavior to someone who walks with Christ. Literally, there are blinking lights, glowing lights, Christmas lights, spotlights and countless lights across the world, but, on top of them, is the light that speaks to us with deep meaning—the light of Christ.

Our celebration of Christmas today draws us to connect our faith experiences in light of the Scriptures, particularly in the historical Jesus of Nazareth. Jesus becomes human like us except for sin so that we can become like him as 'co-creators' in bringing about his kingdom through our witnessing. Because of his birth the fullness of time got its Christian meaning with its full significance in the hope of a glorious future. Like an ever constant present, Jesus brings us to eternity as we become 'partakers of the divine nature.'

Looking at the gospel we find the Johannine presentation of God's plan of salvation, the incarnation of the Son and the redemption of humanity. It is the most editorial action with a language that provides us the promise of eternal life for all those who believe in him. John's theology contains Jesus' divinity and power; witness, light, and believe; and most importantly, as it enters the world of time and space, the Word became flesh (Jn 1:14; 8:58; 16:28; 17:5). He uses the term 'Word' (Logos) to emphasize the pre-existence of Jesus in this world.

We may recall in the OT when God dwelt with the Israelites in the Tent Meeting (Ex. 25:8; Num 35:34). He still does today as he dwells with us, no longer in a tent of animal skins but in the "tent of humanity."[299] It is his incarnation when the Word became flesh and dwelt among us. This is the pinnacle of Johannine theology.

Despite the polemic issue and debate as regards relationship of the Prologue to the whole recount of the gospel, one scholar expressed his view and was held potentially accurate that the first eighteen verses provide us a perspective in understanding the entire book. It is like a microcosm of the whole gospel of John, a synopsis which puts forward the core and substance, along with different themes expressed in Jesus' challenge of discipleship.

Charles Dickens' 'A Christmas Carol,' a 19th century novella published in early Victorian era Britain, is a story of a miserly man, Ebenezer Scrooge and a trio of ghosts (aka the three spirit-guides) i.e. the Christmas past, present and future. It has been viewed as an indictment of nineteenth century industrial capitalism and tells of tribulation of

---

[299]   Mark Escobar. 2007. *On Bits and Pieces—Along with Crooked Lines.* Xlibris Publications, Philadelphia. p 271.

England's poor; his sympathy for the poor, his humiliating experiences in his childhood when he was compelled to work in a factory. He also exposes the flaws of the unfair system of the British government especially when his own father was put in jail.

The Ghost of Christmas Present serves as the central symbol of the Christmas ideal—generosity, goodwill, empathy, and universal brotherhood. To possess riches or to throw a lavish Christmas party is not a moral sin. What matters is when one closes himself to share his wealth with the poor. The religious meaning of Christmas is well accentuated in the story as it favors the plight of the poor.

Like us, as we reflect on what it may tell us in celebrating Christmas in today's context, it is of interest to note that simplicity is the watchword. This quality wells up in the whole panoply of our lives; it is the run-of-the-mill pattern we deal every day. Christ became man so that we could become like him. And our mental review or memorial of him prompts imitation to be ordinary and simple, but focused on treasures of sanctity and examples of virtue.

The Word became flesh and dwelt among us. Despite the fastest growing secularism and moral relativism in today's world, we need to insert ourselves into the orbit of Christ's life; to make him the center of our lives especially in this celebration of Christmas. We need to endeavor more conscientiously in our quest to be transformed into the likeness of Christ. Now as we look upon the scenery in the manger, let us implore God's help to make us simpler and to teach us to cultivate essential awareness of the people around us.

Gilbert Keith Chesterton, an English writer, once commented that many people believe that they are being serious when they are merely being solemn.[300] Let us pray that the God in-flesh may help us cope with the challenges of our times. May God's choicest blessing abound in your families. Merry Christmas!

---

[300] Quoted from Fr Francis Connell, CSSR. <u>American Ecclesiastical Review</u>. Vol. CXXXII, No. 6. Published by The Catholic University of America Press

FEAST OF THE HOLY FAMILY

Readings: Sir 3:2-7, 12-14; Ps 128:1-5; Col 3:12-
21 or 3:12-17; Matt 2:13-15, 19-23

The Flight into Egypt

*"Rise, take the child and his mother flee to Egypt, and
stay there until I tell you. Herod is going to search for
the child to destroy him."* Joseph rose and took the child
and his mother by night and departed for Egypt.

When Christianity entered the world and made its growing
effects on the lives and minds of people, its influence brought
profound connections to Christ's mission. It has a global
scope of primary importance. The inception of the Church
focused upon Christ remained in line with the institution of
the family as a domestic church and the womb of Christian
formation.

St. Augustine, the African saint and bishop of the fifth
century, is also commonly known in the Catholic Church
as Doctor of Grace. His concepts and language centered in
Christ have spiritual character of the Church that has a life
of the future world through good foundations of families.
His personal love for the Church reflects his love for Christ.
And his doctrine on grace has transforming values on all
peoples and families.

As we see now the increasing trends in families,
marriages, and other relationships, the culture of life[301] seems

---

[301] John Paul II writes in Evangelium Vitae: the "role of the family in
building a culture of life is decisive and irreplaceable (n. 92). This
he explains at greater length in several other major documents of
his pontificate, including Centesimus Annus (1991), the Letter to
Families (1994), and the earlier apostolic exhortation, Familiaris

to be experiencing some rough times and moral decadence. In this generation the number of divorces continues to soar, along with abortion and contraception that has spawned infidelities and irreconcilable differences in the breakdown of the family.

Today's feast of the Holy Family reminds us of God's inclusive love for the whole human family. Each liturgical year we read different incidents in the life of Jesus, e.g. the Presentation of the Child in the Temple, Finding of the Child Jesus in the Temple and this time, the Flight into Egypt. It is important to know that the Holy Family is the model for all of us because its mission is identical to what the Church claims in giving witness to the vision of Christ for the world. It teaches us something about his identity and shows us how our lives, too, should be human and Godlike.

We believe that if we want Christ to be born in our families we have to endeavor to give each other that gift of love. This is the reason we are called a family that shares God's love for all the members.

Legends tell us that the Holy Family stayed in Memphis[302] but other scholars said that it's more likely that they settled

---

Consortio (1981) For a profound insight into the development of the pope's ideas from his early, philosophical or poetic writing through the vast body of encyclicals and other teachings, see Kenneth L. Schmitz, 'At the Center of Human Drama: The Philosophical Anthropology of Karol Wojtyla/Pope John Paul II (Washington: The Catholic University of America Press, 1993).

[302] cf. John L. McKenzie, S.J. *Dictionary of the Bible.* The Bruce Publishing Company, New York, NY, 1965, p 564. (Gk Memphis, Hb mop in Ho 9:6, nop elsewhere, represent the Egyptian Menofer), one of the greatest and most ancient cities of Egypt. The site lies about 20 mi S of Cairo on the W bank of the Nile. Memphis was the royal residence during most of the 3rd-4th dynasties, its greatest period, and occasionally up to the 6th. Even after it was no longer the royal residence it was an important city, and its necropolis is large and

in the Jewish colony at Alexandria.[303] Their journey from Bethlehem took at least 12 days and was about 350 miles long. They stayed in Egypt until after Herod's death (which occurred in 4 B.C.), their exile probably lasted about four years, i.e. from 6 to 3 or 2 B.C.

Joseph and Mary have already gone ahead and done their roles following the path of Jesus. The rest is history. In imitating them through their virtues of silence, humility and work[304] we will find some challenges along our way. However, it's our faith and confidence in God's care and providence[305] that he will not lead us where his grace cannot keep us. This is our spirituality of hope.

As St Augustine once stated, "Our hearts are restless until they rest in Thee, Oh God," and each of us shares with the world a universal blueprint for a highly transforming

---

imposing, containing most of the pyramids erected by the Pharaohs for their tombs. It was rebuilt by the pharaohs of the 18th and 19th dynasties. The city declined in importance after the foundation of Alexandria. Today nothing remains of Memphis except a few scattered stones. It is mentioned in Is 19:13; Je 2:16; Ho 9:6.

[303] ibid. pp 20-21. It is a city of Egypt, mentioned in the NT as the home of Apollos, Paul's companion (AA 18:24), and as the home port both of the ship in which Paul was wrecked at Malta (AA 27:6). The Jews of the synagogue are mentioned among those with whom Stephen disputed (AA 6:9). The city was founded by Alexander 332/331 B.C., after whom it was named. It became the greatest intellectual center of the Hellenistic world with its libraries and its assembly of renowned scholars. Here Jews actually came to grips with Hellenistic culture and absorbed more of its thought and its way of life than they knew. In Alexandria the OT was translated into Greek (cf Septuagint). Here also Jewish scholars made efforts to identify their own wisdom and law with Greek philosophy; the most famous of these scholars was Philo, and it is possible that the intellectual currents stirred up at Alexandria.

[304] cf. Paul VI at Nazareth Jan. 5, 1964. LH; Feast of the Holy Family, OR (CCC 333).

[305] It means "seeing before," "planning ahead."

spirituality. One finds a significant blending with life's application to the needs of the human soul. The sacred institution of the family has biblical roots and foundation with God's plan of salvation.

Because of the progress in various disciplines and in our civilization, there is an obvious work of revision or going back to the roots that must yet be done to preserve the sacred institution of the family. Our witnessing and sense of discipline are the essential values that take on this feature of harmony in the family. God bless you.

BIBLIOGRAPHY OF
CITED WORKS

I. SOURCES

Barclay, William. 1955. *The Gospel of John.* 2 Vols. The Daily Study Bible Series. Saint Andrew Press.

____. 1975. *The Gospel of Luke.* Westminster. Philadelphia. pp 203-206.

Barrett, C. K. 1978. *The Gospel According to St John: An Introduction with Commentary and Notes on the Greek Text.* Second Edition. SPCK: London.

Bermejo, Luis M., S.J. 1986. *Body Broken and Blood Shed.* Gujarat Sahitya Prakas, India.

Borg, Marcus. 1995. *Meeting Jesus Again for the First Time: The Historical Jesus And the Heart of Contemporary Faith.* Harper: San Francisco.

Brown, Raymond E. 1997. *Introduction to the New Testament.* Anchor Bible: New York. pp 267-268.

Bultmann, Rudolf. 1971. *The Gospel of John: A Commentary.* Translated by G. R.

Beasley-Murray, R.W.N. Hoare, and J.K. Riches. Blackwell: Oxford.

____. 1979. *The Community of the Beloved Disciple.* Paulist Press. New York

Carson, Donald A. 1978. *The Expositors Bible Commentary: Matthew.* Grand Rapids Baker House. p 131.

____. 1991. *The Gospel According to John.* Inter-Varsity Press and Grand Rapids. Wm. B. Eerdmans Publishing Co., Leicester, England.

Derrett, Duncan, J. 1970. *Law in the New Testament.* Darton, Longman and Todd: London.

Dodd, C.H. 1953. *The Interpretation of the Fourth Gospel.* Cambridge Press University. Cambridge, UK.

Ellsberg, Robert. 1998. *All Saints.* The Crossroad Publishing Company. New York, New York.

Friedman, Richard E. 1997. *Who Wrote the Bible?* Harper Publications: New York. pp 76-78, 92.

Fullenbach, John. *Proclaiming His Kingdom.* Divine Word Publications. Manila. p 190.

Galot, Jean. 1984. *Theology of the Priesthood.* Ignatius Press: San Francisco, California.

Green, Joel B. 1997. *The Gospel of Luke. The New International Commentary on The New Testament.* Eerdsman Publishing Company. p 21.

Jeremias, Joachim. 1966. *The Eucharistic Words of Jesus.* Third Edition. Revised. Translated by Norman Perrin. SCM: London.

Johnson, Luke T. 1977. *The Literary Function of Possessions in Luke-Acts.* Missoula: Scholars. p 140.

Harrison, Roland Kenneth. 1969. *Introduction to the Old Testament.* William B. Eerdsmans Publishing Company. p 802.

Hodgson, L. 1943. *The Doctrine of the Trinity.* London. p 95.

Hultgren, Arland J. 2002. *The Parables of Jesus: A Commentary.* Eerdmans. pp 110-118.

Koester, Craig R. 1995. *Symbolism in the Fourth Gospel.* Fortress: Minneapolis, MN. p 230.

Lewis, C.S. 1980. *The Weight of Glory.* Harper Collins Publisher. New York, NY p 25.

Martin, James, S.J. 2006. *My Life with the Saints.* Loyola Press: Chicago. pp 81-88.

Martini, Carlo Cardinal. 1991. *After Some Years—Reflections on the Ministry of the Priest.* Veritas Publications. Dublin, Ireland. p 69.

McGinnity, Gerard. *Christmen: Experience of Priesthood Today.* Christian Classics. Westminster. p 48.

Mohler, James. 1970. *The Origin and Evaluation of the Priesthood.* Alba House. New York.

Moltmann, J. 1977. *The Church in the Power of the Spirit.* ET. London. p 56.

O'Collins, Gerald. 1987. *Jesus Risen. An Historical, fundamental and systematic examiation of Christ's resurrection*. Paulist Press: New York.

_____. 1988. *Interpreting the Resurrection*. Paulist Press: New York p 9.

Osborne, Kenan. 1988. *Priesthood*. Paulist Press. New York.

Pasco, Rowanne and Redford, John. 1994. *Faith Alive—A new presentation of Catholic belief and practice*. Twenty-Third Publications. Mystic, Connecticut. p 73.

Pentecost, J. Dwight. 1981. *The Words and Works of Jesus Christ*. Grand Rapids: Zondervan Publishing House.

Perkins, Pheme. 1984. *Resurrection—New Testament Witness and Contemporary Reflection*. Doubleday & Company, Inc. Garden City, New York. pp 74-75.

Perrin, Norman. 1977. *The Resurrection Narratives: A New Approach*. SCM Press. London. pp 68, 76.

Ramsey, Arthur Michael. 1966. *The Glory of God and the Transfiguration of Christ*. Longmons Publisher. London, UK. p 144.

Richards, Herbert. 1986. *The First Easter: What Really Happened?* Mystic Twenty-Third Publications. p 66.

Wilkens, Ulrich. 1979. *Resurrection*. St Andrew Press. Edinburg. p 16.

Williams, Robin. 1989. How Does America Hear the Gospel? Grand Rapids, MI: Eerdmans. p 97.

Williams, Rowan. 2000. *On Christian Theology*. Blackwell Publication. Oxford. p 194.

II. REFERENCES

Anstay, Roger. 1975. *The Atlantic Slave Trade and British Abolition, 1760-1810.* Macmillan: London. p 5.

Ben-Dov, Meir. 1982. *In the Shadow of the Temple: The Discovery of Ancient Jerusalem.* Trans. by Ina Friedman. Harper & Row Publishers: San Francisco, CA.

Bernardin, Cardinal Joseph. 1997. *The Gift of Peace.* Loyola Press. Chicago. p 152.

Berenbaum, Michael. 2006. *The World Must Know.* United States Holocaust Museum. p 103.

Catechism of the Catholic Church. 1995. Doubleday Dell Publishing Group, Inc. New York, NY. §1223 Christ's Baptism.

Celebrating the Eucharist. April 25, 2010-August 21, 2010. Liturgical Press. St John's Abbey—Collegeville, Minnesota 56321. p 127.

Clark, John. (Trans). 1975. *St Thérèse of Lisieux's Story of a Soul.* ICS Publications Washington, D.C.

Crosby, Michael H., O.F.M. Cap. 2005. *Spirituality of the Beatitudes.* Orbis Books. Maryknoll, New York, NY.

Edwards, R.A. 1976. *A Theology of Q.* Fortress Publications, Philadelphia.

Ellsberg, Robert. 1998. *All Saints.* A Crossroad Publishing Company. New York. p 5.

Elwell, Walter A. (Edited). 1996. Baker's Evangelical Dictionary of Biblical Theology. Baker Book House Company. Grand Rapids, Michigan.

Escobar, Mark. 2007. *On Bits and Pieces*. Xlibris Publications: Philadelphia. p 116.

Funk, Robert. 1982. *Parables and Presence*. Fortress Press: Philadelphia. pp 29-34.

Galinsky, Karl G. 1975. *Ovid's Metamorphoses: An Introduction to the Basic Aspects*. Berkeley & Los Angeles.

Goodman, Martin David. 1996. *Babatha*. The Oxford Classical Dictionary. 3rd Edition.

Greenblatt, Stephen (Ed). 2006. *The Norton Anthology of English Literature*. Eighth Edition. Vol. B. W.W. Norton and Company: New York, London. pp 19-21 & 160-161.

Hastings, James. (Ed). 1906. A Dictionary of the Bible. S.v. *"Numbers, Hours, Years, and Dates,"* by W. M. Ramsay, extra volume: 473-84.

Just, Arthur A. Jr. 1996. *Luke 1:1-9:50*. Concordia Commentary. Concordia: St Louis.

Kamen, Henry. 1999. *The Spanish Inquisition: An Historical Revision*. Yale University Press: Connecticut.

Kittle, Gerhard. (Ed). *Theological Dictionary of the New Testament*. S.v. elecho, by F. Büchsel.

Liturgical Biblical Diary (365 Days with the Lord). 1998 & 1999. St Paul's Publishing Inc. Makati, Philippines.

Lange, John Peter, ed. *A Commentary on Holy Scriptures*. 25 vols. New York: Charles Scribner, 1865-80; reprint ed., 12 vols. Grand Rapids : Zondervan Publishing House, n.e. Vol. 9: The Gospel According to John, by J. P. Lange. Translated, revised, enlarged, and edited by Philip Schaff.

Luther's Small Catechism. 1986. Concordia Commentary: St Louis. IV:10.

McKenzie, John L., S.J. 1965. *Dictionary of the Bible.* The Bruce Publishing Company. New York, NY.

Metzger, Bruce M. 1998. *Textual Commentary of the Greek New Testament.* Second Revised Edition of the United Bible Societies' Greek New Testament. New York, New York.

Nazianzen, Gregory. 1994. *The Trinitarian Faith.* T & T Clark: Edinburgh. pp 239, 320 ff.

Osiek, Carolyn and Senior, Donald. (Edited) 1988. *Scripture and Prayer.* Michael Glazier, Inc. Wilmington, Delaware. pp 37-38.

Peterson, Richard F. 2000. *Slide, Kelly, Slide: The Irish in American Baseball.* Edited by Charles Fanning. Southern Illinois University Press: Illinois. p 176.

Powers, Ron. 2005. *Mark Twain: A Life.* Free Press: New York.

Schmitz, Kenneth L. 1993. *At the Center of Human Drama: The Philosophical Anthropology of Karol Wojtyla/Pope John Paul II.* The Catholic University of America Press: Washington, D.C.

Schneiders, Sandra M. 1991. *The Revelatory Text: Interpreting the New Testament as Sacred Scripture.* Harper San Francisco: San Francisco, CA. p 153.

Senior, Donald. 1977. *Invitation to Matthew.* Doubleday Image Books: Garden City, New York.

The Anchor Bible Dictionary. 1992. Vol. V. Edited by Walter A. Elwell. Baker Book House Company. Grand Rapids: Michigan.

The Columbia Encyclopedia. 2008. Sixth Edition. Columbia University Press.

Theological Dictionary of the New Testament. 1964. Edited by Gerhard Kittel, Gerhard Friedrich, Geofrrey W. Bromiley. Wm. B. Eerdmans Publishing Co. Vol. 4. pp 733-734.

The Oxford Dictionary of Phrase and Fable. 2006. Oxford University Press.

The World Book Dictionary. 1976. Doubleday & Company, Inc.

Warner, Rob. 1998. *The Sermon on the Mount.* Kingsway Publications. p 42.

Wenham, John. 1974. *The Goodness of God.* Intervarsity Press: London.

Wilke, C. G. 1889. A Greek-English Lexicon of the New Testament. Revised by C. L.

Wilibald Grimm. Translated, revised and enlarged by Joseph Henry Thayer. American Book Company. New York, Cincinnati, Chicago.

III. PERIODICALS

Brotherton, B. *Towards a definitive view of the nature of hospitality and hospitality management.* International Journal of Contemporary Hospitality Management. Vol. 11, No. 4. pp 165-73.

Caldarola, Effie. *Reflection on Turning 60*. The Tablet. Vol. 103, No. 25. September 25, 2010. p 25.

Casey, John. Daily Telegraph. London. December 19, 2001.

Christoffersen, John. *Convicted murderer Hayes says death will be a 'relief'*. The Providence Journal. December 3, 2010. p B1.

Culpepper, Alan. 1991. *The Johannine Hypodeigma: A Reading of John 13*. Semeia 138. pp 1133-152.

D'Auguste, Arielle, DeLalla, Amanda & Hernández. *Let's Celebrate!* Staten Island Advance. December 2, 2007. pp A1 & A4.

DiMarzio, Msgr. Nicholas. *Justice and Forgiveness*. The Tablet. Vol. 103, No. 2. April 17, 2010. p 4.

Donadio, Rachel. *Pope Issues Forceful Statement on Sexual Abuse Crisis*. The New York Times. Vol. CLIX, No. 55, 038. May 12, 2010. p A4.

____. *Flowers, Tears and Rows of Coffins at a Funeral in Italy for Earthquake Victims*. The New York Times. CLVIII, No. 54, 642. April 11, 2009. p A4.

Donahue, John R., S.J. *The Word*. America. Vol. 184, No 14. April 23, 2001.

____. *Reading the Will*. America. Vol. 184, No. 17. May 21, 2001.

Dutton, Denis. *It's Always the End of the World as We Know It*. The New York Times. Vol. CLIX, No. 59, 907. January 1, 2010. p A29.

Editorial. The New York Times. Vol. CLVIII, No. 54, 778. August 25, 2009. p A20.

Faith and Statistics. The Tablet. Vol. 103, No. 4. May 1, 2010. p 11.

Figueroa, Allan Deck, S.J. *You Can't Ignore the Mandate to Evangelize.* The Tablet. Vol. 103, No. 2. April 17, 2010.

Fiorenza, Elizabeth Schüssler. 1995. *Jesus: Miriam's child, Sophia's prophet. Critical issues in feminist Christology.* Continuum. New York. p 126.

Freedman, Samuel G. *Voodoo, a Comfort in Haiti, Remains Misunderstood.* The New York Times. February 20, 2010. p A14.

Friedman, Thomas L. *What's our Sputnik?* The New York Times. Vol. CLIX, No. 54, 922. January 17, 2010. p Wk 8.

Geller, Adam. *Spotlight on Facebook.* The Providence Sunday Journal. October 3, 2010 p B5.

Gibson, David. *Religion is losing ground to spirituality.* San Jose Mercury News. January 15, 2000. p 3E.

Hafner, Katie. *To Deal with Obsession, Some Defriend Facebook.* The New York Times. December 21, 2009. p A16.

Hemmington, N. *From service to experience: Understanding and defining the hospitality business.* The Service Industries Journal. Vol. 27, No. 6. pp 747-55.

Karush, Sarah & Westley, Brian. *Train crash probe focuses on computer flaw.* The Buffalo News. June 24, 2009. p A2.

Kovel, Terry. *Before there was electricity, girandoles helped light in the night.* The Providence Journal. October 9, 2010. p E3.

Lander, Fr. Robert. *Good Literature unveils God's Creation.* The Tablet. Vol. 99, No. 1 April 1, 2006.

Machado, Felix. How do Hindus view Jesus Christ? The Examiner. October 10, 1998.

Miller, John H., C.S.C. *The Theology of the Liturgical Year.* The American Ecclesiastical Review. Vol. CXXXVIII. No. 4. April 1958. p 225.

Oppenheimer, Andres. *Region ignores Venezuela coup threat.* The Providence Journal. November 16, 2010. p B6.

Pope Benedict XVI. *Message for World Day of Migrants and Refugees: Caritas Christi urget nos* (2 Cor 5:14). November 14, 2006. Vatican City.

Pope John Paul II. *Mary is the Virgin Mother of God.* L'Osservatore Romano. September 20, 1995. p 7.

_____. November 22, 2006.

Riggans, Walter. *The Parousia: Getting our Terms Right.* Themelios Journal. Vol. 21. October 1995. pp 14-16.

Rolheiser, Ronald, OMI. *Religious Life in America Faces a Change of Epoch.* Paper prepared for the Inter-American Meeting in Toronto. May 1999. p 13.

Schneiders, Sandra M. 1981. *The Foot Washing (13:1-20): An Experiment in Hermeneutics.* Catholic Biblical Quarterly. 43. p 81.

Stehle, Walter O.S.B. *Learning to Pray.* The American Ecclesiastical Review. Vol. CXXIX, No. 4. October, 1953. p 227.

Stolberg, Sheryl Gay. *For Better and for Worse, Senate has Seen changes in Kennedy's Time.* The New York Times. Vol. CLVIII, No. 54, 781. August 28, 2009. p A15

Tobin, Msgr. Thomas J. *Lessons from the Christian Life of Mother Teresa.* Rhode Island Catholic. p 3.

Urbina, Ian. *Woman Who Killed her 4 Daughters is Given 120 Years.* The New York Times. Vol. CLIX, No. 54, 894. December 19, 2009. p A16.

Van Biema, David & Chu, Jeff. *Does God want you to be Rich?* Time Magazine. September 10, 2006. The Religion Pages.

Vitello, Paul. *Archbishop Earns Praise in First Year, As Tests Await.* The New York Times. Vol. CLIX, No. 55, 011. April 15, 2010. pp A20 & A24.

White, Michael. *Remembering Rostropovich, the Master Teacher.* The New York Times May 13, 2007. Section 2 Arts and Leisure. p 22.

Witherrup, Ronald D., P.S.S. *The Emerging Priesthood.* St Anthony Messenger. March 20010. pp 36-40.

IV. PAPAL ENCYCLICALS

Centesimus Annus (1991). Latin for "hundredth year" which was an encyclical written by Pope John Paul II in 1991 on the hundredth anniversary of Rerum Novarum.

Christus Dominus (1965). Second Vatican Council's Decree on the Pastoral Office of Bishops proclaimed by Pope Paul VI concerning the discipline to be observed with respect to the Eucharistic Fast.

Evangelium Vitae (1995). Written by Pope John Paul II which expresses the position of the Catholic Church regarding the value and inviolability of human life.

Familiaris Consortio (1981). Latin roughly translated as "of family partnership," but titled in English 'On the role of the Christian Family in the Modern World.' It is an Apostolic Exhortation written by Pope John Paul II.

Lumen Gentium (1964). Latin for "Light of the Nations." It is a Dogmatic Constitution on the Church promulgated by Pope Paul VI on November 21, 1964.

V. WEBSITES

http://www.answers.com

http://www.bookrags.com-Parable of the Good Samaritan

http://www.britannica.com/EBchecked/topic/126960/Columbia-Encyclopedia

http://www.cgg.org. Parable of the Good Samaritan.

http://encyclopedia.com

http://www.homilies of Fr Munachi Ezeogu, cssp for Baptism of the Lord.

http://www.tomorrowsworld.org. Richard F. Ames

http://www.wikipedia, free encyclopedia.

INDEX

ABOUT THE AUTHOR

F r. Mark A. Escobar, C.S., born and raised in the Philippines, is a member of the Missionaries of Saint Charles, also known as Scalabrinians. He belongs to the Eastern Province of St Charles which comprises mission territories in the U.S., Canada, Dominican Republic, Haiti, Venezuela, and Colombia. His writings reflect a hodgepodge of experiences with a combination of learning and interest in other disciplines. As a missioner, he holds with St. Augustine that "we must judge our discourses by their effect on our hearers." Charity is his watchword.